KNOWLEDGE MANAGEMENT FOUNDATIONS

About KMCI Press
Powerful Knowledge for Knowledge Professionals

KMCI Press is an exciting publishing partnership that unites the Knowledge Management Consortium International (KMCI), the leading organization for knowledge management professionals, and Butterworth-Heinemann's Business group and Digital Press imprints, one of the premier publishers of knowledge management books.

KMCI Press publishes authoritative and innovative books that educate all knowledge management communities, from students and beginning professionals to chief knowledge officers. KMCI Press books present definitive and leading-edge ideas of the KMCI itself, and bring clarity and authoritative information to a dynamic and emerging profession.

KMCI Press books explore the opportunities, demands, and benefits knowledge management brings to organizations and defines important and emerging knowledge management disciplines and topics, including:

- Professional roles and functions
- Vertical industry best practices and applications
- Technologies, including knowledge portals and data and document management
- Strategies, methodologies, and decision-making frameworks

The Knowledge Management Consortium International (KMCI) is the only major not for profit member organization specifically for knowledge management professionals, with thousands of worldwide members including individuals in the professional and academic fields as well as leading companies, institutions, and other organizations concerned with knowledge management, organizational change, and intellectual capital.

Other titles published by KMCI Press include:
The Springboard, How Storytelling Ignites Action in Knowledge-Era Organizations by Stephen Denning
Knowledge Management Foundations by Steve Fuller
Knowledge Management and Enterprise Portals by Joseph Firestone
World Congress on Intellectual Capital Readings edited by Nick Bontis

KNOWLEDGE MANAGEMENT FOUNDATIONS

STEVE FULLER

University of Warwick, UK

KNOWLEDGE
MANAGEMENT
CONSORTIUM
INTERNATIONAL

BUTTERWORTH
HEINEMANN

Boston   Oxford   Auckland   Johannesburg   Melbourne   New Delhi

Copyright © 2002 by Butterworth–Heinemann

&. A member of the Reed Elsevier group

Library of Congress Cataloging-in-Publication Data
Fuller, Steve.
    Knowledge management foundations / Steve Fuller.
      p. cm.
    Includes bibliographical references and index.
    ISBN 0-7506-7365-6 (pbk.: alk. paper)
    1. Knowledge management. I. Title.
  HD30.2 .F86 2001
  658.4′038—dc21   2001049937

British Library Cataloguing-in-Publication Data
A catalogue record for this book is available from the British Library.

The publisher offers special discounts on bulk orders of this book.
For information, please contact:
Manager of Special Sales
Butterworth–Heinemann
225 Wildwood Avenue
Woburn, MA 01801-2041
Tel: 781-904-2500
Fax: 781-904-2620

For information on all Butterworth–Heinemann publications available, contact our World Wide Web home page at: http://www.bh.com

10 9 8 7 6 5 4 3 2 1

Printed in the United States of America

TABLE OF CONTENTS

Introduction, ix

1

WHAT KNOWLEDGE MANAGEMENT HAS
MANAGED TO DO TO KNOWLEDGE   1

1. Much Ado about Knowledge: Why Now?, 2
   1.1. Historical Myopia as a Precondition for Knowledge Management, 5
   1.2. What's in a Name?: "Knowledge Management," 12
2. Knowledge and Information: The Great Bait and Switch, 16
3. The Scientist: KM's Enemy Number One?, 20
4. The KM Challenge to Knowledge in Theory and Practice, 23
   4.1. KM and the End of Knowledge in Theory: The Deconstruction of Public Goods, 23
   4.2. KM and the End of Knowledge in Practice: The Disintegration of the University, 30
5. Back to Basics: Rediscovering the Value of Knowledge in Rent, Wage, Profit, 36
6. The Epistemic Empire Strikes Back: Metapublic Goods and the Injection of Academic Values into Corporate Enterprise, 44
7. Squaring the KM Circle: Who's Afraid of Accelerating the Production of New Knowledge?, 49

v

2

MAKING KNOWLEDGE MATTER: PHILOSOPHY, ECONOMICS, AND LAW   57

1. The Basic Philosophical Obstacle to Knowledge
   Management, 58
   1.1. The Philosophical Problem of Knowledge and
        Its Problems, 61
2. The Creation of Knowledge Markets: The Idea of an
   Epistemic Exchange Rate, 67
   2.1. An Offer No Scientist Can Refuse: Why Scientists
        Share, 72
   2.2. Materializing the Marketplace of Ideas: Is
        Possessing Knowledge Like Possessing Money?, 75
3. Intellectual Property as the Nexus of Epistemic Validity
   and Economic Value, 81
   3.1. The Challenges Posed by Dividing the
        Indivisible, 82
   3.2. The Challenges Posed by Inventing the
        Discovered, 88
4. Interlude: Is the Knowledge Market Saturated or
   Depressed?: Do We Know Too Much or Too Little?, 93
5. Recapitulation: From Disciplines and Professions to
   Intellectual Property Law, 96
6. The Legal Epistemology of Intellectual Property, 98
   6.1. Two Strategies for Studying the Proprietary
        Grounds of Knowledge, 105
7. Epilogue: Alienating Knowledge from the Knower and
   the Commodification of Expertise, 106

3

INFORMATION TECHNOLOGY AS THE KEY TO THE KNOWLEDGE REVOLUTION   116

1. Introduction: From Epistemology to Information
   Technology, 117

2. The Post-Industrial Dream: The Intellectualization of Information Technology, 125
3. Society's Shifting Human-Computer Interface: An Historical Overview, 137
4. From Expertise to Expert Systems, 143
   4.1. A Brief Social History of Expertise, 143
   4.2. How Knowledge Engineers Benefit from the Social Character of Expertise, 145
   4.3. The Lessons of Expert Systems for the Sociology of Knowledge Systems, 151
   4.4. Expert Systems and the Pseudo-Democratization of Expertise, 154
   4.5. Recapitulation: Expertise as the Ultimate Subject of Intellectual Property, 161
5. Why Even Scholars Don't Get a Free Lunch in Cyberspace, 167
   5.1. A Tale of Two Technophilosophies: Cyberplatonism versus Cybermaterialism, 169
   5.2. The Publishing Industry as the Cyberscapegoat, 174
   5.3. Adding Some Resistance to the Frictionless Medium of Thought, 178
   5.4. Why Paperlessness Is No Panacea, 183
   5.5. Does Cyberspace "Deserve" Peer Review?, 187
   5.6. Conclusion: Purifying Cyberplatonism's Motives, 189
6. Postscript: Capitalized Education as the Ultimate Information Technology, 191

4

A CIVIC REPUBLICAN THEORY OF KNOWLEDGE MANAGEMENT   196

1. The Historical and Philosophical Bases of Civic Republicanism, 197
2. A Distinguished False Lead: Michael Polanyi's "Republic of Science," 203

3. In Search of Republican Vehicles for Knowledge
   Management, 211
   3.1. Knowledge Worker Unions, 212
   3.2. Consensus Conferences, 213
   3.3. Universities: The Ultimate Republican Institution, 216
4. Historic Threats to the Republican Constitution of the
   University, 220
5. The Challenge of Contract Academic Workers to the
   University's Republican Constitution, 225
6. Conclusion: A Civic Republican Agenda for the Academic
   CEO of Tomorrow, 229

APPENDIX: WHAT'S LIVING AND DEAD IN PEER-REVIEW PROCESSES?   232

1. Introduction: The Scope of Peer Review, 232
2. Defining Peers, 235
3. Recruiting Peers, 238
4. Systematically Recording Peer Judgments, 241
5. Ethically Monitoring Peer Judgments, 242
6. "Extended Peer Review": The Universal Solvent?, 245
7. Does Peer Review Have a Future? Implications for
   Research and Policy, 248
   7.1. Methodological Note, 251

CONCLUSION: THE MIXED ROOT METAPHOR OF KNOWLEDGE MANAGEMENT   252

REFERENCES   254

Index, 270

INTRODUCTION

Knowledge Management Foundations attempts to place knowledge management ("KM" to its friends) on a secure intellectual footing. Unlike most others who have written on this topic, I have been primarily oriented to the institutions traditionally dedicated to knowledge production—that is, universities—whose maintenance has been largely dependent on significant state subsidies. The idea that privately owned corporations might be also in the business of knowledge production is a recent development that raises a host of questions about the exact nature of knowledge in our times. Thus, I proceed by asking what the management mentality does to knowledge, rather than vice versa. It means that my analysis tends to adopt the knowledge worker's perspective, as opposed to the manager's. If knowledge management teaches nothing else, it is that these two perspectives easily rub against each other.

To be sure, knowledge management's challenges are not entirely unwelcomed. As knowledge production has come to involve more people in more expensive activities, the relationship of benefits to costs looms ever larger. Academics are not especially adept at handling this issue, having come to expect indefinite funding for their inquiries. Nevertheless, the knowledge management literature presses the case for knowledge producers to justify themselves with a freshness—indeed, a rudeness—that has not been seen since Jeremy Bentham's original defense of utilitarianism. However, a fine line separates demystification from disempowerment, especially if the power relations among the relevant parties are not closely monitored. This book treads this fine line. Knowledge workers must recognize both their internal differences and their accountability to those who pay their way. However, such recognition need not lead to the mass exploitation—or proletarianization—predicted by Marxists. Nevertheless, it *does* mean that knowledge workers see themselves as engaged in a common enterprise *simply by virtue of producing knowledge*. Ironically, the knowledge management literature currently tends to obscure this viewpoint—but not surprisingly, considering the little that professors, industrial researchers, and IT specialists naturally share by way of worldview or work setting.

This book begins by considering the historical and philosophical origins of knowledge management, and the ways it has transformed our understanding of what knowledge is. This transformation has generally gone unappreciated by academics, even economists. Two signs of the times provide the focus for *Chapter 1*. One is the subtle shift in knowledge from a public to a positional good, one whose value is directly tied to its scarcity. The other is the KM classification of universities as "dumb organizations" (where a McDonalds franchise is a "smart" one). To be sure, these tendencies have been present throughout most of history, but KM explicitly justifies them. However, there are also opposing tendencies, whereby an academic orientation to knowledge production (the "Executive Ph.D.") has begun to infiltrate business as a stabilizing force. Together these two tendencies point toward a major rethink about what exactly is the value of producing knowledge. *Chapter 2* probes more deeply the philosophical, economic, and legal peculiarities of knowledge that— up to this point—has made knowledge resistant to a KM-style treatment. *Chapter 3* focuses on how information technology has broken down this resistance, even though much of the IT revolution can be understood by extending a standard Marxist analysis of industrial labor to knowledge work. Yet IT enchantment may be found even in the inner sanctum of the academy, as exemplified by my extended debates with "Cyberplatonists," featured in the second half of that chapter. In *Chapter 4*, I formally consider the political economy that is needed for underwriting the autonomous pursuit of knowledge— partly to counteract some of the more corrosive KM tendencies. Here I explore the virtues of the elusive brand of politics known as "civic republicanism," which historically combined the best elements of liberalism and communitarianism. Significantly, republicans prefer the word "governance" to "management." I discuss how universities as a form of organization have come closest to institutionalizing the civic republican ideal. In the *Appendix*, I explore in depth the issues surrounding the present and future of that characteristic form of academic knowledge production, the peer review process. In the *Conclusion*, I observe that the difficult questions raised by knowledge management ultimately rest on the rather contradictory terms in which we normally conceptualize knowledge. In that respect, the field is worthy of much deeper thought than it has so far received.

Before we embark on this intellectual journey, I would like to thank a variety of people who represent the full range of those concerned with knowledge management: Steffen Bohm, David Boje, Ahmed Bouzid, Steve Cavaleri, Daryl Chubin, Jim Collier, Art Diamond, Sir Brian Fender, Stevan Harnad, Tomas Hellstrom, Merle Jacob, Hidetoshi Kihara, Kristian Kindtler, Rob Kling, Ron Kostoff, Stephanie Lawler, Brian Loader, Roy MacLeod, Harry Marks, Philip Mirowski, Glynthea Modood, Michael Perelman, Philip Pettit, Sujatha Raman, Greg Ransom, Francis Remedios, Floyd Rudmin, Harry Scarbrough, Esther-Mirjam Sent, Nico Stehr, Jacky Swan, Ed Swanstrom, Stephen Turner, Bjorn Wittrock, and Tarcisio Zandonade. In addition, I would like to acknowledge the support of the U.K.'s Economic and Social Research Council for the work discussed in the Appendix.

1

WHAT KNOWLEDGE MANAGEMENT HAS MANAGED TO DO TO KNOWLEDGE

1. Much Ado about Knowledge: Why Now?   2
   1.1. Historical Myopia as a Precondition for Knowledge
        Management   5
   1.2. What's in a Name?: "Knowledge Management"   12
2. Knowledge and Information: The Great Bait and Switch   16
3. The Scientist: KM's Enemy Number One?   20

1

4. The KM Challenge to Knowledge in Theory and Practice   23
   4.1. KM and the End of Knowledge in Theory: The
      Deconstruction of Public Goods   23
   4.2. KM and the End of Knowledge in Practice: The
      Disintegration of the University   30
5. Back to Basics: Rediscovering the Value of Knowledge in
   Rent, Wage, Profit   36
6. The Epistemic Empire Strikes Back: Metapublic Goods and
   the Injection of Academic Values into Corporate Enterprise   44
7. Squaring the KM Circle: Who's Afraid of Accelerating the
   Production of New Knowledge?   49

1. MUCH ADO ABOUT KNOWLEDGE: WHY NOW?

"Knowledge management," "knowledge society," and not least the burgeoning employment prospects of "chief knowledge officers" ("CKOs") are signs of our times. To the naïve observer, it is perfectly obvious that knowledge has always played an important role in the organization and advancement of society. In that sense, saying that we live in a "knowledge society" would seem to be no more informative than saying that we live in a "power society" or a "money society" or a "culture society." But perhaps "knowledge" here is really an instance of what rhetoricians call *catachresis*, i.e., the strategic misuse of words, a euphemism for something a bit unsavory. After all, that knowledge would need to be literally "managed" suggests that its growth should not be left in a wild state: at best it remains unused and at worst it is wasted. Yet, this managerial mindset goes against the grain of the last 2500 years of Western thought, which has valued the pursuit of knowledge "for its own sake," regardless of its costs and benefits.

People who claim to know something about KM must decide whether the field is more about *knowledge* or *management*. The dark secret of this field is that its name is an oxymoron, for as soon as business enters the picture, the interests of knowledge and management trade off against each other. After all, why spend valuable resources generating new knowledge, if one can simply try to do what one has always done, only more efficiently? To be sure, rising to the level of efficiency demanded of the market can take different forms. It may take the Taylorist route of increasing the level of surveillance on one's own workers, so that more of the fruits of their labors are reaped by their corporate employers. Alternatively, it may involve acquiring a better understanding of the market itself. In short: What do consumers want? Who, if anyone, is currently providing it? Or, more ambitiously: What can consumers *be made* to want?

It is only in response to these questions that knowledge is of interest to management. In that respect, "knowledge management" is little more than talk about ordinary management in a world that has become a little too complex for traditional managers to handle. However, complexity is primarily a mathematical feature of reality, referring to an increase in the number of dimensions that need to be taken into account. We can acknowledge that our world has become more complex without necessarily concluding that it demands a qualitatively different mode of analysis. Managers who remain skeptical of the value of investing in people and machines designed to provide something called "knowledge management" figured this out a long time ago.

We are used to thinking that knowledge is produced by hard work that is never fully rewarded, the fruits of which are nevertheless distributed as widely as possible. For economists, this is what distinguishes knowledge as a *public good*. However, from a KM standpoint, it is not a very economic scenario. It would be better for the reverse to occur. Effort toward innovation would then be discouraged except where profits are likely to follow. This would license, on the one hand, the redundancy of research staff and, on the other, the acquisition of intellectual property rights. In both cases, capturing knowledge takes precedence over cultivating it.

Generally speaking, the competitive advantage likely to be gained from the introduction of a new product largely depends on one's ability to create a demand for it, which usually has more to do with an ability to second-guess consumers than anything truly revolutionary in the product itself. Thus, relatively small innovations can end up making major profits for big companies, while truly radical innovations can be easily captured or ignored. And if the fate of non-petroleum-fueled cars is any indication, some innovations may even be captured *in order to be* ignored.

These features of the *Realpolitik* of KM acquire a special poignancy in the country from which I write, the United Kingdom. It begins to explain why the recent surge in the number of British scientific publications and patents has failed to enhance our national competitiveness in global markets. Even if there is some truth to the widespread view that scientists and businesspeople do not communicate with each other very well, a deeper problem is that businesspeople regard the need for new knowledge as the moral equivalent of a necessary evil: the more necessary, the more evil. Economists often fail to recognize this point because of the rather patronizing attitude towards business that is enshrined in their "constrained optimization" model of rational action. In this model, the average corporate executive appears as a harried and impatient person—a "bounded rational" agent, in Herbert Simon's terms—who must strike a balance between doing what is best in the short and long terms (Fuller 1985). This may involve curtailing the work of the Research and Development ("R&D") division. However, had the corporation a limitless supply of time and resources, it would (allegedly) increase its R&D investments and eventually reap the corresponding benefits, since new knowledge is presumed to be the royal road to an increased market share.

The rise of knowledge management reveals that "the average corporate executive" does not think like this at all. Indicative is the difference in the biological imagery to which the economist and the KM specialist typically appeal. Economists regard new knowledge as spontaneously generated, much like a mutation that eventually becomes the basis for a new species. Despite their pessimism about the prospects for controlling the growth of knowledge, economists are generally optimistic that such uncontrolled growth will ultimately result in overall good. In contrast, knowledge managers regard the uncontrollable character of knowledge growth as itself a problem. Where economists imagine a proliferation of new variations and species, knowledge managers see only potential weeds that crowd out the effort needed to maximize profitability. Where economists see "factors of production" in the staff and equipment of the average knowledge-intensive firm, knowledge managers see "conspicuous consumption," the cost-effectiveness of which is presumed dubious, unless proven otherwise.

Difference in historical perspective plays an important role here. Economists' views of knowledge remain anchored in the Industrial Revolution of the late 18th and early 19th century, when capitalized innovation did indeed result in a general expansion of markets and increase in wealth—at least in the Europeanized world. However, KM is anchored in the "information explosion" of the late 20th and early 21st century, in which corporations are struggling to cope with overflowing databases, the care of which has been left to a highly skilled but mobile labor force.

But knowledge management is equally about academics whose employment prospects have been improved since the 1980s by moving from the arts and sciences faculties to the business schools. This move reflected the global success of capitalism (a.k.a. USA) over socialism (a.k.a. USSR) that marked the end of the Cold War. Here it is worth recalling that, generally speaking, the expansion of the arts and sciences faculties in universities in the 19th and 20th centuries had been nation-building exercises motivated by the prospect of citizen mobilization in time of war. The humanities provided instruction in the values that needed to be upheld; the social sciences taught the relevant mechanisms of social control; and the natural sciences contributed to the consolidation and upgrading of the nation's infrastructure and defense system. However, in times of peace, these disciplines potentially created obstacles to commerce by reifying differences that could be otherwise negotiated away in the free exchange of goods and services. Thus, from a strictly capitalistic standpoint, language differences between trading partners are not indicative of vast cultural chasms that require many years of experience—or advanced academic degrees—to fathom. Rather, they provide opportunities to construct more efficient forms of communication, what linguists call "pidgins," that circumvent the need for all this learning. KM continues this "if it's good for academia, it's bad for business" mentality—only now within academia itself.

These observations about the origins of knowledge management are complicated by a couple of factors. The first pertains to the field's historical myopia, the second to the arbitrariness of the field's name.

1.1. Historical Myopia as a Precondition for Knowledge Management

Even those academics who in the 1980s were driven by "market conditions" into business schools were taken by surprise by the incursion of capitalist values into their own workplaces. I refer here not only to the increased need for "external" (i.e., non-university) sources of income to validate a "demand" for one's research, but also the use of production and consumption metrics to judge research quality— that is, the number of papers and/or patents produced and the frequency with which they are cited. However, academics have tended to interpret this situation as heralding the emergence of a new post-industrial order, the *knowledge society* (Stehr 1994), in which "knowledge" is the new "capital" and "knowledge management" the science of this revolutionary order. Seen through these rose-tinted spectacles, knowledge now matters to business in ways it never has before.

Unfortunately, this vision is persuasive only to those with a short historical memory. Ever since Joseph Schumpeter (1961) introduced the "entrepreneur" as the lifeblood of capitalism in 1912, there has been a general appreciation of the centrality of new knowledge —a.k.a. "innovation"—to capital accumulation. However, the legendary entrepreneur championed by Schumpeter was not an academic specialist but a "self-made man" whose confidence was matched only by his determination. The entrepreneur was more Edison than Einstein: a master of induction, not deduction. (In fact, Schumpeter's favorite example was Henry Ford, who, unlike Edison, managed to incorporate his innovations into a sustained profit-making institution.) But nowadays *everyone* is more educated. The great entrepreneur of our times, Bill Gates, was a Harvard dropout, not a semiliterate journeyman. And, of course, the people who work for Bill Gates have at least a bachelor's degree. Given this shrinkage in social distance between academia and industry, it is easy for academics to imagine that business has (finally!) come to realize the value of knowledge to enterprise. This explains the rather sanguine outlook of most of the popular and academic KM literature.

As the reader will have already gathered, my attitude is more skeptical. A concept that informs my skepticism and plays an important explanatory role in the pages that follow is the *positional good* (Hirsch 1977). KM's most lasting contribution to our understanding of the nature of knowledge may be its practical demonstration that, other things being equal (i.e., no special effort to institutionalize knowledge as a public good), knowledge is naturally a positional good: Its value is directly tied to its scarcity, such that the more people who possess it, the less valuable it is. This begins to explain the ease with which management gurus have established themselves as theorists and vendors of "intellectual capital" (Stewart 1997). Indeed, the so-called KM revolution is best understood as the extension of fairly conventional management principles to a more demanding class of producers and consumers. What makes them so demanding? I shall focus mainly on how knowledge workers differ from manual laborers, at least as portrayed in the traditional management literature, and then end with a discussion of consumers.

The appeal to common goals in labor–management negotiations—everyone's interest in keeping the factory open—can no longer be taken for granted in the case of knowledge workers. A scientist who finds the corporate workplace oppressive may take leave to a university or perhaps even start his own company. To be sure, this lack of commitment and ease of mobility among knowledge workers can be used to management's advantage, as corporations increasingly shift to "just-in-time" and "outsourcing" production strategies, and otherwise flexibly adapt to changing market conditions. However, the downside is that it becomes harder to motivate worker loyalty when it is needed. The old threats and bribes do not work as well anymore. In terms of management strategy, then, there has been a paradigm shift in the preferred school of behavioral psychology. Heavy-handed, Pavlovian classical conditioning has yielded to the subtler Skinnerian form of operant reinforcement that aims not to make the workers better (in spite of themselves) but to discover (and reward) the good they naturally do.

Moreover, the problem of motivating knowledge workers affects union organizers just as much as managers. Unions traditionally leveraged worker solidarity to ensure the welfare of anyone working in a given trade. But knowledge workers are no more likely to show solidarity with fellow knowledge workers than with the managers who employ them. This problem has dogged the history of scientific professionalization. Despite the best efforts of several eminent scientists, no large scientific labor union has ever survived for very long. Indeed, scientists have never been able even to agree on a code of professional conduct. Thus, restrictions on the use of humans (and animals) in experimental research have had to be imposed on scientists by their managers, i.e., administrators and legislators. The most successful example of union-style solidarity among knowledge workers has probably been the securing of tenure in academia. Yet, as post–Cold War market conditions force new academically trained researchers and teachers into short-term contracts that involve shifting between institutions, both in and out of academia, tenure as a symbol of "academic freedom" appears more as an unearned privilege than a mark of collective identity.

In one sense, the situation of knowledge workers has not changed. They are still largely "alienated" from their labor in Marx's original sense of having little control over how their products are used. But this is a price knowledge workers are often quite happy to pay for retaining control over the actual conduct of their work. Here management has learned a valuable lesson from the U.S. atomic bomb project, which combined exceptionally high funding for very talented people with low day-to-day accountability of their activities. In the end, the goods were delivered. The lesson runs deeper. When managers interfere with the conduct of knowledge work, knowledge workers have the ability to bite back and interfere with managerial work. Indeed, most scientist-led calls for greater public accountability have been motivated by the perception of state interference with the conduct of *their own* work (e.g., surveillance, coercion), which then spills over into more inclusive concerns about the infringement of civil rights. The managerial solution to this problem is captured in the U.S. poet Robert Frost's memorable line: "Good fences make good neighbors." In KM lore, Frost's principle surfaces in the need for management to provide a friendly "self-organizing" environment that enables knowledge workers to report when they feel ready. (Correspondingly, managers should prepare to cut their losses if the report is not satisfactory.) Knowledge workers are themselves portrayed as psychologically more complex than manual laborers, sporting powers of "reflexivity" lacking in more primitive employees. This is code for the fact that knowledge workers are relatively detached from corporate goals, yet capable of preventing those goals from being realized.

In this context, the Taylorist "scientific manager" brandishing stopwatch and clipboard does not produce the best results. Instead, management must resort to less obtrusive means, especially the employment of ethnographers whose status is not higher but equal to or, better still, lower than that of the knowledge workers they observe and report back on. The presumption here is that knowledge workers—and, to a certain extent, consumers—operate in ways that are mysteriously superior to those of management. Fathoming these ways would (presumably) lead to increased profit margins. At the very least, the resort to subtle means shows that managers are just as alienated from their workers as vice versa. Such *double alienation* is necessary for KM to acquire its luminous status. Of course, this state of affairs may simply reflect that managers now employ workers and serve customers more sophisticated than they are. It would not be the first time in the history of capitalism that a "knowledge gap" has emerged. The very fact that businesspeople, traditionally not known for their literary interests, have turned many self-help management books into bestsellers suggests that they do not quite believe that native wit and practical experience are sufficient to see them through the next shareholders' meeting. Indeed, the mass-marketed self-help management book was born of the 1929 New York stock market crash, when it became blatantly obvious that "producers" were a class divided against itself. In Marxist terms, the owners of the means of production—the shareholders—suddenly realized that they did not know how their agents—the managers—were handling their investments.

The first modern management guru, Peter Drucker, emerged from this traumatic episode and has successfully exploited its potential recurrence for the better part of a century. Drucker's own innovation was to anticipate that the gap between knowledge workers and their managers would come to resemble the original one between managers and owners that led to the 1929 crash: a case of the same shoe now being on the other foot. However, Drucker never lost sight of the fact that knowledge workers are still workers. Thus, his longstanding dislike of both academia and middle management can be easily understood as part of a strategy to ensure that knowledge workers remain relatively atomized and hence more easily shaped to the will of corporate policymakers. On the one hand, universities tend to undermine the loyalty of knowledge workers, much like guilds and unions, by promoting performance standards (a.k.a. "validity" and "reliability") that increase the costs of knowledge work in ways that their corporate employers would prefer to avoid (e.g., the purchase of state-of-the-art equipment, longer and more elaborate experimental trials). On the other, the presence of intermediate corporate levels tends to hybridize the role of manager and knowledge worker, which in turn threatens to take corporate policy "off message," as managers come to think more like knowledge workers. Better, then, to leave knowledge workers formally detached from the management structure, while encouraged to communicate their findings and concerns to managers in a relatively unmediated fashion. In that case, managers can be assured of having a clear view of corporate interests when dealing with these communications (Drucker 1988).

This "management at a distance" approach is often portrayed as indicative of the respect that management accords knowledge workers, as opposed to the more "hands-on" approach applied to even skilled manual laborers. However, this impression needs to be tempered by another implication of the distancing move, namely, that the KM literature tends to treat knowledge workers as if they were conveyors of precious metals that management then needs to extract from their less than precious bodies, especially through the arts of *knowledge engineering* and the design of customized computers known as *expert systems*. In terms of the factors of production, knowledge workers appear more as raw materials than labor.

Arguably this move is a step in the direction of dehumanization, but interestingly it tends not to be perceived this way—perhaps because knowledge workers identify more with the specific (cerebral) character of their work than with the very fact that it is work. In any case, KM is peppered with metaphors from chemistry that regard the fact that knowledge workers "know more than they say" as "ore" that comes to be "purified" once knowledge engineers articulate and extend it (Nonaka 1991). The ethnographers involved in knowledge engineering tend to be enthusiastic about this cycle of cognitive extraction, purification, and synthesis for reasons unrelated to the overall corporate strategy in which their work fits. Ethnographers are usually hired to help render knowledge workers more accountable or even redundant, but they themselves are fascinated by the opportunity to fathom knowledge workers as a subculture whose practices elude the larger corporate culture. This curious symbiosis between ethnographers and managers is central to the trumpeted success of Xerox PARC as a long-term exercise in knowledge management (Brown 1991).

The alchemy of knowledge management, then, lies in the ability to combine people of rather complex and often opposing motives to deliver the traditional goods of management, namely, higher profit margins. As I have been suggesting, the overall thrust of empirical KM research is toward increasing the manipulability and disposability of knowledge workers. We shall return to this theme in more detail in Chapter 3, as we examine information technology as KM's revolutionary principle. However, some influential KM research cuts against this general tendency. I refer here to a body of work emanating from the Harvard–MIT axis in Cambridge, Massachusetts, spearheaded by Chris Argyris and Donald Schon, and updated and popularized by Peter Senge (Argyris 1957, Argyris and Schon 1978, Senge 1990). This work, associated with the concept of "organizational learning," stresses the need for melding managerial and worker perspectives into a common mindset. Here knowledge workers appear intellectually open (and hence accountable) only to each other but not to managers or clients. In this context, KM becomes an exercise in encouraging these captive elites to extend their ethic of openness to the larger business community, during which the knowledge worker's perspective would (one hopes) come into alignment with management's (Argyris 1991). I shall not formally address this strand of the KM literature because Drucker, in his Machiavellian way, may be right that the long-term interests of business are not really served by having knowledge workers think more like managers. Nevertheless, I strongly endorse the general point that the ethic of openness needs to be distributed more widely. I shall develop this point in Chapter 4 under the rubric of a civic republican approach to knowledge management.

Finally, knowledge workers are not the only complicated beings in the KM universe. So, too, are knowledge consumers. Nevertheless, knowledge managers have tried to stick close to Drucker's (1954) maxim: "There is only one valid definition of business purpose: to create a customer." Admittedly, the "hidden persuaders" of the large advertising agencies can no longer so easily induce consumer demand from their skyscraper offices on Madison Avenue (cf. Galbraith 1967). But this fact is far from mysterious. If it is possible to deconstruct magic after repeated exposure to a trick, why should not a similar cognitive awareness emerge in the case of commercial advertising? Thus, in our "post-Fordist" world of "flexible capitalism," mass marketing has yielded to more customized forms of hidden persuasion and subliminal seduction that address various levels of consumer sophistication. Alongside the usual bombardment of mass media are invitations to more "participatory" and "user-centered" forms of product design—usually in relation to new information technology—that appeal precisely to those consumers who regard themselves as sophisticated (cf. Greenbaum and Kyng 1991). Once again, ethnographers turn out to function well as facilitators, since by fixating on the local victories that discerning users score over arrogant software designers, they ignore the more systemic power relations between producers and consumers that remain largely untouched. The thin line dividing participation from cooptation is thus missed.

A reality check here is Karl Polanyi's (1944) version of market socialism, which called for "consumer collectives" to tie market prices to values that can be realized only by virtue of being part of a community (e.g., a religion or social movement). In that case, consumers do not face producers as atomized individuals but as members of an organized group with sufficient market leverage to negotiate the terms on which new products are introduced. Anyone who has witnessed the ventriloquism that passes for market research in focus groups will realize how far we currently are from Polanyi's ideal.

1.2. What's in a Name?: "Knowledge Management"

Strictly speaking, the mass academic exodus to the business schools occurred in *anticipation* that capitalism would triumph over socialism. The turn to KM began in the early 1980s, just as Ronald Reagan and Margaret Thatcher adopted the final hard-line Western stance that coincided with the internal collapse of the Soviet regime. I say "coincidence" deliberately, since it is superstitious to think that the politically conservative and economically liberal ideology associated with Reagan and Thatcher had much to do with—or, more importantly, is vindicated by—the fall of the Soviet Union. Had the Democrats prevailed in Washington and Labour in London during this period, Moscow would have probably suffered the same fate. But then we would have traced the Soviet demise to its failure to provide adequate welfare for its population, not its repression of the free exchange of information. In that case, we would have called the field under investigation in this book "welfare management" rather than "knowledge management."

Indeed, the welfare and knowledge management perspectives were born joined at the hip in the 18th century European Enlightenment. During this period, political theorists began to argue that there was a more integral connection between a state and its inhabitants than previous theorists had thought: A ruler should not simply keep the peace; s/he also had to provide for their welfare (Manicas 1986, 26ff). Statecraft thus had to go beyond the usual threats and deceptions, since rulers were now expected, as Adam Smith would say, to increase the wealth of their nations. This historic change of attitude had three important consequences. First, it led to a managerial conception of the state, in which economic matters acquired a public significance that had been previously left in the hands of private households and corporations. Second, it fostered a more discriminating sense of citizenship as "contribution to society," especially for purposes of raising and distributing revenue. Finally, it led to the systematic collection of data about people's lives, culminating in a hardening of social categories (into classes and even races), which were then projected backward as having been implicit throughout history.

The defining moments in the state's reconstitution as welfare manager were the American and French Revolutions in the final quarter of the 18th century. Both were instigated by middle-class taxpayers incensed by the state's fiscal mismanagement. The generation following these revolutions witnessed the emergence of the original knowledge management gurus, Henri de Saint Simon and Auguste Comte, who designed schemes to harness innovations in science and technology to the state's newly acquired welfare functions. To be sure, these functions were seen as directly benefiting the middle class and only indirectly those below them. Nevertheless, the legacy of these gurus remains in the continuing ideological resonance of their coinages, "socialism" and "positivism." Perhaps of even deeper significance has been that representation of data known as "statistics," a slightly shortened version of "state-istics." Not surprisingly, among social scientists, there has been a strong positive correlation between faith in the state's powers and reliance on statistical data as "indicators" of larger socioeconomic tendencies. Thus, those skeptical of the authority of statistics, such as followers of the liberal political economist Friedrich von Hayek (1952), have wanted to draw a sharp distinction between "knowledge" and "information." Knowledge is a property of individual minds that largely reflects their unique circumstances, whereas the information provided by statistics is at best a crude summary of the subjective states of knowers that cannot be reliably used to base large-scale social policy. (We shall see in the next section that KM has tended to undo this distinction.)

As it happens, the expression "knowledge society" also has a dual origin in welfare and knowledge management, but this time in the second half of the 20th century. It is normally traced to two rather different social thinkers who nevertheless are also credited with having first identified the "postmodern" condition: Daniel Bell (1973) and Jean-Francois Lyotard (1983). Bell's image of "intellectual technologies" enabling an increasingly observant administrative state to curb the excesses of advanced capitalism was clearly grounded in Keynesian economics and the subsequent growth of what the sociologist Alvin Gouldner (1970) memorably called the "welfare–warfare state" of the Cold War era. Bell's "intelligent system" was a top-down processor, be it the central government or a computational model of the mind. Whatever else one might say about Bell's vision of "post-industrial society," it was designed in large part to "rationalize" or "contain" the effects of capitalism, so that it produced a sufficient level of prosperity without destabilizing the balance of power between and within nations.

However, the end of the Cold War has yielded a new vision of the knowledge society. From this more Lyotardian standpoint, Bell is a bit of an embarrassment. What he regarded as signs of intelligent life in the social system are now seen as misguided acts of will to disrupt knowledge's naturally fragmented and fluctuating state. Indeed, the dominant image of this revised knowledge society is that of the market, a parallel distributing processing unit, to quote the corresponding model of brain. Computers are themselves envisioned as many personal terminals connected together in a network rather than all to one mainframe generator. Even computer languages are now valued less for their algorithmic powers than for the conceptual spaces left open by their "incompleteness" and "undecidability," which, in turn, demand the "interactivity" of the user. Not surprisingly, then, Hayek (1948), as Keynes's main opponent, was among the very first to have interrelated the political, economic, and psychological aspects of this new "self-organizing" image of the knowledge society.

The historical trajectory of the knowledge society is not quite so simple as a reversion from central planning to devolved control. Otherwise, something called "knowledge management" would never have come to be all the rage. Here we do well to distinguish three ways of characterizing social knowledge (or labor, for that matter), which together are indebted to Hayek (1948, 83–6), that early devotee of Hayek, the phenomenologist Alfred Schutz (1964, Prendergast 1986), and Hayek's colleague Fritz Machlup (1984, 186–9): (i) *dispersed*; (ii) *distributed*; (iii) *divided*. The list proceeds in order of knowledge's increasing role in stabilizing society.

(i) Lyotard's image of the knowledge society comes closest to a knowledge dispersion, in which a competitive labor market reduces "skill" to scarce locally relevant knowledge, the value

of which may be expected to change (and may even be converted to non-human capital) according to market conditions.
Thus, your knowledge is most valuable if it complements that
of others in your immediate situation, thereby enabling all of
you to collaborate in activities that will benefit each of you
differently. This is what Castells (1996) has dubbed our
"network society."

(ii) Socially distributed knowledge implies somewhat less flexi-
bility, as the spatio-temporally situated character of knowledge reinforces a common cultural identity among people
located together that resists attempts at standardization,
homogenization, and globalization.

(iii) In this scheme, the division of labor appears, contrary to its
classical sociological image as the vanguard of modernization,
as a strategy designed to arrest the natural flow of knowledge
by locking people into fixed status positions (a.k.a. "classes").
Only now the capitalist factory replaces the feudal estate
as the model of the well-ordered society. "Disciplines" and
"professions" have traditionally enforced a division of labor
among knowledge workers. The recent extension of intellectual property legislation may represent an ironic step "back
to the future," whereby many of the feudal elements of social
divisionism receive a new lease on life.

In this context, it is significant that the first modern management
guru, Peter Drucker, was a younger contemporary of Hayek, Schutz,
and Machlup. Like them he studied political economy with Ludwig
von Mises at the University of Vienna in the interwar years. Mises
was the center of one of the two main "Vienna Circles" that flourished in the 1920s. Like the more famous circle that included Ludwig
Wittgenstein, this one was also concerned with laying micro-
foundations for science. But their focus was the social, as opposed
to the natural, sciences. Where Wittgenstein's group looked to symbolic logic, Mises' looked to situated experience. Moreover, whereas
Wittgenstein's group was locally known as the "Red Vienna Circle"
because of the known socialist commitments of its leading members,
Rudolf Carnap and Otto Neurath (though not Wittgenstein himself),
Mises' group had a decidedly bluer complexion, broadly committed
to the liberalism of classical political economy. In particular, they
were highly critical of Weimar Germany's tendency to reduce democ-

ratization to mass mobilization, which in turn imputed a spurious cognitive superiority to organized groups over situated individuals (cf. Cartwright et al. 1996; Peukert 1993, Chapter 8).

2. KNOWLEDGE AND INFORMATION: THE GREAT BAIT AND SWITCH

"Knowledge" and "information" have virtually had to reverse meanings to arrive at knowledge management's baseline assumptions. This transformation has removed much of the contemplative and even ethereal quality of classical philosophical conceptions of knowledge, thereby contributing to the incisive and critical spirit of knowledge managers. But at the same time, it has introduced a coarseness into the handling of its putative object, knowledge, often by reducing it to information. This should raise the alarm for those interested in the future of organized inquiry.

In the Middle Ages, "information" was, as the original Latin suggests, the process by which forms were transferred (or "communicated") from one material thing to another. Things were thus "informed" in the course of acquiring distinct identities. The image goes back to Plato's creative deity who functioned as the "Ultimate Informant." A secular version of this vision survives in the idea that "genetic information" is copied in the course of reproducing the species. As for "knowledge," it was the mind's representation of this process, which was usually understood in relatively passive terms. Knowledge was the result of the mind's receptiveness to what lies outside it. The type of discipline needed to acquire knowledge was the removal of obstacles to reception, including false ideas and prejudices. It is a discipline most familiar today from the contemplative philosophies of the Orient (which is now thought to have been a source of Plato's own thought). Yet, it continued to capture the Western imagination well into the modern period. The founder of modern rationalism, Rene Descartes, underwent this discipline to arrive at what he took to be the foundations of knowledge, "Cogito ergo sum" ("I think, therefore I am"). Even modern empiricism—which is normally seen as counterposing experience and contemplation—has treated valid ideas as the product of robust *impressions* left on the mind, which again implies that knowers are glorified receptacles, or mere "buckets," as Karl Popper (1972) said in disdain.

Indeed, rationalism and empiricism turn out not to be so far apart, if Descartes' revelation is treated as an impression that God left on his own properly disciplined mind.

What is missing from this classical conception of the relationship between information and knowledge? To both experimental scientists and knowledge managers, the obvious answer is the lack of any context of *action* to motivate the search for knowledge. However, scientists and managers see this lack in rather different ways. Presented with the classical picture, scientists would suspect its overly trusting view of reality, as if the misconceptions of would-be knowers provide the only obstacles to acquiring knowledge. Rather, it may be that reality also conceals its secrets, such that a receptive mind will not necessarily end up learning them. Once these suspicions are raised, it is common to use the word "nature" to refer to those features of reality that lie outside our grasp. Thus, we must invent means of interrupting nature's schemes, thereby forcing its secrets to be revealed. This was the advice offered by Francis Bacon at the dawn of modern rationalism and empiricism in the 17th century, the period that came to be known as the "Scientific Revolution." Although the advice fell on deaf ears, it motivated the likes of Isaac Newton to develop what has become the major research paradigm in the experimental approach to the natural sciences.

To be sure, experimental scientists and knowledge managers share an active orientation to knowledge. Nevertheless, their goals could not be more opposed. Newton conducted experiments in order to get a glimpse of regular patterns in nature that would otherwise be concealed in what William James called the "blooming, buzzing confusion" of everyday experience. Action in a controlled laboratory environment was thus merely a means to acquire a state of knowledge not so very different from what the ancient and medieval philosophers had sought. What Plato called "forms," Newton called "laws." In contrast, knowledge managers see the sorts of experiments that scientists do in a rather different light. Experiments are short-term investments designed to increase the likelihood of success of some larger strategy, such as market domination. In this context, "information" is simply any return from these investments that reduces the level of uncertainty in the strategist's subsequent course of action. It is modeled on a signal detection task, such as troubleshooting products in a factory's quality control check or spotting enemy aircraft on a radar screen. "Knowledge" is defined complementarily as the background mentality that enables the strategist to act decisively upon this information.

Economists are familiar with the stripped-down definition of *information* as whatever an agent needs to determine her market strategy (cf. Schiller 1988). It can be understood in terms of what an agent needs either (i) to *consume* or (ii) to *produce* before deciding on a course of action.

(i) As an act of *consumption*, the search for information takes resources that are then no longer available for pursuing the chosen course of action. This is Herbert Simon's (1981) problem of bounded rationality, and it is perhaps here that the difference between the epistemologist and the economist is most apparent. The main reason that the epistemologist stresses quality control in the search process is that she presumes that a more methodical search will lead to knowledge that will enable the agent to perform better. In contrast, the economist presumes no such neat link between the quality of information and the quality of action—and hence she does not make the quality of the agent's search her overriding concern (Fuller 1993a, 198ff).

(ii) As an act of *production*, the search for information involves the construction of mediating instruments—so-called information and communication technologies—that enable not only the current agent to achieve the current goal, but also other agents to achieve related goals. The idea here is that, short of perfect information about each other's moves, if agents try to pursue their goals directly, they will probably interfere with each other's efforts, which render them less efficient than had they first pursued a common goal—a reliable medium for the exchange of information—and then pursue their own respective personal goals. On this view, the search for knowledge emerges in much the same way as the institution of *money*, a point first explored in detail by the German sociologist Georg Simmel (1978, Chapter 6), a point to which I shall return in Chapter 2.

From a philosophical standpoint, this conflation of knowledge and information is unabashedly "relativist," in the sense that there is no standard of validity beyond the context that calls for knowledge. Thus, knowledge is whatever enables an agent to choose between various ways of investing her efforts, assuming the optimal use of resources. The thoroughness of the agent's search and the reliability of her findings are not questioned. Whereas an epistemologist would advise the agent to hold off from any decision until "all the evidence is in," the knowledge manager would steer the agent away from regarding the search process as an end in itself, recalling that the agent is motivated to acquire knowledge only in order to eliminate undesirable courses of action. After all, the search itself involves consuming the same resources—time, money, effort—that the agent will subsequently need for other purposes. Once the agent learns enough to eliminate all but one option, the search is complete (cf. Stigler 1961). Still harboring philosophical scruples, economists prefer to call this "difference that makes the difference" for action "information" rather than "knowledge." But from a KM standpoint, name-calling is less important than figuring out how to lower the cost of future searches.

This equation of knowledge and information brushes aside several questions: Must the agent be able to expressly recognize the information as a piece of knowledge, say, by articulating it as part of a theory? Is it even necessary that the agent embody the information in her proper person, as opposed to, say, in some other agent or machine at the agent's disposal? These questions define a sphere of inquiry that cuts across economics, political science, and psychology. It is bounded by, on the one hand, the "principal-agent theory" (Guston 2000, Chapter1) and, on the other, the creation of "smart environments" from "offloaded" intelligence (Norman 1993). In short, whenever expedient, the efficient agent lets someone or something else do one's own thinking. That "something else" may even turn out to be the *law*.

Generally speaking, the very buying and selling of goods impose additional costs that are normally transferred to the price the goods can fetch at market. These are *transaction costs* (Lepage 1987, a popular extension of the pioneering work of Ronald Coase in this area). Thus, an elaborate legal system develops to regularly redistribute the costs and benefits of the market's activities. It covers, among other things, maintenance of the trading site, advertisement of the market's existence and contents, and even quality assurance of the goods traded. The point is to render the market predictable, so that agents are encouraged to return and expand their trading interests. For example, modest payment for a trading permit may relieve the trader of the burden of having to check the quality of the goods for himself. Economists often refer to this as the "internalization of externalities," a process which, according to Douglass North, was more important for the rise of capitalism in the West than the mere increase in productive capacities (North and Thomas 1973, De Soto 2000). As we shall see in Chapter 2, perhaps the most important part of this elaborated legal system is *intellectual property law*, which imposes, in the name of an inventor or author, a regulated fee on those interested in building on her innovation for purposes of developing their own products. The stability and growth characteristic of modern capitalist economies arguably stem from the delicate balance of incentive and reward fostered by intellectual property law.

3. The Scientist: KM's Enemy Number One?

The contrast in the action orientation of experimental scientists and knowledge managers should alert us to the unholy alliance lurking behind any corporation's R&D division, regardless of the resources and freedom lavished upon its employees. Scientists regard knowledge as an end in itself, whereas managers regard it as a means toward market-driven ends. Thus, absent some striking discovery or invention that quickly enables a corporation to improve its market share, scientists and managers often find themselves at loggerheads. Indeed, a minor scandal of knowledge management is that corporations routinely flourish—even today—without spending much on R&D. From a managerial standpoint, scientists want to waste endless time and space searching for the ultimate truth, whereas from a scientific standpoint, managers want something that will work just long enough to make a killing in the market. Of course, each side has demonized the other's utopia perfectly, but luckily ours is a world of negotiated settlements. Scientists have been known to persuade managers (who have not been already persuaded by the KM literature!) that robust investment in research is an insurance policy against the effects of long-term market competition.

To appreciate the awkward status of scientists in the KM universe, it is worth recalling how "scientist" came to denote someone professionally engaged in the systematic pursuit of knowledge, a.k.a. "science." When William Whewell introduced "scientist" into

English in the 1830s, he had to overcome the time-honored objection enshrined in the first line of Aristotle's *Metaphysics* that knowledge is something anyone with sufficient leisure at his or her disposal can—indeed, should—pursue. The suggestion that salaried specialists are uniquely entitled to the mantle of science was initially received with as much skepticism as the idea that only professional athletes have a serious interest in physical fitness. As it happens, Whewell, Master of Trinity College Cambridge, was partly reacting to the recent coinage of "artist" to capture those trained in "mechanics colleges" (precursors of the British polytechnics), who were contributing more palpably to the ongoing Industrial Revolution than university graduates. If it now seems odd that people called "scientists" and "artists" originally competed for the same social and economic space, simply consider that until the end of World War II (when a period specifically called the "Scientific Revolution" was coined), the Italian Renaissance was normally portrayed as the pinnacle of *both* science and art, as exemplified by that fading cultural icon, Leonardo da Vinci.

The origin of the word "scientist" raises some very large questions about the political economy of knowledge production. Before Whewell, knowledge was not something systematically acquired in order to save time or make money. On the contrary, it took up time (that was otherwise not productively employed) and spent money (i.e., wealth that was above what was needed for maintaining one's household); hence, it was the quintessentially leisured pursuit. Indeed, it would not be far-fetched to envisage such pursuits as a high-grade form of *gambling*: Sometimes the hours conducting experiments and observing nature turned up something genuinely useful, but for the most part it was a hit-or-miss affair that attracted only the most "speculative" of human capital investors. Typical was early Royal Society member Robert Boyle, a gentleman–farmer who lived off his inheritance while engaged in scientific pursuits that would lay the foundations of modern chemistry. In Whewell's own time, this lifestyle was pursued by Charles Darwin, whose failure as a medical student was more significant as a loss of face than of income.

To be sure, the life of inquiry was pursued by more than curious men of leisure. Those who suffered a decline in family and personal fortunes have also been prime candidates for assuming the risks that have occasionally been issued in scientific innovations. For example, Galileo's career approximated that of the entrepreneur who, in

Joseph Schumpeter's classic phrase, "creatively destroys" markets (Brenner 1987). As for that greatest of scientists, Isaac Newton, he was the model for Whewell's professional scientist. Newton, of relatively humble origins, was one of the few early Royal Society members who had to draw a regular salary from a university in order to survive. Yet, even he wrote *Principia Mathematica* in his spare time. He needed external funding only to publish his arcane and hefty tomes, not to conduct the research reported in them. A measure of the long-term significance of Whewell's semantic innovation is that most professional scientists today find themselves in a situation that is the exact *opposite* of Newton's: If one can find the money to do research in the first place, the publishers are more than happy to oblige in communicating its results.

At the popular level, KM's rise can be seen as a backlash against professionalism in the pursuit of knowledge—but without the interest in reviving the original amateur ethic. At a popular level, the KM mentality resonates with the perceived lack of scientific genius in our time. We are more impressed with such early 20th century physicists as Einstein, Bohr, and Heisenberg, for whom the chalkboard was the laboratory, than with the battery of physicists continuing their work on multibillion-dollar particle accelerators today. We even rank those seat-of-the-pants discoverers of DNA's structure, Watson and Crick, over that well-financed and methodical mapper of the human genome, Craig Venter, even though the latter has enabled the promise of biotechnology to become a reality. Perhaps genius will not be ascribed to people who require enormous resources *prior* to the production of new knowledge. To be sure, considerable resources—both economic and cultural—may be needed *after* a putative breakthrough to enable it literally to "break through" existing scientific and social practices. Indeed, there may be a trade-off here. After all, once the human genome was mapped, relatively little had to be spent to publicize its boon to medicine.

In other words, a "most bang for the buck" principle seems to rule our intuitive judgements of genius. Television producers know this all too well. It explains why viewers are more impressed by a John Doe who invents something that stumps the experts than by a battalion of well-financed lab scientists who arrive at some equally counterintuitive and probably better grounded discovery. But the consequences of requiring payment for research run deeper than the topic of the next science documentary. If the people who are regularly paid to produce knowledge find publication relatively easy, then it should come as no surprise that the ratio of useful to useless research turns out to be unacceptably low, at least to the untrained eye. The knowledge manager promises to sort out this situation.

4. The KM Challenge to Knowledge in Theory and Practice

As a way into the radical shift that KM has introduced into academic conceptions of knowledge, consider the original statement of *social epistemology*, a research program I designed to answer the question: How should knowledge production be governed, once we admit that it has many of the same characteristics of other organized social activities, specifically that knowledge is produced by fallible and biased agents who pursue conflicting goals against the background of various resource constraints (Fuller 1988, 3)? My formulation presumed that the most knowledge should be produced at the lowest cost, a principle that conformed to the so-called constrained optimization model of rational action found in neoclassical economics. Like most other philosophers and economists attracted to this principle, I interpreted it as providing guidelines for an absolute increase in society's knowledge stock. Yet, the principle can be read as more concerned with the *productivity* than the sheer production of knowledge. Thus, if you want "more bang for the buck"—and not simply more bangs or more bucks—then you may wish to terminate further research investments, once the rate of return starts to be too low. This alternative interpretation of the constrained optimization model turns out to be KM's own. Its radical implications for the intellectual and institutional dimensions of knowledge production will be explored below.

4.1. KM and the End of Knowledge in Theory: The Deconstruction of Public Goods

Economists, all too much like philosophers, easily assume that what is best for knowledge is best for business. Unfortunately, this academic conceit carries little weight with professional knowledge managers. Indeed, the seemingly liberating quality of knowledge management thinking largely rests on an image of knowledge as dangerous if allowed to grow wild. At a hands-on level, this reflects the "search and retrieval" problems that corporations face when huge investments in computers fail to improve their ability to access salient information in a timely manner (Scarbrough and Swan 1999). At a more abstract level, it helps explain the unflattering reduction of knowledge to "information" often found in the literature. In terms of the Australian economist Colin Clark's (1957) influential trichotomy, knowledge managers invoke metaphors drawn from the *primary* sector of the economy—knowledge is thus "captured," "mined," and "cultivated." It is most decidedly *not* "manufactured" (a *secondary* sector metaphor familiar to Marxist and social constructivist accounts of science) and, only when necessary, "delivered" as a service (a *tertiary* sector metaphor that had been popular with Daniel Bell and many of the original knowledge society theorists).

Knowledge managers are mainly interested in exploiting existing knowledge more efficiently so as to capture a larger share of the markets in which they compete. A concern for producing more knowledge and distributing it more widely merely subserves that goal. Indeed, knowledge management may be seen as being mainly in the business of manipulating scarcity, at either the supply or the demand side of the exchange equation. Knowledge management strategies tend either to restrict the production of knowledge and open up its distribution, or vice versa. Thus, knowledge managers are urged to adopt a strategy of "outsource or specialize" for their firms: that is, either rent forms of knowledge that others can produce more cheaply or own forms of knowledge that others cannot (and subsequently will not) produce more cheaply (Stewart 1997, 90–1).

As a global knowledge strategy, an example of the former route is requiring credentials for employment, while extending access to those credentials to anyone able and willing to go through the trouble of acquiring them (e.g., a university education). Since the number of positions remains scarce relative to those eligible to fill them, the global result is a more focused and competitive labor market. For an instance of the general strategy of opening up knowledge production, while restricting its distribution, consider the rent-seeking incentives behind the pursuit of intellectual property (Machlup 1984, 163ff). As we shall see in the next chapter, with the liberalization of patent law, the easiest way down this route is to privatize something that was previously treated in the public domain and thereby avoid the uncertainties of invention altogether.

To appreciate the *Realpolitik* attitudes of knowledge managers, we need look no further than the difference between their and most economists' view of scientific innovation in wealth production. Economists tend to treat innovation as an unalloyed and often unanalyzed good, whereas businesspeople regard it as good only insofar as it helps their firm maintain or increase its competitive advantage in the market. Generally speaking, the competitive advantage likely to be gained from the introduction of a new product—including a knowledge-based product—largely depends on one's ability to create a demand for it, which usually has more to do with an ability to second-guess consumers than anything truly revolutionary in the product itself. The idea of *social capital* captures this magical ability to get "the most bang for the buck" because of one's position in the market (Coleman 1990, Chapter 12). Thus, relatively small innovations can end up making major profits for big companies, while truly revolutionary innovations can end up being ignored or "captured" by more market-savvy competitors because of the innovators' marginal status.

Because innovation turns out to be such a risky means of securing larger profits, companies have been traditionally reluctant to devote too much of their operating budgets to R&D. The most cost-efficient operation gets the biggest bang from the smallest buck, which means—in knowledge terms—that one exploits what one knows better than one's competitors and blocks all attempts to supersede that knowledge. This point is typified by the business strategy that would have a company devote considerable attention to acquiring intellectual property rights for existing innovations, regardless of whether the company in question actually originated the innovations (Stewart 1997, Chapter 4). In this respect, any technique specifically designed to accelerate the growth of knowledge potentially poses a challenge to the business community as fundamental as that to the scientific community. For if philosophers (and most economists) of science believe that the intrinsic unpredictability of new knowledge renders a planned increase in innovation close to a logical impossibility, the average corporate executive is willing to grant the possibility of such planning but then go on to question its cost-effectiveness as a business strategy.

To be sure, economists often do not seem to believe they have a quarrel with the business approach to innovation policy. However, this may be wishful thinking born of the idealization methods of economics. Economists tend to take the relationship between innovation and market advantage as given, the only remaining question being how much time will pass before the innovation provides adequate returns on an initial investment of resources. Thus, to the economist, businesspeople often appear impatient, albeit perhaps justifiably so, since the average corporate executive must manage other short-term issues alongside the long-term concerns represented by the company's R&D division. But were the company equipped with an indefinite timeframe and corresponding resources, it would eventually reap the benefits of its original R&D investments: so say the economists.

Unfortunately, this patronizing appeal to the constrained optimization model does not capture how the business world sees matters. For them there is nothing especially sacrosanct about knowledge that makes it worthy of indefinite promotion. If anything, in lines of what I shall later call the "profit-oriented" model, the need for knowledge in business is always the moral equivalent of a necessary evil. In striking contrast, economists generally locate the value of new knowledge in some conception of "natural" scarcity associated with its origins, typically in self-selected communities or the minds of exceptional individuals, neither of which are transparent to publicly accessible forums. Consequently, tacit knowledge is valued more highly than explicit knowledge—the "something extra" that explains the difference between innovative and routinized economic systems once the usual factors of production have been taken into account. But once tacit knowledge is codified, according to this view, it no longer offers a competitive advantage. In that sense, it becomes a *public good* (Dasgupta and David 1994). This has made economists generally skeptical about the possibilities for managing, cultivating, or expediting the growth of knowledge. Indeed, they tend to treat new knowledge as occurring just as "naturally" or "spontaneously" as climatological changes, which also affect a society's productive capacity in significant yet largely unforeseeable ways.

However, knowledge managers are unimpressed by the bruteness of this conception of nature, be it human or physical. Regarding knowledge as part of the primary sector of the economy, they see it as a natural resource worthy of cultivation. Of course, like natural resources, the exploitability of a piece of knowledge is never known in advance. But by the same token, effort may be focused on developing replacements for resources that could run out in the long term—hence the emergence of computerized expert systems and biomedical syntheses of genetic materials as growth areas in knowledge-based industries.

In this respect, the KM movement can be seen as the final stage in the retreat of knowledge's status in the economy from a public good in the tertiary sector to a natural resource in the primary sector. This devolution is captured by the following narrative. In the beginning, when economists first started to think about knowledge in economic terms, knowledge was regarded as a "public good," which meant that once knowledge is produced, more than one person can consume it at the same time (Samuelson 1969). There are two important versions of this idea. The first is the *ethereal good*, in which once it is produced, consumers of the good incur no additional costs (Thompson 1982, Bates 1988). The second is the *collective good*, according to which it would cost more to restrict consumption of the good than to allow its free use; moreover, any cost imposed on consumers would not result in a palpable gain for producers (Olson 1965). On either reading, one is invited to imagine that, once discovered, knowledge spreads naturally, only to be arrested by artificial means. Clearly, the public good conception has aimed to approximate the classical philosophical ideal of knowledge as universal not only in applicability but also accessibility.

Unfortunately, the appeal to a distinct category of "public goods" rests on a semantic trick, since even though producers of these goods cannot reap all the benefits of their products, additional effort is still needed to enable that knowledge to benefit *everyone* (cf. Machlup 1984, 121–159). (A free rider should never be confused with a universal subject.) The collective goods version already draws attention to the problem, since according to Mancur Olson, they are maintained by keeping the access costs low for collective members and high for non-members: i.e., tax breaks for the natives and high tariffs for foreigners. In other words, the "universe" covered by the knowledge good is relative to a particular community, whose collective identity is reinforced by the presence of the good. Thus, an insight that originally took a genius, such as Einstein's theory of relativity, is supposedly now accessible to *anyone who can read a physics textbook*. The highlighted phrase reveals the hidden access costs of public goods (cf. Callon 1994). Einstein's efforts to arrive at relativity theory appear significantly greater than a student's efforts to understand it, only if it is presumed that the student already brings to the physics text the relevant background knowledge. But as a matter of fact, this background knowledge often does not come cheap (e.g., a university physics degree) or even well-marked in the text (e.g., obscure allusions and jargon). A text in relativity theory may thus be likened to a mass-produced toy, which costs little to purchase but then requires additional costs to be assembled.

The economic mystique of knowledge largely rests on keeping these access costs hidden. It is underwritten by the commonsense intuition that the "hard work" of invention or discovery comes with the original development of an idea, and that the subsequent work of transmitting, or "distributing," the idea to others is negligible by comparison. Economists tend to neglect the costs of distribution in these contexts because they talk about knowledge *production* in terms of the material good embodying the knowledge (e.g., Einstein's original articles), whereas they talk about knowledge *consumption* in terms of the knowledge "contained" in the material good (e.g., Einstein's ideas). Given this asymmetrical treatment, it is not surprising that knowledge has often struck economists as an enigma. But the puzzle is dissolved, and knowledge starts to look more like other goods, once the distribution of a knowledge good is included as part of the good's overall production costs. In that case, knowledge is necessarily knowledge *for someone*. As we shall see in Chapter 3, the advent of customized expert systems takes that additional step.

In short, the maintenance of public goods requires considerable work to ensure that everyone potentially has access to the goods. Provision for education and dissemination—normally tasks undertaken by the state bureaucracy—is the source of these hidden costs. They remain hidden because economists tend to conceptualize public goods in an equivocal fashion. *Prima facie*, the nature of the good itself is specified "objectively," while the value derived from the good is specified "subjectively" (Bartley 1990, 47–50). However, a clue to the problem with this interpretation is that the only aspect of subjectivity that interests public goods theorists is that one's possession of them can be described without reference to anyone else's possession, in which case such goods would appear to be *divisible* and hence quintessentially *private*.

Consider this point in light of a paradigm case of a public good. Although a town commons is supposed to be a public good, for all of the town's residents to benefit from the commons, they must *inter alia* occupy different plots at the same time or the same plot at different times. The semantic trick here involves conflating a distinction originally drawn by the Polish logician Stanislaw Leszniewski as part of a solution to Russell's paradox (Smith 1994, 213–225). The distinction contrasts the *distributive* and the *collective* interpretation of class terms. The key term in the logic of classes is "membership," which may be interpreted in two ways. "John Doe is a member of the public" may mean either that John is one instance of what "the public" signifies (distributive) or that he is a proper part of the thing called "the public" (collective). In that case, *a public good can be understood as a collectively defined product whose use is defined distributively.* Logicians nowadays would put the matter more harshly: the concept of public good results from equivocating between the "intensional" and "extensional" definitions of "good." Armed with such equivocation, one can reclassify virtually anything as a public good. That there happen to be relatively *few* public goods (at least of interest to economists) thus reflects some deeply held prejudices—masquerading as ontology—about the sorts of things that everyone should be compelled to maintain so that anyone can have access to them.

The equivocation between the distributive and collective interpretations of class terms obscures two sorts of devaluation that may befall public goods, each attributable to a kind of "overuse." For simplicity's sake, let us return to the town commons. On the one hand, overuse may imply that the plots are becoming dirtier and hence returning smaller benefits to users; on the other, overuse may result in each plot becoming smaller through an increase in the number of users sharing the commons simultaneously. In the one case, repeated usage degrades the good; in the other, increased division does so. These overuses become evident once public goods are also seen as positional goods, since their value can be ascertained only once one knows how many others possess the good. The bare fact that many benefit from a public good may lower its value for a potential consumer of that good. Thus, there are two ways by which the democratic extension of higher education may erode higher education's value as a public good: either as larger course enrollments lower the quality of instruction or as a larger number of academic degree-holders lowers the competitive advantage one receives from the degree.

Why has the equivocal character of public goods gone relatively unnoticed up to now? One reason may be that economists take for granted the background welfare-state conditions that have enabled such goods to appear "public." If public goods are akin to the prover-bial frictionless medium of intellectual exchange, then the welfare state contributes the relevant *ceteris paribus* clause. After all, absent regular government provision for activities such as park maintenance and educational quality assurance, the value afforded by the town commons and the university system would quickly devolve accord-ing to market-driven norms: those who can pay could gain access to an excellent private good; those who cannot would have to settle for an inferior product. Following Schumpeter (1950), it has become increasingly clear that what pass for "public goods" are part of the state's strategy for facilitating the circulation and accumulation of capital, at the same time buffering the citizenry from its worst effects. Little surprise, perhaps, that the knowledge manager's demystifica-tion of public goods occurs at a time when many national govern-ments are failing to serve both capital and citizens within tighter budgetary regimes and an ideological climate that precludes the most obvious solution, namely, higher taxes on the private enterprises that most directly benefit from a healthy supply of public goods, espe-cially education (cf. O'Connor 1973).

4.2. KM and the End of Knowledge in Practice: The Disintegration of the University

Joseph Schumpeter (1954, 536) usefully highlighted two alterna-tive goals for political economy that were hotly debated in the late 18th and early 19th centuries. They are captured by two Greek coinages of the period: *chrematistics* and *catallactics*. The former concerned the sheer accumulation of wealth, and the latter the ratio-nal organization of exchange relations. In this context, Adam Smith can be understood as having argued the delicate thesis that the "wealth of nations" is best pursued as a long-term strategy, the short-term focus of which is state provision of a free labor market that enables people to discover how they are most productively employed. In short, a catallactic orientation is a better means to chrematistic ends than the direct pursuit of chrematistics. Thus, Smith was unim-pressed by the displays of wealth that characterized the great Eastern empires and had been mimicked by Spain and France in their nation-building efforts from 1500 to 1750. In these cases, too much signifi-cance was attached to either the sheer quantity of bullion in the treasury (regardless of how it was spent) or the amount of goods produced (regardless of how many were sold).

Were Smith resurrected today as a KM guru, he would say that the state needs to invest in institutions that facilitate the development and mobility of human capital. Indeed, he might well warm to the phrase "social capital." In any case, he would steer his clients clear of policies that smacked of *academic bullionism*, namely, the sheer accumulation of "big names" at universities whose enormous salaries and discretionary time allow them to generate a load of publications, while doing nothing to nurture local talent or even to ensure that the big names' productivity has maximum impact—say, by establishing links with state, industry, or even other academics with the capacity of extending and applying the big names' ideas. In the long term, this expenditure on big names is more likely to be judged an instance of conspicuous consumption than a productive investment. This is not surprising, since academic bullionism began as a consequence of the literal form of bullionism that Smith originally targeted in *The Wealth of Nations* (1776).

Spain lavished much of the wealth it gained from New World precious metals on its university system, which by 1600 had consisted of 32 institutions (a figure matched by Germany in 1900) with 3% of males in attendance (a figure matched by the United States in 1900). The result was the world's first knowledge society: Its labor market had become so competitive that doctorates were required for entry into key state and church administrative posts (Collins 1998, 581–2). Many failed job seekers, such as Miguel de Cervantes, went on to found the Golden Age of Spanish literature by marketing their academic training to a more popular audience, thereby straddling the classical definitions of history and poetry. (Today that genre is called the novel.) Spain was also the largest publisher of academic works, most of which were scholastic syntheses that came to symbolize "useless learning" in the emerging Scientific and Industrial Revolutions. Indeed, the demonstrable waste of resources that characterized Spain's original knowledge society promoted an image of universities as bastions of decadent conservatism. This image began to change only in the early 19th century, when Wilhelm von Humboldt established the University of Berlin as an institution expressly devoted to the dissemination of *new* knowledge.

This cautionary tale of the first knowledge society should remind us that whether an expenditure counts as an instance of investment or consumption depends on the perceived returns. An antipathy to universities is one of the few sentiments common to the revolutionary European philosophers, scientists, and inventors who lived in the 200 years prior to Humboldt's institutional renovation. Virtually all, at some point, expressed a desire to see all the scholastic tomes eaten by worms, engulfed in flames, or otherwise erased from historical memory. For them, universities represented a waste of talent and effort that was an affront to humanity. Interestingly, a very similar attitude to one readily found in Galileo, Bacon, Descartes, and Hume was also found among the Muslims who legendarily torched the Library of Alexandria in 641 A.D. (Fuller and Gorman 1987). Before Edward Gibbon's revisionist account in *The Decline and Fall of the Roman Empire* (1788), this episode had been emblazoned in the Western psyche as the paradigm case of religious fanaticism triumphing over enlightened learning. As it happens, the celebrated Library was little more than an unorganized warehouse of stockpiled books. It did not so much advance human knowledge as demonstrate the wealth of the Pharaohs who could afford to acquire these books. Egypt's Muslim conquerors regarded this gesture as a blasphemous use of our God-given powers. Islam's own seminal contribution to KM was the deployment of its trading language, Arabic, to consolidate the Greco-Roman intellectual heritage for purposes of elaboration and evaluation. This was its ultimate legacy to the original European universities, whose charters enabled the autonomous pursuit of knowledge in a way that had been prohibited under Islamic law.

Knowledge management updates the spirit that led to the burning of the Library of Alexandria and the stigmatizing of universities during the Scientific and Industrial Revolutions. An ironic consequence of the traditional belief that knowledge is produced and consumed rather differently from other material goods is that its indefinite pursuit has been presumed to be an unmitigated good. This has led to a set of knowledge policies that, from a KM standpoint, look nothing short of superstitious (Fuller 1997, Chapter 4). The dogma of "trickle-down effects" (from knowledge production to economic well-being) codifies this superstition. Even the founder of "scientometrics," Derek de Solla Price (1978), had already seen that the best predictor of a research-intensive society is electricity consumption per capita—not, say, income per capita. (Think about the costs of maintaining research facilities, especially after the computer revolution.) In other words, a Martian scanning Earth's economic indicators would naturally conclude that so-called knowledge production is designed to show off how much wealth nations can afford to *waste*. ("Knowledge accumulation" would be a better phrase.) To be sure, this was Aristotle's original point about leisure as a prerequisite for pure inquiry, which Michael Polanyi (1957, 1962) promoted to a moral imperative, given the temptations to harness knowledge production to military–industrial concerns. Yet, knowledge managers fail to be impressed, and universities as the principal knowledge-producing institutions in modern society have responded unimpressively.

In the words of former *Fortune* editor Thomas Stewart (1997, 76), universities are "dumb organizations" that are "high on human capital" but "low on structural capital": A fast food chain such as McDonalds is a "smart organization" because it makes the most of its relatively ill-trained staff by maximizing the interconnectivity of the staff's activities. Business as usual in academia proceeds almost exactly in reverse, which is why its well-educated staff must be specifically required, if not begged, to attend department meetings and declare office hours. Thus, from a KM standpoint, the traditional university is a whole that is much less than the sum of its parts, and academic administrators are little more than high-paid custodians of car parks, classrooms, and other campus facilities. Imagine a firm whose goals are dictated almost entirely by the various trade unions from which its labor force is drawn. Each union has the final say on the performance standards to which its members are held. Management ensures that the firm's employees do not interfere with each other's work, without aspiring to any greater level of cooperation and coordination of effort. If we replace "trade union" with "academic discipline" or "professional association," the firm starts to look like a university.

However, universities have begun to take the "dumb organization" label to heart by modeling themselves on McDonalds' performance measures and the conclusions drawn from them. McDonalds famously records its success on its "golden arches" signs, not in such conventionally economic terms as profits, but the number of products sold—or rather, "served," which evokes (without demonstrating) the idea of "satisfied customers." This practice, limited to U.S. outlets, is a brilliant stroke of public relations in a country that fancies itself full of "informed" consumers. The genius of this move is to appeal to a quantitative indicator that can never decrease, yet at the same time it can suggest room for improvement. The downside of such an open-ended metric is that it can easily become an end in itself, which is precisely the situation in which British academia finds itself today. Unlike the United States, whose educational sector is constitutionally devolved to a mix of public and private institutions, the United Kingdom largely follows the European pattern of state centralization. Whereas the McDonalds mentality has typically entered U.S. education through the hiring of professional managers at particular institutions, in 1988 it became the official U.K. policy for higher education's accountability to the taxpayers. Thus, every 4–5 years, the United Kingdom is subjected to the Research Assessment Exercise (RAE), which ranks every discipline in every university. The result is a set of academic "league tables"—the implied metaphor is from football—that ranks every department at all of the U.K.'s 100-odd universities. These are then published in the leading broadsheet newspapers and become the basis for student choice, corporate sponsorship, and most of all, state funding.

In some respects, the RAE has been a clear success. Few academics have complained about it, which may be explained by the U.K.'s seemingly limitless sense of gamesmanship. (In the U.S., someone would have by now found something sufficiently unjust about the RAE's implementation to bring a lawsuit that would have halted the exercise.) Moreover, the U.K.'s research productivity has increased and become more prominent internationally. Indeed, the exercise is now emulated by other countries in need of an academic audit. It has even spawned, within the U.K., a periodic exercise in "teaching quality assessment" (TQA). Yet, whatever their respective merits, the RAE and TQA have little, if anything, to do with each other. The TQA is driven by a desire to maximize the number of highly skilled workers. And if well-trained workers continue to be paid less in the U.K. than in other parts of the world, TQA should contribute to an effective global market strategy. The motives behind RAE are more elusive, since a high rate of scientific publications and patents is more a striking indicator than an underlying cause of a nation's wealth. In the symbolic world of politics and public policy, this is not a trivial point but one worth keeping in perspective. In effect, the RAE is about the cultivation and identification of knowledge products that are "high quality" in a sense not unlike that of an unalloyed precious metal.

In short, because of some lingering superstitions about the instantaneous impact of new knowledge on social and economic well-being, an academic bullionist model of universities coexists with some KM-style knowledge policies. Thus, in his 1999 keynote address to the annual meeting of the Higher Education Funding Council of England, the United Kingdom's minister for science and technology (and heir to a major supermarket chain) Lord David Sainsbury praised academics on the following grounds: The United Kingdom has 1% of the world's population, does 6% of the world's science, produces 8% of the world's scientific publications, and gets 9% of the world's scientific journal citations—this despite a 20% reduction in government spending on scientific research over the last 10 years (i.e., since the end of the Cold War). Instead of querying the logic that links these statistics (e.g., is the accumulation of publications and citations anything more than bullionism?) or perhaps recommending that U.K. academics could make good use of *more* research funding, Sainsbury concluded that the results justified the continued use of RAE-led competitive rationing as a national funding policy, without necessarily increasing the overall pot of funds.

The problems with Sainsbury's assessment are manifold but not uncharacteristic of contemporary confusions over how exactly one assesses the state of knowledge production. I can only list the problems here, but together they provide a strong argument for knowledge management returning to basics:

1. Even academics working in public institutions are increasingly reliant on private funding for their research. Indeed, many are now virtually self-funding, often obtaining more than they would from public sector agencies. Yet, however helpful this development is to balancing state budgets, it does not constitute increased "productivity" as measured by "the most bang for the buck" principle.
2. But even if we accept that British research activity has become more productive, that may be an artifact of researchers being paid wages that are low relative to the quality of the work they do. After all, even in our high-tech world, most research expenditure is still for labor. A revisit to Marx's theory of surplus value may not be amiss here.
3. To what extent does funded research contribute to "human capital development," i.e., seeding the next generation of

researchers—say, through quality undergraduate education and graduate training—or, for that matter, the next generation of informed non-specialist consumers of new research?

4. Lacking a clear productive relationship between academic publications and economic well-being, perhaps the major long-term benefit of an increasingly competitive system is the unintended one of people exiting the mainstream knowledge production markets (i.e., academic appointments) in order to establish their own niches which, as with the Scientific and Industrial Revolutions, eventually "creatively destroy" those markets: Is the next Cervantes to be found among science-fiction writers and cyberwarriors?

5. BACK TO BASICS: REDISCOVERING THE VALUE OF KNOWLEDGE IN RENT, WAGE, PROFIT

Clearly we need to take a step back—indeed, to the beginning. Consider knowledge production from the three sources of income originally stipulated by Adam Smith: *rent*, *wage*, and *profit*. There are a couple of ways of motivating the relationship between these three entities, which are compared systematically in Figure 1.1. The first is to envisage them as forming an idealized historical sequence from pre-capitalist to capitalist modes of value assignment. The second involves focusing on their respective attitudes toward *time* as a measure of value. In the jargon of welfare economics, rent-seeking "discounts" the future in favor of the past, in that payment is made for things already done, even if that deters the ability to do something else later. In contrast, profit-seeking discounts in reverse, as it favors ongoing and likely future returns at the expense of past investments. Finally, wage-seeking sticks to the classical ideal of the labor theory of value, whereby one is simply paid for what one actually does, without reference to what has been or is likely to be done.

Rent is traditionally associated with income from land, but it carries some additional connotations. The payment of rent typically implies the need to remove a barrier in the way of achieving one's goals. For example, before setting up a factory, one must first pay rent on the land where the factory is to be built. Economists have traditionally disliked rent as a source of income because landowners do not need to do anything productive in order to exact rents from tenants: they simply need to own the land and perhaps maintain it

SOURCE OF INCOME	RENT	WAGE	PROFIT
FRAME OF REFERENCE	"Science" (a body of knowledge)	"Scientist" (the professional)	"Scientific" (the character of things)
KNOWLEDGE IS . . .	What you build on	What you do	What you provide
VIRTUE OF KNOWLEDGE	Authority	Craft	Efficiency
EPISTEMOLOGY	Foundational	Practical	Instrumental
AIM OF KNOWLEDGE	Power through craft	Craft at the expense of power	Power at the expense of craft
"DIVISION OF LABOR" MEANS	Expert deference	Team cooperation	Comparative advantage
LABOR MARKET STRATEGY	Restrict entry	Promote entry and restrict exit	Promote exit
PAYMENT FOR KNOWLEDGE	Grant (for past performance)	Salary (for ongoing work)	Prize (for finished product)
"PROGRESS" MEANS	Completing a world-picture	Refining a tradition	Diffusing an innovation
"NATURE" MEANS	Property to be staked out	Raw material to be shaped	Obstacle to be overcome
THE EFFECT OF CODIFICATION ON KNOWLEDGE	Adds value by explaining craft	Orthogonal to craft's tacit nature	Subtracts value by cheaply replacing craft
ECONOMIC ABSTRACTION	Tribute	Labor	Utility
LIMIT CONCEPT	Credentials	Artisanship	Automation

Figure 1.1.
Three potential sources of value in knowledge production

at a level that is attractive to potential tenants. As long as producers do not already own land, and land is scarce, it will be rational for landowners to charge them rent. Of course, the *rentiers* may not wish to lease the land at all. In that case, they refuse to create the conditions for economic growth because they are under no pressure to risk potentially unreliable tenants. Analogously, economically secure academics—say, career civil servants whose livelihood is based on the training and examination of the new generation of recruits to their ranks—are not especially motivated to overturn existing knowledge regimes. This has often been cited as an important factor in explaining why the politically and economically more advanced societies of China and India did not foster the climate of innovation that eventuated in Europe's "Scientific Revolution" (Collins 1998, Chapter 10).

From a KM standpoint, the need to qualify in academic forms of knowledge in order to gain professional accreditation—be it business, engineering, law, or medicine—may be seen as a form of intellectual rent that is imposed on the student (cf. Tullock and McKenzie 1975). Is knowledge of economics really necessary to succeed in business? Is physics necessary to succeed in engineering? Is biology necessary to succeed in medicine? Until the early 20th century, the answer to all these questions was no. But now the answer is yes, because one is not "licensed" to practice these professions, unless one first has acquired the relevant university training. In the past, professionals were known for their track record; now increasingly it is for their credentials (Collins 1979). In a sense, one could tell the story of the rise of academic power in the 20th century as a matter of turning ever larger portions of everyday life into intellectual real estate to which academic disciplines hold the deeds. The map of this real estate is often called a "world-picture" that allows access to a "domain of reality." (Note the spatial metaphors associated with this conception of knowledge.)

But it would be a mistake to regard epistemic rent-seeking as entirely a matter of academics restricting the entry of non-academics to their ranks. A version of the same practice transpires inside academia, albeit more subtly, since academics are trained, in effect, to pay rents before they are formally demanded. I refer here to that abstract act of tribute involved in crediting another academic with part of one's own work in the form of a citation (Fuller 1997, Chapter 4; Fuller 2000a, Chapter 5). As in Mafia-style relations, preemptive payment is often intended less as ancestor worship than as insurance against future harm in the peer review process, a point to which I shall return in the next chapter.

Notwithstanding the apparent cynicism of my remarks, the pursuit of academic knowledge is not entirely reducible to rent-seeking, since it is not clear who would take a personal interest in upholding standards in the knowledge that is allowed to circulate around society, were it not for academics. Left to their devices, businesspeople and other professionals may prefer a free market environment, where knowledge claims are made willy-nilly and the consumer is simply told "Let the buyer beware!" This function of academic knowledge corresponds to the historic role that aristocratic landowners have played in conserving the land from corner-cutting factory-builders and housing developers. One can think of the important roles played by state-commissioned academic laboratories in testing products before they are marketed and informing the patent office on how (if!) an invention can be understood as the application of known scientific principles (Fuller 2000a, Chapter 6). Some of this perspective survives in the cultivation of "metapublic goods," which are discussed in the next section.

Wage is income paid according to the amount of labor performed. Although presumably this labor is performed in aid of making goods that can then be sold at market, the crucial feature of wages is that they are paid simply for doing the work, regardless of the price at which the goods are sold. When people talk about the pursuit of knowledge as "an end in itself," the wage conception is normally implied. In contrast with the rent-seeking landowner image, the wage conception is associated more with farmers who enjoy getting their hands dirty in the art of raising crops, regardless of how much land they own or how much their crops fetch at market. Scientific work is often discussed in these terms, especially given the unpredictable relation between the effort expended in the laboratory and the ultimate impact of the knowledge produced in that setting. In this respect, Max Weber's (1958) exhortation to new recruits to the academic ranks, "Science as a Vocation," is a classic expression of what I am calling the wage orientation.

Economists have observed that the differences in salary among academics is not as wide as the differences in their research productivity would predict: strong producers do not usually earn that much more than weak producers (Frank 1984). Indeed, an awareness of this fact helps explain the attraction that the world of science parks, intellectual property, and related business ventures has held for more entrepreneurial scientists. The usual justification for salary compression is that academics primarily pursue knowledge because that is what they want to do, not because they intend to come up with lucrative findings, etc. In addition, since academic markets are defined more vaguely than commercial markets, there is no clear measure of value, or "bottom line," that determines the worth of a particular piece of academic knowledge. Finally, there is a long tradition—perhaps superstitious—that claims that some of the most important findings are made as a by-product of inquirers just following their curiosity without any preconceived goals. All of this points to the wage conception.

It is important to appreciate the difference between the wage and rent conceptions of knowledge because academics like to see themselves in terms of the former, not the latter. Consequently, modes of payment that formally acknowledge social capital, and hence reward credentials or past achievements, are often subject to controversy within the academic community. For example, grants for research are typically made on the basis of one's reputation in the field, which tends to reinforce the distinction between the "haves" and "have nots" in academia: if you have not already done something significant, you are unlikely to get a grant to do something significant. Rarely are grants given simply for the quality of the proposal alone. The grant system thus operates—often quite explicitly—to promote and inhibit certain lines of inquiry, depending on their relationship to what has already been done. For that reason, less orthodox academics often forgo the usual grant agencies and seek private funding, which tends to be awarded in a more overtly speculative fashion, in the spirit of a venture capitalist or prospector.

This brings us to the third form of income, *profit,* which is traditionally the return on the investment of land and labor, as determined by the price that goods fetch at market. The basic idea is that you manage to get back something more than you originally put in. The "scientific" way to pursue profit is to defer any discounting of the future, by spending the time now to understand something deeply, so that you can act more efficiently in the future. Of course, trial-and-error can often produce the same results as scientifically informed inquiries, but usually it takes longer, since the innovator cannot take advantage of the organized memory of academic knowledge—and often this extra time is not available. From a business standpoint, the problem may boil down to knowing enough of the language that academics use to be able to access what one needs to know. In that case, great value should be placed on people who can "decode," "translate," and otherwise remove the linguistic barriers to accessing academic knowledge. With this aim in view, Executive Ph.D. programs, co-sponsored by academia and business, have emerged that are designed to equip middle managers with the research skills needed to exploit the commercial potential of the knowledge base contained in the scientific literature. (I shall raise countervailing dimensions of these programs in the next section.)

Clearly, the value that the profit-seeker places on knowledge is the most removed from the academic ethos. To see just how non-academic it is, consider the various ways in which one might place a value on knowledge of arithmetic. For the profit-seeker, the value of arithmetic is as a systematic form of calculation that provides significant shortcuts to counting. The next logical step for the profit-seeker is to figure out how to mechanize this knowledge, so that people do not have to do the arithmetic themselves, but can delegate it to a piece of technology. Although it might initially take a while to develop such a technology, the effort would be endlessly repaid in terms of the amount of time and energy saved whenever a calculation needs to be made. For the profit-seeker, then, knowledge is quite literally a necessary evil: the more necessary, the more evil—hence, the impulse to move it out of the mind and into the environment. Perhaps the purest case of the profit-seeker's approach to knowledge is Donald Norman (1993), the cognitive scientist who popularized the design of "smart environments" that enable people to "offload" routine knowledge from their brains to their surroundings so they can think about emergent issues.

Rent- and wage-seeking knowledge producers see the matter much differently. For the rent-seeker, the codification of arithmetic means that one does not fully understand how to calculate if he or she does not know the fundamental principles that render the calculations valid. Acquiring this knowledge entails taking courses and passing examinations in arithmetic. The wage-seeker is interested in arithmetic as an inherently valuable mental skill, regardless of the uses to which it can be put. Indeed, the wage-seeker is likely to discover paradoxes and puzzles by pursuing the logic of arithmetic thought wherever it may lead. Nevertheless, both the rent- and the wage-seeker want to ensure that those interested in arithmetic undergo formal training. Consequently, both would regard the profit-seeker's interest in mechanizing arithmetic as potentially depriving them of their livelihood, much as automation has historically made redundant much of the industrial labor force. In other words, the profit-seeker is rewarded solely for actual results, not for sheer effort or past track record. However, she may benefit from rent- and wage-seeking knowledge producers—the former providing quality control checks and the latter a sense of exploratory openness—that may otherwise be crowded out by the competitive environment of the marketplace.

The unique contribution of Western science to knowledge production has been to enable the scientist's craft to maintain its autonomy against tendencies toward devolution to either a priesthood (i.e., rent-driven) or a technology (i.e., profit-driven). The university is the institution most responsible for enabling scientists to stay the course, but its restraining power has been considerably eroded in recent years through the introduction of market forces. On the one hand, education is devolving into a credentials mill; on the other, research is devolving into intellectual property. As a result, that archetypal knowledge producer, the academic scientist, is becoming a role divided against itself.

Of course, science may internally manifest profit-seeking or wage-seeking tendencies but appear to be primarily rent-seeking with respect to the larger society. In other words, whatever competitiveness exists *within* science may be offset by the barriers that prevent people from entering the competitive field. The cost of acquiring the right credentials most immediately comes to mind. At the beginning of the 20th century, it was still common for amateurs to contribute to scientific journals—much less so today.

However, in some important respects, the rent-seeking tendencies of science have yielded to the profit paradigm, as universities increase their dependency on researchers and teachers on fixed-term contracts. The "harder" sciences tend to bear the brunt of the contract researchers, whereas the "softer" sciences absorb more of the contract teachers. The difference reflects the source of income: lucrative grants versus student enrollments. Both types of knowledge workers are oriented more toward delivering their goods and services *just-in-time* than developing long-term skills likely to result in an improvement of the academic base, something knowledge managers deride as *just-in-case* knowledge (Stewart 1997, 131). The latter is meant to conjure up an Alexandrian image of libraries as warehouses full of stockpiled knowledge products for which there is no clear immediate demand. Not surprisingly, library budgets have been generally cut, and more academic journals require an author-generated subsidy for publication.

Figure 1.1 summarized the sources of income in classical political economy as three potential sources for assigning value in knowledge production. Despite their palpable differences, all three perspectives accept the validity of the Baconian equation, *Knowledge Is Power.* However, each interprets the equation differently. When knowledge is a source of rent, power is exerted as a delaying or inhibiting factor in others' action. When knowledge is a source of profit, power resides in the ability to remove barriers to action. And when knowledge is a source of wage, power coincides with the control that knowledge producers have over their own collective activity. To be sure, any form of knowledge contains power in all three senses, since any knowledge-producing community is simultaneously maintaining its position in the present (wage), displacing others who occupied its position in the past (profit), and preventing others from occupying its position in the future (rent). However, depending on the non-epistemic goals of the community, any one of these three orientations may come to predominate over the others.

Given the negative value normally attached to rent-oriented forms of knowledge, I should observe that even here much depends on the exact source of rent. Before natural science research cost taxpayers so much that universities could demand overheads to fund disciplines with less lucrative research prospects (i.e., the humanities and social sciences), universities had been seen largely as teaching institutions. It was almost only as an afterthought that universities allowed researchers to gather together. Over time this has enabled professional academic associations—or at least recognized disciplinary identities—to exert perhaps an undue amount of moral pressure on university administrators (cf. Fuller 1993b, 48–55). When knowledge managers dub universities "dumb organizations," they are merely tapping into this history. From their standpoint, a university looks like a firm with no ends of its own, other than the ones that representatives of various areas of work (labor unions?) negotiate among themselves. But as it turns out, the call to fiscal responsibility is forcing universities to take greater control of their own fates. That in itself is not a problem. Problems can arise, however, if universities model their cost-accounting procedures too closely on what they imagine a knowledge manager would do under similar circumstances.

6. THE EPISTEMIC EMPIRE STRIKES BACK: METAPUBLIC GOODS AND THE INJECTION OF ACADEMIC VALUES INTO CORPORATE ENTERPRISE

KM's "brave new world" appears to be one in which knowledge production is deprofessionalized and perhaps even de-skilled, as the teaching and research functions of the university are subjected to increasingly polarized demands. All of this is in the name of the profit orientation to knowledge. For some this institutional meltdown is returning us to the liberating conditions of the original Industrial Revolution. Yet, there is also reason to believe that both business and government are slowly rediscovering what academics have traditionally done better than anyone else, namely, give a shape and direction to entire bodies of knowledge. As we shall now see, these two tendencies are not completely opposed.

In the annals of knowledge management, much is made of the fact that James Watt perfected the steam engine with hardly any formal academic training. Much less is made of his correspondence with Edinburgh University chemist Joseph Black, who helped Watt understand why certain prototypes of the engine did and did not work. Whatever the virtues of "trial-and-error" learning, it is difficult to deny that access to an organized collective memory base can help economize on time and effort—especially when, as in the Watt–Black exchange, no consultancy fees are charged. Closer to our own time are the industrially funded teams that brought to life such interdisciplinary fields as molecular biology and artificial intelligence. Knowledge managers stress the frustration that the pioneering scientists felt within the disciplinary confines of their home universities, without giving proper due to the subsequent establishment of university departments and academic degree programs, which ultimately ensured that these fields remained in the public domain as scientific knowledge, rather than being converted into trade secrets and other bits of intellectual real estate.

The combination of efficiency, systematicity, and publicity highlighted in these historical cases points to the institutional uniqueness of universities. They are virtues that even business has begun to appreciate, as firms suffer from *corporate amnesia* (Kransdorff 1998), the negative by-product of quickly formed, flexibly organized associations of providers and clients. Although the existence of these nimble networks has enabled the business community to adapt to a changing competitive environment, the only knowledge traces they leave are those embodied in their constitutive nodes and joint products. But once a network's mission is accomplished, its human nodes simply disperse and connect with other nodes to form new networks in pursuit of new projects. The precedent for this diabolical situation is captured by the phrase "market failure," which is the economist's way of talking about goods that markets fail to generate because no one finds it in their interest to produce them. This is because the cost of producing the goods can never be completely recovered in profits. In welfare economics, market failure defines the frontier that justifies state provision of public goods. Similarly, we may speak of the role of universities in redressing *network failure* by reproducing and extending knowledge that might otherwise be lost through network dispersion.

Knowledge managers have yet to realize the full significance of universities in this capacity because they tend to diagnose network failure much too locally, as mere instances of "knowledge hoarding." The idea here is that companies become dependent on the services of certain employees—often IT personnel—who do not make their knowledge directly available. We are asked to envisage these human nodes as blocking the flow of information in the network by refusing to share what they know with the other nodes. Thus, the knowledge hoarder appears as a moral failure who needs to be taught greater concern for her colleagues. Little is said about the emergence of knowledge hoarding as a defensive strategy for remaining employed or even employable in the knowledge economy's volatile labor market. The KM targeting of the individual knowledge hoarder aims to ensure that firms receive an adequate return on their "knowledge investments," as measured by the clients, contacts, or Web links that employees accumulate. It is very much the point of view of managers trying to keep their firms afloat. However, from a more global perspective the tendency of knowledge to escape from its formative networks may be seen as a positive market mechanism for counteracting the *corporate hoarding* of knowledge, which could result in that ultimate blockage of free exchange, a monopoly.

In a related context, Michael Perelman (1991) has introduced the concept of *metapublic goods*, which attempts to resurrect some key features of public goods in a market where the leading producers exert imperfect control over the flow of their goods, so that free riders and pirates flourish in a parallel "black market." The most realistic setting for "creative destruction" of an existing market—and hence the production of new knowledge—is where a barrier is placed to achieving ends by the usual means, which then demands that one come up with legal or illegal alternative means. The most obvious barrier is the temporary monopoly afforded to a patent holder, but it may be simply the fact that knowledge is transmitted neither instantaneously nor intact; rather, its transmission requires effort on the part of both sender and receiver, which is not always completely successful. Of special relevance here are two groups: (a) those who fail to receive the message intended for them and (b) those who receive the message despite its not being intended for them.

The trial-and-error character of these efforts indirectly generates its own knowledge base, a metapublic good. The more people involved in this process, the smarter the collective. This process is epitomized by the activities surrounding software piracy. These goods may be generated in two complementary ways: on the one hand, the manufacturer (say, Microsoft) does not catch the bugs in its latest software, but a self-organized user group does and then takes the initiative to remove them; on the other, instead of dispersing or even regulating the user group, the manufacturer exploits the group's findings in designing new software. In short, metapublic goods flourish because it is more cost-effective for corporations to learn from pirates than to prosecute them for piracy.

As my last comment suggests, metapublic goods differ significantly from public goods in that their provision is not maintained by the state. Rather, metapublic goods are unintended consequences of market activity that market leaders can then strategically convert to the usual divisible goods. Universities may be able to counteract this tendency and thereby perform a crucial role in the maintenance of metapublic goods. In other words, universities institutionalize *knowledge escape* so as to redistribute the corporate advantage accumulated in a firm's staff, databases, and intellectual property. Classically this task has involved synthesizing disparate cases from their original contexts of discovery and inferring larger explanatory principles, which are then subject to further study and ultimately dissemination through teaching and publication. This was certainly William Whewell's original vision of the "scientist's" profession. Nowadays these activities extend beyond contemplating the design of nature to "troubleshooting" and "reverse engineering" products to enable their improvement and even replacement (Fuller 2000a, Chapters 6, 7). *In short, universities function as knowledge trust-busters whose own corporate capacities of "creative destruction" prevent new knowledge from turning into intellectual property.*

But academia can penetrate corporate knowledge practices beyond being an institutionalized "loyal opposition" to the marketplace. Perhaps the most hopeful sign is the establishment of the Executive Ph.D. as a degree program in business schools. The pilot for this program, appropriately called "Fenix" ("phoenix"), began as a joint venture between the highest levels of academia and business in Sweden. (The Web site is http://www.fenix.chalmers.se.) Academia is represented by the Chalmers University of Technology (Sweden's answer to MIT or Imperial College) and the Stockholm School of Economics. Business is represented by most of the major Swedish multinational corporations, including Volvo, Ericsson, and AstraZeneca. The premise behind this program is that the business world is much too dynamic today and hence needs to recover the qualities of mind that have enabled academics to sustain collective bodies of knowledge that not only survive changes in fashion, but also provide standards for evaluating new forms of knowledge. Being on top of the latest trend makes good business sense only if the trend is likely to leave a lasting trace. Otherwise, one risks wasting effort now and suffering obsolescence later—"overadaptation" in the jargon of evolutionary biology. Moreover, as corporations come to regard themselves as potential victims of a mobile labor force, they have begun to appreciate the standpoint of the "knowledge disadvantaged," which in turn renders the public-good conception of knowledge more attractive than perhaps it previously seemed.

Business initially wanted to tap into what was imagined to be an unfathomed wealth of knowledge lodged in esoteric texts and inscrutable databases. Thus, "advanced research skills" were seen as enabling middle managers to subject the scientific literature to such favored KM activities as "mining" and "prospecting." However, as the Executive Ph.D. program has evolved, the sense of what counts as "metal" and "ore" has shifted from a hardcore KM orientation to one more attuned with academic values. Indeed, some have claimed that the Executive Ph.D. might create a "virtual academic commons" (Hellstrom 2002) in the business world. The clearest example of the relevant gestalt switch is the move away from thinking that some brute sense of "information" is the metal that needs to be extracted from its orelike theoretical and methodological encasement. Instead, these budding "doctors of business" come to regard this encasement not so differently from how stock market analysts think of "fundamental" indicators. One learns not to be too impressed by a striking research result, unless one is in a position to judge the robustness of the theory and method that inform it. Judgments of this sort usually involve some knowledge of the history of the research field in question.

An easily overlooked feature of the Executive Ph.D. program is that its academic staff consists mainly of contract researchers who were drawn into paid collaboration with business because of the paucity of regular academic posts. Often the collaboration results in the contract researcher adopting habits associated with the business world, notably a penchant for problem-oriented thinking aimed at practical short-term solutions. This can then make it difficult for the contract researcher to become reintegrated into academic culture, once a regular post opens up, and at a deeper level can engender hostility to the distinctive institutions of that culture, such as peer review, tenure, and the value of basic research. However, the exact opposite occurs as well, whereby the staff of the Executive Ph.D. program serve as *de facto* academic ambassadors and perhaps even colonizers (Jacob and Hellstrom 2000). Thus, business doctoral students acquire habits of mind that were not part of their undergraduate degree training (usually in narrow technical subjects) and that have not been especially fostered in the business environments where they have been working. These include a tolerance, respect, and capacity for sustained reading, rigor, abstraction, synthesis, and criticism.

Indeed, the Executive Ph.D. program addresses the problem of corporate amnesia quite literally by teaching students how to institutionalize a corporate conversation that continually rehearses the history and re-plots the aims of the organization in light of current practice. At a metaphysical level, this conversation constructs what might be called the "subjectivity" or "conscience" of the firm. In practice, it amounts to keeping written records of corporate goals that can be used to evaluate subsequent performance and changes of the collective mind. Regardless of the firm's actual market performance, an academically informed corporate subjectivity would adopt the standpoint of a player who has yet to win. Thus, one would aim, not for conservative adjustments to the current market paradigm, but to "creatively destroy" the paradigm by introducing new products that force competitors to rethink their market strategy.

The spread of Executive Ph.D. programs will not necessarily rescue academia from KM's tendency toward bottom-line thinking. After all, the contemporary university does suffer from a fundamental structural weakness. The teaching function, which is organized in terms of rigidly defined departments, works at cross purposes with the research function, which favors largely self-organizing interdisciplinary teams. There is no doubt that this tension has only worsened in recent years. Research activities—be they in the lab or in the field —have required more time and space away from the preparation and delivery of courses. It may well be, then, that knowledge managers will persuade universities of the cost-effectiveness of allowing research to migrate off their grounds. In time research would become completely outsourced to facilities specially tailored to the needs of major clients. Academic employees would be then left with the perennial job of filling classrooms. But by the time this scenario comes to pass, one may hope that there will be enough holders of Executive Ph.D. degrees in public and private sector administration to undo the damage that will have been done.

7. Squaring the KM Circle: Who's Afraid of Accelerating the Production of New Knowledge?

That innovation can reconfigure markets for purposes of unleashing new sources of wealth is as old as capitalism itself. What is relatively new—and still controversial—is the idea that the production of new knowledge should be promoted explicitly and always. For example, two economists who have been among the most astute theorists of innovation, Thorstein Veblen and Joseph Schumpeter, were suspicious of both the motives and consequences of the promiscuous pursuit of new knowledge. Veblen (1904) saw endless innovation as motivated by "businessmen" (i.e., the corporate marketing division) who persuade investors to prefer the future over the present, thereby undermining the value of what workers currently do. For his part, Schumpeter (1950) saw the relationship between innovation and corporate survival as akin to that of charisma and routinization, according to Max Weber. In other words, persistent market instability will eventually lead the state and industry to agree to discourage speculative investments in new knowledge. In Veblen's telling, endless innovation is unfair to the ordinary worker; in Schumpeter's, it is systemically unsustainable. Nevertheless, the Holy Grail of contemporary knowledge management is that knowledge growth can be deliberately accelerated.

To be sure, this goal also flies in the face of philosophical wisdom, which claims that, as a matter of principle, scientific progress cannot be predicted or planned. This "principle" is typically presented as a matter of logic, but it is better seen as a matter of ethics. The main issues concern whether (or under what conditions) one *ought* to accelerate knowledge growth—not *whether* it can be done at all, since the answer to that question is clearly *yes*.

Skepticism about the predictability of knowledge growth was born of extreme tendencies exhibited by capitalist and socialist regimes that first became clear in the 1920s. They are associated with so-called *self-fulfilling* and *self-defeating* prophecies, which occur whenever a prediction functions as a communication to those whose behavior is being predicted, who can then respond by either enabling or disabling the prediction's realization. In this way, we can explain both the fluctuation of prices in the open market and the single-mindedness of social policies in an authoritarian regime. Specifically, we can explain, on the one hand, how fortunes were made and lost through speculation, culminating in the stock market crash of 1929 that launched the Great Depression, and on the other, Soviet and Nazi beliefs in the laws of history that motivated atrocities that would have been unthinkable, had their perpetrators not thought they knew which way the future pointed.

The basic argument against the possibility of planned knowledge growth is simply that *by definition* a genuine scientific discovery cannot be predicted or planned. Those who claim otherwise are therefore dealing in hype. This susceptibility to hype was born of the 1920s, the first great period for stock speculation purportedly based on scientific innovation (Chancellor 1999, Chapter 7). Yet, often the innovations were not forthcoming—though they managed to generate major investments in the interim—or their significance was oversold by advertising agencies, whose recent emergence presupposed that products had become too sophisticated to sell themselves. In the latter case, the "innovation" may have merely added a wrinkle or an efficiency to an already existing demand for a good or service.

In addition, the skeptics usually make certain assumptions about the nature of reality:

(A1) Our inquiries initially have a low probability of capturing the aspects of reality that interest us.

(A2) There is a direct correlation between the significance of a scientific discovery and the degree of surprise it brings to those who make it. In other words, a quantum leap in knowledge growth should always be counterintuitive to those who have been monitoring the course of inquiry.

Nevertheless, even if assumption A1 is true, it does not follow that assumption A2 is also true. To think that it does is to deny that people collectively learn from particular discoveries so as to improve their ability to make discoveries in the future. Once this point is granted, the main logical objection to accelerating the growth of knowledge is overcome. Speculative investments on prospective revolutionary breakthroughs are thus not irrational. Kuhn (1970, Chapter 11) has observed that scientific revolutions tend to be "invisible" because they are generally recognized as such only after the fact. Of course, it is hard to ignore a controversy while it is happening, but the overall direction of its resolution is known only in retrospect, once official histories of the episode are written which distinguish clear winners and losers. These verdicts track the students, professorships, and other academic resources the various sides managed to accumulate in the process. Moreover, there is typically some mystery as to what the controversy that resulted in the revolution was really about— beyond simply the distribution of social, political, and economic resources to the next generation of inquirers. Since official histories are calculated to place the winners in the most favorable light, they often ignore the fundamental issues that originally divided the disputants.

In this context, Fuller's (1988, Chapter 5) "social epistemology" develops Kuhn's concept of *incommensurability*, the non-negotiable differences that lead to the winner-take-all outcomes of scientific revolutions. But unlike Kuhn, I argue that these differences are not deeply metaphysical but themselves artifacts of an institutionalized communication breakdown between kindred intellectual factions, which in principle can be either maximized or minimized, depending on what we know and want out of our knowledge claims. (For an innovative and systematic use of computer simulations to track the relationship between communication network formations and knowledge distribution, see Carley and Kaufer 1993.) In other words, the "unpredictability" of radical scientific change may be purely a function of our ignorance of how our own knowledge processes work, rather than a sign of some unbridgeable disparity between our state of knowledge and the nature of reality. If we knew our own knowledge processes better, we might not be so surprised by what is and is not possible. In that sense, a high incidence of first-order revolutionary breakthroughs could be treated as symptomatic of low control over second-order knowledge processes.

If scientists were regularly compelled to declare shifts in their research commitments—and not only through a self-selecting, partly devolved, semi-secret peer review system—then revolutions could be standardized as periodic election-like events, the outcomes of which would provide regular feedback to remove the surprise and disruptiveness that characterize revolutions. It would not simply be left to the vicissitudes of the stock market. Indeed, this sublimation of the revolutionary impulse by the electoral process is one of the great innovations of civic republican democracy from which science as socially organized inquiry might learn. (I explore this civic republican alternative in Chapter 4: cf. Fuller 2000a, Chapter 8.)

However, a potential casualty of this institutional innovation may be that science itself no longer appears to exhibit striking innovation. The reason, of course, is that scientists would be regularly invited to consider altering their inquiries, rather than having to bear the burden of forcing innovation on a system that refuses to change course unless its guiding principle has failed on its own terms. The need for heroics would be thereby eliminated. Indeed, Kuhn himself distinguished scientific from artistic revolutions precisely on these grounds, suggesting that only science—by virtue of its normally monolithic paradigm structure—had proper revolutions that overturned an existing order. In contrast, so-called artistic revolutions have merely demonstrated the ability of a countercurrent to survive alongside the dominant one (Kuhn 1977, 225–239). Applying this insight from science, politics, and art to business, the implication is clear: *The desire for and recognition of innovation increases as normal market conditions approach monopoly.*

A more sophisticated argument against planned knowledge growth is that even if someone thought he or she could predict or plan scientific progress, humans are free to determine whether or not it happens. This argument also makes some assumptions of its own:

(B1) The people whose behavior is predicted or planned know that their behavior has been predicted or planned.

(B2) Those people are in a position to prevent or, in some other way, divert what others have predicted or planned.

Note that B1 and B2 are independent claims. For example, I may know that you have predicted something about me, yet I may be in no position to do anything about it. We see this whenever a physician diagnoses someone with a terminal illness. That possibility cuts against self-defeating prophecies. Conversely, I may be able to prevent your prediction from coming true without realizing it, perhaps because my behavior may not be as consistent as you (or I) think, for example, because of unforeseen interactions between genetic dispositions and behavioral patterns. That cuts against self-fulfilling prophecies.

The advancement of social science research has not tended to increase the number of self-fulfilling and self-defeating prophecies. This is because people exposed to knowledge claims about themselves typically cannot relate the concepts used in those claims to anything they feel they have power over. Often this is because people do not know how to reorganize themselves in the relevant ways, either as collectives (in response to socioeconomic predictions) or as individuals (in response to health predictions). But sometimes people simply do not understand the claims. In that respect, when the knowledge claims of social scientists go over the heads of lay people, the latter are behaving rather like the animals and things that are incapable of grasping what natural scientists say about them. Moreover, that is often a necessary (though not sufficient) condition for those claims being true—because if people knew what was being asserted about their situations, they might take steps to either enhance or diminish the truth of those assertions. The classic case of the latter was

Bismarck's creation of the world's first social security system for industrial workers specifically in order to preempt Marx's prediction that the proletarian revolution would originate in Germany.

In short, new knowledge *can* be predicted—but only given a strict boundary (hierarchy?) between the knowledgeable and the ignorant. The difference between socialism and capitalism as policy regimes lies in how the boundary is drawn. If socialism institutionalizes the boundary *a priori*, capitalism allows it to emerge *a posteriori*. In this respect, the central planner and market speculator are two sides of the same coin. The former knows at the outset that his knowledge is superior (and has the political might to make it so), whereas the latter takes risks to discover whether his is. That speculator *par excellence* George Soros (1998) has argued that capitalism tolerates a dangerous level of uncertainty in the name of greed, gamesmanship, and the pursuit of novelty. In contrast, socialism's strong suit has been its ability to contain this volatile side of humanity, albeit often at the cost of stifling innovation and inhibiting risk-taking altogether (Schumpeter 1950). Knowledge management, then, is about planning for what might be called "tolerable variation" or "sustainable change" in the firm, state, university, or any other organization. Fuller (2000c) uses the term *reversibility*, which Karl Popper (1957) originally adapted from thermodynamics. The basic idea is that, as opposed to the popular economic doctrine of the "path dependence" of scientific and technological change, "progress" would be measured by the increased receptiveness to changing a course of action once its negative consequences have outweighed its positive ones for sufficiently many over a sufficiently long period.

This principle of knowledge policy reversibility, which Popper himself dubbed "negative utilitarianism," brings us to two explicitly *ethical* objections to deliberate attempts to accelerate the growth of knowledge.

1. The most efficient ways to learn more about reality—especially social reality—always seem to involve violating the integrity of human beings. The horrors of Nazi science come to mind most readily. But we could equally include, say, traditional religious objections to opening corpses for medical and scientific purposes.
2. Any new discoveries made by a knowledge acceleration scheme would benefit those who made (or funded) the discoveries, at

the expense of others, which may in turn adversely affect power relations in society.

There are substantial historical precedents for both objections, but they do not imply that the knowledge growth cannot, or even should not, be accelerated. All they imply is that the appropriate background social conditions must first be in place, so as to prevent the occurrence of these adverse ethical consequences. Just as the Great Depression led to the establishment of regulatory bodies (e.g., the U.S. Securities and Exchange Commission) to monitor stock market activities, something similar may be needed once knowledge acceleration becomes a financially viable practice.

So far I have only cleared a space for programs designed to accelerate the growth of knowledge. I have yet to justify the *desirability* of such programs. In terms of the *Realpolitik* of capitalism, such a program would be no more radical than Frederick Winslow Taylor's original program in "scientific management." Taylor assumed that normal performance is not necessarily the best possible and that those who do the work are not necessarily in the best position to judge how to improve its performance. The point now would be to transfer these insights from the industrial to the scientific workplace (cf. Fuller 1993b, 307–311). Research in the sociology and social psychology of science generally shows that scientific innovation is mostly determined by the organization of the scientific work environment (Shadish and Fuller 1994). This is because even individuals with scientific training are subject to the same sorts of biases and incapacities as ordinary reasoners (Faust 1985, Arkes and Hammond 1986). What has been traditionally called "the scientific method" is nothing more than an abstract characterization of how people and things need to be arranged in order for the whole to be greater than the sum of its parts (Fuller 1993a, Fuller 1994a).

Presumably, then, the rate of scientific knowledge production can be increased by applying this method to science itself. But in order to ensure the success of such a knowledge acceleration program, potential managers and investors should bear in mind three things:

1. The confidence and trust of the scientific community need to be secured. Scientists must come to see it as in their own interest to cooperate with knowledge acceleration schemes. This may be the main negative lesson of Taylorism, which failed because

it appealed to management by going over the heads of the very workers who would be most directly affected by its scientific approach. A similar skepticism and resistance explains why scientists have been relatively uncooperative with psychologists and sociologists interested in studying their patterns of work and reasoning. To date, most studies with an explicit interest in improving scientific performance have been done on either computer simulations (Fuller 1995) or so-called "analogue populations" (e.g., students are given problems that resemble scientific ones: cf. Tweney et al. 1981). There have also been many insightful comparative studies of knowledge production based on ethnographic and historical methods, but these rarely draw any lessons for how knowledge production may be improved (e.g., Pickering 1992). They tend to assume that what is, is good enough.

2. As the pursuit of scientific knowledge has become more expensive and its prospect of improving wealth production more evident, scientists are being increasingly pressured—by both the public and private sectors—to improve their rate of return on investment. Thus, it is only a matter of time before the scientific community is forced to take seriously the issue of accelerating knowledge growth in a way they have not had to in the past. This undermines the objection raised in point 1.

3. The ultimate significance of a scientific innovation cannot be reduced to the competitive advantage it brings one in the marketplace—at least in the relatively short-term sense in which one normally speaks of "competitive advantage." The competitive advantage one gains from new knowledge largely depends on one's ability to create a demand for it (Drucker 1954). It probably has more to do with one's understanding of the market than anything truly revolutionary in the innovation itself. In this respect, the possibility of accelerating knowledge growth is no less a challenge to the business community than to the scientific community.

2

MAKING KNOWLEDGE MATTER: PHILOSOPHY, ECONOMICS, AND LAW

1. The Basic Philosophical Obstacle to Knowledge
   Management   58
   1.1. The Philosophical Problem of Knowledge and Its
        Problems   61
2. The Creation of Knowledge Markets: The Idea of an
   Epistemic Exchange Rate   67

2.1. An Offer No Scientist Can Refuse: Why Scientists
     Share   72
2.2. Materializing the Marketplace of Ideas: Is Possessing
     Knowledge Like Possessing Money?   75
     2.2.1. Knowledge's Likeness to Money   76
     2.2.2. Knowledge's Unlikeness to Money   79
3. Intellectual Property as the Nexus of Epistemic Validity
   and Economic Value   81
   3.1. The Challenges Posed by Dividing the Indivisible   82
       3.1.1. The Challenge to Attributions of Validity   82
       3.1.2. The Challenge to Attributions of Value   86
   3.2. The Challenges Posed by Inventing the Discovered   88
       3.2.1. The Challenge to Attributions of Validity   88
       3.2.2. The Challenge to Attributions of Value   89
4. Interlude: Is the Knowledge Market Saturated or
   Depressed?: Do We Know Too Much or Too Little?   93
5. Recapitulation: From Disciplines and Professions to
   Intellectual Property Law   96
6. The Legal Epistemology of Intellectual Property   98
   6.1. Two Strategies for Studying the Proprietary
        Grounds of Knowledge   105
7. Epilogue: Alienating Knowledge from the Knower and the
   Commodification of Expertise   106

1. THE BASIC PHILOSOPHICAL OBSTACLE TO
KNOWLEDGE MANAGEMENT

The Western philosophical tradition has not made life easy for
knowledge managers. It has tried to make knowledge seem as immaterial and asocial as possible. Knowledge producers have trained and
worked in places quite removed from the producers of other goods
and services. (The locations of the original universities—Oxford,
Cambridge, Paris, Bologna—in medieval city centers are the revolutionary exceptions to the rule; cf. Fuller 1997, Chapter 5.) Philosophical talk about knowledge has perennially had a self-contained
and abstract quality divorced from any clear spatio-temporal, let
alone causal, frame of reference. Even our everyday talk about
knowledge equally being "in" brains, books, databanks, and vast
communication networks continues this line of thinking, since if

knowledge seems to be everywhere, then it is effectively nowhere—at least when it comes to issues relating to "knowledge management." Not surprisingly, the processes and products of knowledge have been subject to their own idiosyncratic forms of evaluation that escape more ordinary analyses of costs and benefits. Consequently, "validity" and "reliability" have acquired technical meanings in philosophical reflections on the scientific method that enable one to possess a perfectly "valid" and "reliable" knowledge system without having a clue about how it may be maintained, extended, or even applied.

We generally think about knowledge as being *about* things, but rarely is knowledge itself conceptualized as a thing. Historically, this has been due to the conceptual difficulties supposedly involved in treating knowledge as something both *in* and *about* the world (Fuller 1992b). More metaphysical ways of making this point have included: How can the whole (i.e., the world) be represented by one of its parts (i.e., knowledge)? How can "the view from nowhere" (i.e., the objective standpoint associated with knowledge) be located somewhere (e.g., in particular beliefs and theories)? It would seem that if knowledge is roughly defined as a faithful representation of reality, then it is essential that neither it nor reality be contaminated by the fact that reality is being represented. Thus, philosophers since Plato have imagined knowledge as immaterial propositions that "transcend," or have no causal interaction with, the material reality they represent. This explains why such surrogates for knowledge in the different branches of the discipline—most notably "beliefs" (in epistemology) and "theories" (in philosophy of science)—are just as difficult to pin down to bits of worldly matter as were Platonic propositions. Are beliefs to be found in my brain as well as in my mind? In what sense do the physics textbook and Newton's *Principia Mathematica* express the same theory of classical mechanics? Even assuming that philosophers could agree on the best method for getting the right sort of beliefs or theories, where should the policymaker then look to see whether that method and those beliefs or theories are being promoted? In short, what are the empirical indicators of knowledge?

The cardinal intuition that informs philosophical approaches to knowledge is captured in the following paradox: *If genuine knowledge is universally applicable, should it not then also be made freely available to everyone—and not just to "those who know"?* Addressed in this paradox is what economists call the *indivisible* character of knowledge as a public good. The paradox has been intensified in the 20th century with a division of intellectual labor that has increasingly separated students of *power* (law, ethics, politics, social theory) from students of *knowledge* (logic, metaphysics, epistemology, philosophy of science). This division is most vividly felt in the bristling effect that the identification of knowledge and power continues to have. Even those who accept the equation *knowledge = power* vary their stance, depending on whether they are talking about the "knowledge" or "power" side of the equation. Philosophers have tended to focus on the *production of knowledge* but the *distribution of power*, wishing an accumulation of knowledge but a diffusion of power. But is this goal coherent?

Most philosophers have wanted to see power equitably (if not equally) distributed among society's members; hence the perennial debates over "the just society." Yet, relatively little attention has been paid to how the just society might be brought about materially. Exactly who would pay and who would benefit? The form of power that would have to be produced and deployed in the course of diffusing power has hardly figured in the evaluation of rival distribution schemes. Here our paradox rears its ugly head. The most natural way to diffuse power in a society would be to make claims to epistemic authority publicly scrutable and, thereby, accountable to as many people as possible, which would tend to eliminate esoteric discourses and arcane techniques that only the few are in a position to master. Yet, these discourses and techniques are precisely the items that are responsible for the distinctive character of knowledge. Once they are eliminated, knowledge loses its special "representational" or "referential" power set apart "objectively" from the rest of the world. Moreover, this point cuts across the "two cultures" divide between the arts and the sciences: on the one hand, say, ancient and medieval hermeticists whose epistemic authority rested on the mastery of texts written in an untranslatable language of *prisca sapientia* ("pristine wisdom"); on the other, those who, in a more modern vein, claim that the expensive technologies involved in laboratory experiments can resolve scientific disputes with a finality that could never be achieved by verbal reasoning alone (cf. Shapin and Schaffer 1985).

The fervor with which philosophers have wanted to shield knowledge from public scrutiny has fluctuated over the centuries, but, generally speaking, their efforts have reflected a dual fear of what would happen to knowledge if rendered public (i.e., *vulgarization*) and what would happen to people if rendered knowledgeable (i.e., *demonization*). If there is an issue that joins the classical endpoints of the Western philosophical tradition, Plato and Nietzsche, it is this one.

1.1. The Philosophical Problem of Knowledge and Its Problems

According to a still widely accepted definition, first propounded by Plato in the dialogue *Theatetus*, and famously developed by Descartes, knowledge is "justified true belief" (Chisholm 1966). Epistemologists spend much of their time arguing about the proper explication of the three component terms in the definition: *justified*, *true*, *belief*. Moreover, the definition is meant to carry normative force, which is to say, a standard against which candidate cases for knowledge can be evaluated. The cases evaluated are mostly hypothetical tales about individuals being in certain states of mind as a result of certain things happening in their environment (cf. Pollock 1986). The individuals are typically described as being in a particular state of knowledge (or not), regardless of the epistemic states of other individuals and without consideration of the technologies available to the individual for mediating her cognitive capacities (cf. Fuller 1992b). Now, an ordinary citizen worried about the diverse impacts of knowledge on society—via communication networks, databanks, expertise, books, and the like—will quickly notice that some rather obvious features of the modern knowledge enterprise are perversely missing from the abstract and atomized character of the classical approach. To heighten the intended contrast, I shall express it as a scholastic dialectic, in which the "thesis" is represented by classical epistemology and the "antithesis" by its materialist alternative, developed in this chapter.

(1) *Thesis*: The fixation on the bare "having" of knowledge puts knowledge in the same category as antiques and other collectible items that accrue value to their owners simply in virtue of their continued possession. Specifically, like collectibles, knowledge is pursued for its own sake, and hence, value is accrued through continual reflection on the object of knowledge, which in turn serves to personalize its significance of the object for the knower (cf. Belk 1991, Will 1988).

Antithesis: The value of knowledge lies not in its mere possession, but in the range of possible uses and users for it, a.k.a. "power." Even the slogan "knowledge for its own sake" is shorthand for the uses that can be made of knowledge to produce still more knowledge. However, the idea of knowledge as "instrumentality" pulls in opposing directions (cf. Abelson 1986 on "beliefs"). On the one hand, it suggests that knowledge is a "mere" means adapted to the accomplishment of some end, but then fully consumed, or at least forgotten, once the end is achieved (cf. Bem 1967). This view runs completely counter to the classical approach. On the other hand, the instrumental character of knowledge points to the need to conserve the knowledge one acquires for appropriate moments of use. This view converts the classical emphasis on the subsistence of knowledge across contexts of use into a realization that such subsistence must be actively maintained. As economists (e.g., Sowell 1987, Chapter 4) put it, *process costs* must be calculated: that is, the cost of using a bit of knowledge *now* (say, as an explicit warrant for some other knowledge claim) to one's ability to use it *later*. In this sense, knowledge, like power, must be possessed so as to be *reusable* (Fuller 1992a), and must therefore display a certain "rarity" in its actual deployment (cf. Foucault 1970). The Polish economic psychologist Leon Litwinski referred to this attitude of cognitive possession as "relaxed attention." It is the basis of the Christian Democratic notion of property as "stewardship," the desire to make something one's own in order to preserve it for the right purposes (cf. Rudmin 1990). This entire line of thought raises an interesting set of questions about the status of knowledge claims as they are forgotten, attacked, or simply repeated (cf. Abelson 1986). Indeed, the epistemology of public opinion suggests that the burden of proof borne by a piece of knowledge may change simply as a result of a shift in the frequency and distribution of its utterance, even without the introduction of new evidence (Noelle-Neumann 1982; Fuller 1988, Chapter 9).

(2) *Thesis*: Only individuals possess knowledge and they do so if, and only if, they have appropriate access to it. Thus, beliefs must be justified in order to count as knowledge. In other words, my personal claims to knowledge rest largely on my ability to present reasons for beliefs that function as a kind of "proof of purchase" (hence, epistemologists refer to reasons as "warrant" for a belief). Someone else

who avowed the very same beliefs, but without the proper reasons in hand, would not be said to possess knowledge.

Antithesis: If knowledge is a kind of property, then it is collectively owned, which raises a whole host of typically unasked questions about the nature of both the "collective" and the "ownership." When a scientist lays claim to a discovery, she has, in effect, yielded an epistemic profit from capital she borrowed from the community that must ultimately confer value on her work. But who are the members of this community? Simply those who themselves might have made the discovery, or anyone whose livelihood might be changed as a result of the discovery, or, as in the Social Democratic conception of "social talent," everyone whose livelihood had to be changed in order to enable the scientist to make the discovery? To be sure, increasing the store of knowledge products is a risky venture, as there are no foolproof epistemic investment strategies. For example, many of the features of 17th century political thought that are now regarded as central contributions to the liberal constitutional tradition were, in their day, rhetorical miscalculations that prevented, say, Hobbes and Locke from communicating effectively with their intended audiences (Skinner 1969). Indeed, the scientist may well succeed in adding to the storehouse of knowledge without exactly knowing how or why (cf. Rothschild 1973, on the contradictory inferences that producers can draw from sales patterns in the market). And so, while the citation pattern of journal articles reveals a long-term tendency toward stabilizing, perhaps even stereotyping, the significance of a piece of research (e.g., it turns out to be cited because of its "exemplary" use of a particular methodology), it remains unclear how this process actually takes place, especially given that an article often turns out to be citation-worthy on grounds other than those intended by its author (Cozzens 1985).

(3) *Thesis*: Knowledge is ideally a "mirror of nature" (Rorty 1979) which, in principle, can be obtained without the knower significantly intervening in the causal order. Indeed, part of what has classically conferred on beliefs the status of knowledge is their remaining true even without the intervention of the knower (cf. Hacking 1983, Part I).

Antithesis: Knowledge costs time, effort, and money to produce, because everything that can convey knowledge requires the transformation of matter, be it as a residue of some process (e.g., an "expert" handling of some situation) or as a more self-contained product (e.g., a book or an invention). This point was easier to appreciate at the start of this century than now. Back then, epistemology had been "naturalized," which to say, that knowing was treated as a way of doing things in the world (cf. Fuller 1992b, 1993a). Distinctions between theory and application, fact and value, were routinely not drawn. As it happens, science was also seen as an unequivocally positive force in society. However, with the advent of World War I, and the clear involvement of scientists in the escalation of military destructiveness, epistemologists found it essential to protect value-free theoretical science from its value-laden technological applications. While shielding science from political critique, this distinction—the hallmark of the transition from pragmatism to positivism in American philosophy—unwittingly served to revive the disembodied, alienated image of reason characteristic of the classical approach to knowledge (cf. Kolakowski 1972).

(4) *Thesis*: The diversity of materials capable of containing knowledge implies the existence of a knowledge "content" (often called "propositions" or simply "truths") that transcends and persists over changes in container. On the one hand, this idea underscores the extent to which no specific causal intervention is deemed necessary for knowledge acquisition. On the other hand, to follow Marx, it also exhibits the type of reasoning that led to the commodification of money in capitalist exchanges, so that just as capitalists came to exchange goods simply in order to accumulate money as an abstract quantity, so, too, epistemic agents are portrayed as exchanging claims and practices in order to accumulate knowledge as another sort of abstract quantity.

Antithesis: Given its multiply embodied character, knowledge is better seen as an exchange function than as a single substance (cf. Cassirer 1923). Knowledge is distinguished from other goods by both its versatility and its efficiency in exchange, which help explain why philosophers have perennially marveled at science's ability to explain the widest range of phenomena by appealing to the fewest principles possible—a feat that many thought had been accomplished with the emergence of classical mechanics in the 18th century (cf. Oldroyd 1986). A particularly concrete case in point is "organizational learning," which occurs when a firm is able to perform an increasing number of functions by performing each one at a lower cost (cf. Argote and Epple 1990, Engestrom et al. 1990).

(5) *Thesis*: Because of their immaterialist conception of knowledge, philosophers have tended to conflate the *identification* and the *elimination* of false beliefs—as if an identified falsehood would *ipso facto* self-destruct (Fuller 1993a, 115–120). This problem afflicts both objectivist and relativist epistemologies. In particular, relativists typically portray the adoption of knowledge claims as a matter of free choice and voluntary control of the community of knowers, without taking into account that the pursuit of earlier knowledge claims, even if later formally abandoned, nevertheless continues to exert control on future developments. In short, relativism, though often advertised as a social epistemology, lacks any sense of historical or institutional memory (cf. Douglas 1987, Middleton and Edwards 1990).

Antithesis: Like other mass-produced and widely distributed products, the consumption of knowledge is difficult to control. Once a claim or practice has been taken to carry enough epistemic authority to license the circulation of other knowledge products in society, special, often violent, efforts are needed to remove that authority. A formal demonstration of the falsity of the claim or practice is usually not sufficient. Texts must be censored, confiscated, and perhaps even destroyed (cf. Jansen 1988). People must be discouraged from embodying such falsehoods, which may require special instruction, incarceration, or brainwashing. Part of the longstanding hostility that philosophers have had to historical consciousness lies in the assumption that any knowledge that is allowed to persist beyond its moment of validity will eventually be recycled through the knowledge system and thereby undermine any genuine intellectual progress (cf. Fuller and Gorman 1987). Informing this assumption is the idea that the sciences do not sufficiently monitor the circulation of their products. However, as some legal theorists (especially Huber 1990) have realized, it is not clear that the solution is to make scientists accountable to some "higher court" that, in effect, invests in the lay public the authority to decide the applicability of technical theories in complicated situations. Under these circumstances, given the law's tendency to relativize the differences between contesting parties, it is all too easy for judges and juries to grant unfounded speculation the same epistemic status as established hypotheses. In essence, lay people tend to confuse an equal opportunity to voice one's opinion with an equal chance of one's opinion being correct. Consequently, they ignore degree of probability by treating all less than certain forms of knowledge as equipossible (cf. Gigerenzer and Murray 1987, Chapter 5). An alternative solution may be for the courts to simply provide a forum in which scientists can themselves routinely sort out their epistemic differences as they bear on public policy. This would, of course, subject the courts to the normative judgments of the scientific establishment, but it would still leave untouched the important issue of accounting the consequences of less than perfect—albeit probable—science that are absorbed by unsuspecting third parties in the normal consumption of goods and services (Page 1990).

(6) *Thesis*: Philosophical definitions of knowledge offer grounds for evaluating and criticizing people's beliefs without necessarily offering any guidance on improving them. This has had the effect of reducing classical epistemology to a philosophical parlor game with little impact on the actual conduct of research. Moreover, matters are not helped by philosophers making it a necessary condition of epistemological inquiry that the social functions of knowledge *not* be raised. Thus, epistemologists typically end up placing a greater value on "useless truths" than on "useful falsehoods."

Antithesis: A normative orientation succeeds if it improves the practice it is designed to govern. In that case, enforcing (or "operationalizing") the norms of knowledge production should, in the long term, lead to better knowledge products. Clearly, talk of "better" here entails consideration of the ends that are served by producing various kinds of knowledge. At this point, knowledge management gets a foothold in epistemological discussions.

(7) *Thesis*: The pursuit of knowledge is inherently without resolution. No constraints are placed on the sorts of claims and practices that can in principle count as knowledge, even though the standards set up by classical definitions of knowledge cannot be met by the sort of claims and practices that typically do pass for knowledge; hence the so-called problem of skepticism.

Antithesis: Knowledge is a complex form of power that entails self-restraint. In order to inquire into anything at all, one must refuse to inquire into almost everything. This peculiar sense of empowerment results from the limited capacities of individuals and societies to inquire into very many things at once (Thorngate 1990, cf. Collins

1998). This even extends the idea of cognitive stewardship introduced in Antithesis 1. But more important are the various social exigencies that bias inquiry in specific directions, ultimately forcing resolution on even the most abstract of matters. Although philosophers of science typically inquire into *which* theory is chosen, a more materialist inquiry would ask *when* theory choices are made, especially if, as Serge Moscovici's research on small group persuasion suggests, he who controls the moment of decision also controls the decision that is made (Levine 1989). Much external history of science supports this social psychological tendency. A vivid case in point is the so-called Forman Thesis, which argues that German physicists in the late 1920s lined up behind an indeterminist interpretation of quantum mechanics because of the financial and political pressure exerted by the dominant irrationalist elements of Weimar culture, even though the conceptual and empirical argument pro and con indeterminism had not changed substantially (cf. Fuller 1988, Chapter 10).

2. THE CREATION OF KNOWLEDGE MARKETS: THE IDEA OF AN EPISTEMIC EXCHANGE RATE

If knowledge is never quite as immaterial as philosophers would like, perhaps it can be *dematerialized*. Followers of Karl Popper, especially the epistemological anarchist Paul Feyerabend (1975), have thus insisted that all genuine claims to knowledge must be rendered in a form that would open them to criticism in the largest public forum possible. They would make knowledge less powerlike by introducing what may be called a *criterion of substitutability*. The more ways there are to embody the same piece of knowledge, the less opportunity there is to use that knowledge as an instrument of power, since it becomes accountable to a wider range of standards. Does this mean that genuine knowledge is *dis*empowering? Not exactly, since each knowledgeable agent is indirectly empowered by being immunized against certain power relationships that are based on corresponding forms of ignorance or lack of access. Thus, if I learn something about my situation that only you previously knew, then I can control your ability to exercise power over me. The criticizability principle caters to this intuition. It amounts to the ability to "reverse engineer" something that contains knowledge, so as to transfer its contents to a new (and perhaps improved) container

(Davidson 1989). Does my newfound "meta-power," then, divest you of the privileged epistemic access that originally enabled you to control me? Yes, but this rescinded privilege is converted into a form of knowledge that jointly enlightens both of us, so that the limitations inherent in my original advantage can be used to enable us both to progress together.

The criterion of substitutability can be cast in economic terms. When an agent receives a product in an economic system, she is reproduced as *both* producer and consumer. From the economist's standpoint, substitutability arises as consumers discover new ways of satisfying a need that was previously in the hands of a single producer. In monopoly conditions, consumers think that they need the monopolist's product *per se*, not something that is functionally equivalent. However, with the introduction of rival producers into the market, the monopolist's product comes to be seen as replaceable. Thus, the production of less expensive and more generally available goods is fostered. Indeed, it would be fair to say that consumer discrimination in the market *produces efficiency* (cf. White 1981). The knowledge embodied in this process is as an *exchange rate*, which the philosopher would, in turn, gloss as a *translation manual* (Quine 1960).

Both ideas raise questions of whether the rate of exchange (or rules of correspondence in a translation manual) is fixed and who fixes it. (Some limitations of the exchange-translation analogy are explored in Fuller 1988, 139–162; also Fuller 1993a, 186–191.) In many respects, the philosophical ideal of knowledge as universally translatable content is captured much better in the economy by the maintenance of foreign exchange rates than in real knowledge transactions, which more closely resemble bartering, with its lack of globally monitored standards for exchanging one sort of good with another. For example, when a psychologist and a neuroscientist pool their resources, the result is not a reduction of their two jargons to an epistemic Esperanto, but rather what linguists call a "pidgin" designed to facilitate their knowledge transactions, without much concern for whether the two sides have the same understanding or even place the same value on the transactions.

Although many things can be gained by conceptualizing knowledge transactions (translations) as market processes (exchanges), a sense of stable order is *not* one of them. However, the fact that markets do not tend toward stable equilibria (except under idealized conditions) does not imply that they are completely indeterminate.

On the one hand, parallel distributive processing models of the brain have recently inspired a spate of market-like models of group memory processes in social psychology (cf. Middleton and Edwards 1990), whereas, on the other hand, a 50-year tradition of studying "organizational learning" in industrial administration has appropriated cognitive psychology principles to model a firm's decision-making under market conditions (cf. Argote and Epple 1990, for most recent findings). There has even been a major philosophical attempt to regard linguistic communities as subject to similar instability by acknowledging the importance of language to the maintenance of social identity, while denying that languages are sufficiently well bounded to contain distinct theories of meaning (Davidson 1986; Fuller 1988, 73–98).

To be sure, there has been continual resistance in the history of economic thought to the idea that money has a fixed value independent of its purchasing power; hence the antipathy to currency exchange regulation. The history of this opposition, and how it was finally overcome with the institution of a gold standard and then a paper currency market, should be examined in light of analogous opposition to *reductionism* as a philosophical program to organize the sciences in the 19th and 20th centuries. Corresponding to a nation's currency possessing a value independent of its purchasing power, reductionist philosophers have tried to confer on the language of a particular science—usually, physics—an epistemic value independent of what its users normally communicate about the domain defined by the language. Thus, the reductionist is typically not satisfied with the fact that psychological discourse works just as well for psychologists as physical discourse works for physicists. In addition, she yearns for an "epistemic gold standard" with which the two can be compared, evaluated, and ultimately integrated into one world knowledge system. Lacking such a standard, the epistemic value of interdisciplinary exchange can suffer.

For example, just as there has been a tendency in free foreign exchange for "weak" currencies to hoard as much "strong" currency as possible without reckoning the long-term economic prospects of the strong-currency countries, there has been an equal tendency for "softer" social sciences (sociology, political science, anthropology) to convert their claims into ones made by the "harder" social sciences (psychology, economics) without assessing the long-term epistemic prospects for those claims in the harder science (cf. Dogan and Pahre

1990, Chapter 18). Perhaps the most notorious case of the specious attachment to physics as the "hard currency" of science is the continued reliance of economists on equilibrium models that are drawn from energy-based physics, circa 1860, the dawn of the "marginalist revolution" (Mirowski 1989). But even in our own day, rational choice theory has become a full-blown paradigm in sociology and political science (e.g., Coleman 1990) just at the time that its empirical foundations are being challenged by psychologists and even some economists (e.g., Lea et al. 1987).

A fruitful way of regarding the positivist project of reductionism is as a strategy for saving many of the classical intuitions about knowledge's immaterial character without having to posit some ethereal realm of "forms," "ideas," or "propositions" (cf. Nagel 1961). Thus, instead of defining knowledge as something inherently *immaterial*, reductionism defines it as *multi-material*—more precisely, as a set of correspondence rules that describe the rates at which the different material embodiments of knowledge can be exchanged. Thus, reductionists typically claim that the sciences can be arranged in a hierarchy of explanatory and descriptive inclusiveness: sociology, psychology, biology, chemistry, with physics being the most inclusive "reducing" science. The positivists, be they 19th-century followers of Auguste Comte or 20th-century followers of Rudolf Carnap, wanted the subordinate sciences to model their claims and methods as closely as possible on those of physics (Kolakowski 1972).

Talk of "epistemic exchange rates" can help illuminate this vision if we imagine the academic disciplines as a marketplace in which each disciplinary practitioner—called a "scientist" for short—is endowed with certain material resources. These resources have the character typically attributed to them by economists. In particular, they are "scarce" (i.e., finite) and "divisible" (i.e., what I give to you I then have less of by exactly that amount). However, instead of restricting this materialist analysis to such basic production values as time, labor, and capital, knowledge itself is translated into complexes of these values. Thus, the discipline "physics" is shorthand for a complicated system of transforming time, labor, and capital into certain products: texts, technology, microparticles, and, not the least, physicists. An individual physicist is herself a scarce and divisible resource, the exact limits of which have been studied by cognitive scientists under the rubric of capacities for "processing," "storage," and "retrieval" (cf. Gigerenzer and Murray 1987).

A curious feature of the rise of the special sciences over the past 150 years is that the spontaneous rate of epistemic exchange between the sciences has approximated the positivist's reductionist program, even though both scientists and philosophers have regularly criticized the authoritarian impulse that lay behind the program (cf. Dogan and Pahre 1990). For example, sociologists and political scientists spend more time coming to grips with what economists and psychologists say than vice versa, and psychologists and economists try to incorporate biological notions into their research, while biologists rarely repay the compliment. Moreover, everyone seems to worry about the implications that the latest findings in particle physics might have on their own work, while physicists remain notoriously ill informed (yet highly opinionated) about matters outside their field. Indeed, the reading public is implicitly reductionist, given that the best-selling popular science books are grounded in the "harder" sciences, despite their remoteness from people's everyday concerns. Stephen Hawking's *A Brief History of Time* (1988) is the market leader here.

The history of gold's emergence as the international standard of currency exchange during the past 150 years proves instructive. Here, too, is a case in which a rate of exchange could not be fixed by explicit agreement among the relevant parties, yet it nevertheless came to take effect as each party individually calculated its own interest. A crucial part of the puzzle was the difference between the image of gold in the popular imagination of the time and the arguments to which the conveners of the world trade congresses appealed (cf. Gallarotti 1995). By analogy, positivist appeals to the epistemic power of physics, namely, its elimination of metaphysical entities and its grounding in repeatable basic observations, were almost the very opposite of what scientists took to be the strengths of that field, namely, its ability to penetrate the nature of reality, often on the basis of one carefully crafted experiment (cf. Aristotle's *epagoge*, the process by which an essence is perceived in an exemplary instance; cf. Oldroyd 1986, Chapter 1). For working scientists, then, the lure to exchange one's own project for that of the physicist was founded less on the mass of data generated by physics than on the efficiency with which the field generated that data. A short-term investment would presumably yield the long-term benefit of avoiding mindless fact collecting. Economists have probably most explicitly engaged in this epistemic exchange (Mirowski 1989).

A fleshed-out story of how physics came to be the gold standard of science would require an analogue to the commodification of the exchange unit itself—some abstract quality like "method"—that scientists from the special sciences deemed each other to possess to varying degrees. Ideally, there would be a Marx-like story to tell about how method, originally pursued as a means to an end, came to be pursued as an end in itself, thereby becoming the universal currency of science. Recalling Marx's (1970, especially p. 110) classic discussion of the universalization of the commodity form, in early capitalism agents sell in order to buy, and money is simply the means by which the use value of goods is represented in exchange. However, as this process acquires its own momentum, agents can remain in the market only if they buy in order to sell. Thus, goods become mere means for the accumulation of money, which, in turn, obtains a value independent of the utility of the goods it can buy. Similarly, reductionist philosophers have wanted to reverse the focus on scientific language from a mere vehicle for the transaction of information among members of a disciplinary community to something whose ultimate value lies in revealing the direction of epistemic progress. This captures "positivism" in a nutshell.

2.1. An Offer No Scientist Can Refuse: Why Scientists Share

The French sociologist Pierre Bourdieu has promoted a version of the exchange model of the knowledge system by proposing an elementary unit of analysis, *credit*, which is the amount of a scientist's time, labor, and capital that she is willing to divert from her own research in order to contribute to the research of another scientist (cf. Bourdieu and Passeron 1977). This exchange of credit may take several forms, ranging from simply reading the other scientist's work and citing it in one's own work to subsuming one's own work under the other scientist's research agenda. Taken together, these exchanges constitute "cycles of credibility" (Latour and Woolgar 1979). Thus, you are a more "credible" scientist than I if I cede more credit to you than you to me. In that sense, the rate of exchange between you and me is a measure of the relative reducibility of our respective research programs to each other's.

However, these tributes of credit are not done out of charity. The exchange of one's own trajectory for that of another involves a temporary state of subordination, but one which the subordinated scientist anticipates will enhance her own epistemic credit rating in the long term (Kelly 1989). In the terms introduced in Chapter 1, cycles of credibility are designed to make the rent-seeking aspects of knowledge production more dynamic by injecting a (financially) speculative dimension that brings organized inquiry closer to a profit orientation. After all, there is always some uncertainty about the outcome of tying one's own agenda so closely to that of another. Indeed, the harder sciences tend to have both the most clearly defined and the most rapidly changing research frontiers (De Mey 1982, 111–131).

Sociologists such as Robert Merton (1973) have made much of the fact that scientists (at least before our era of intellectual property) have freely shared data with and given credit to colleagues. It has been taken as evidence for a higher ethical sensibility that governs the conduct of scientific inquiry, comparable to the seemingly unselfish "gift-giving" of native tribes (cf. Hagstrom 1965). However, the spontaneity of the exchanges implied here is severely misleading. An historically more perspicuous judgment is that these exchanges have occurred under threat of sanctions. When the first scientific societies were founded in the 17th century, the threats were reciprocal, as scientists often presented the fruits of their inquiries in each other's presence (Shapin 1994). However, these clear invitations to conformity (cf. Asch 1987, Fuller 1994a) yielded to subtler means that are reflected in the stratified citation patterns of articles written by scientists who hail from, and were trained at, a variety of institutions. As we shall now see, a proximal and reciprocal threat has been replaced by a distal yet common one.

To their credit, economists do not immediately turn to the ethics of altruism when agents cede part of their market advantage for no clear return. Thus, Arthur Diamond (1996) has argued that scientists' sharing behavior amounts to paying protection money so that their colleagues will not deny their grants, spread slander, or—worst of all—ignore their work altogether. These "acts of kindness" are not done in the spirit of generosity and respect, but rather in fear of what might result if the relevant gifts are *not* given. Yet, ironically, this is enough to convince economists that sharing is more rational than it first seems. However, a more pathological diagnosis is called for, if scientific communication is reducible to an elaborate protection racket that reinforces a certain power structure, causes a certain amount of misrepresentation of one's own research history, and creates a level of anxiety—especially among less powerful

researchers—that can compromise their innovativeness and indepen-
dence (Fuller 1997, Chapter 4; Fuller 2000a, Chapter 5).

Be it rational or irrational, this phenomenon is not unique to
science. Rational choice theorists call mutual protection rackets
"inscrutable markets" because of the high costs involved in determining the quality of the transacted goods (Gambetta 1994). Thus,
a shopkeeper may not know for a fact that the local Mafia boss will
kill his business if he fails to pay protection money. Yet, since the
boss has a reputation for being able to carry out such threats, it
would be too risky to test the hypothesis. So, the shopkeeper pays
the money, and presumes that the continued success of his business
is due to the Mafia boss looking favorably upon him. Inscrutable
markets work optimally as long as no one doubts the Mafia boss's
powers, and hence no violence breaks out. After all, even if the Mafia
boss were to win during a violent exchange, he would have had to
deplete some resources, not least his reputation for keeping the peace.
This would subvert the rationality of the mutual protection racket,
the point of which is to use undischarged threats to immunize agents
against the urge to disturb the status quo.

Mutual protection rackets work as long as the racket is closed. For
example, the Mafia thrived because the Sicilian law enforcement
agencies were relatively ineffective in protecting the villagers. The
shopkeepers had no other source of protection than the Mafia. Similarly, some scientific specialties are dominated by a few "big men,"
which makes it unlikely that a young or low-status researcher will
make headway in the field unless she appeases them in various ways,
however much she may abhor their actual positions. However, nowadays scientists are less willing to share data because they are finding
alternative outlets for their work in the private sector—often because
they are forced to do so by their corporate employers. Thus, science's
mutual protection racket is beginning to break.

Indeed, the emergence of intellectual property regimes in scientific
knowledge production is implementing the kind of formal codes that
typically drive out inscrutable markets for law enforcement. Nevertheless, some see this development as no more than abandoning the
frying pan for the fire. An omen in this respect is the recent settlement
by transnational pharmaceutical companies to provide South Africa
with drugs for the treatment of AIDS at discount prices, in exchange
for South Africa not developing its own biomedical industries (Smith
2001). Although reported as a victory for South Africa (home to 15%

of AIDS sufferers worldwide), the settlement effectively strengthens the drug manufacturers' control of the market by driving out potential local competitors. The threat in this newly capitalized science, then, is not in terms of violence but in terms of affordable goods.

Finally, in science, one must distinguish sharing *credit* from sharing *data*, though a similar story can be told of each. Scientists often lavishly cite precedents, corroborations, and analogues to their own work—not necessarily because they were materially dependent on the cited works (in fact, they may not have even read what they cite), but because the authors of those works (or their students or followers) expect to see their work cited. Such citations then function as protection, in case someone from the camp of one of the cited authors should be a peer reviewer of the citing scientist's work. Of course, you may be lucky and never get one of those authors, but is it worth the risk of a bad grant decision and perhaps long-term, albeit subtly expressed, enmity from colleagues? In the case of sharing data, if you do not make your data public until the time your research is completed, then others who are doing similar research may refuse to share with you in future, when their data turn out to be relevant for your work. Again, you can take a calculated risk, but are you likely to do so?

2.2. Materializing the Marketplace of Ideas: Is Possessing Knowledge Like Possessing Money?

The sociologist Georg Simmel's (1978) classic work *The Philosophy of Money* (originally published in 1904) provides a transition from the sociology of knowledge to the considerations we have been so far raising. In Chapter 6, Simmel draws several analogies between *disciplined knowledge* (or, when discussing individual knowers, the "calculative intellect") and money as media of exchange. We have just seen that if "having knowledge" is equated with being given credit, then knowledge is being implicitly treated as an economic measure, an admittedly imperfect indicator of how one yields one's time and space to another. In addition, by comparing disciplined knowledge to money, Simmel draws simultaneous attention to the historically contingent character of science and capitalism as epistemic and economic forms, respectively.

Folk conceptions of knowledge mark an important psychological difference between knowledge and money in terms of the initial *default setting* that characterizes possession of these two things. Whereas you are presumed not to have money unless you can demonstrate that you possess it, you are normally presumed to be knowledgeable in a situation unless your ignorance is explicitly demonstrated. This is why economic transactions require the money and goods "up front," whereas epistemic ones normally transpire through reciprocal attributions of intelligence (based on mutual respect and trust: Shapin 1994). To be sure, this difference is not an absolute one. Indeed, it has been relativized through the co-development of science and capitalism over the past 300 years. As a result, the qualities traditionally associated with money and knowledge have interpenetrated each other. On the one hand, fluctuations in the investment values of an increasingly credit-based economy can make it difficult to demonstrate your exact state of wealth at any given moment. On the other hand, the rise of disciplined bodies of knowledge has enlarged the sphere in which one regularly needs to account for one's knowledge explicitly through formal exams and empirical tests. Indeed, it is precisely this blurring of the traditional difference between money's explicitness and knowledge's tacitness that has made Bourdieu's model of the knowledge system as cycles of credit/credibility seem so plausible. Nevertheless, as a general rule, in both economic and epistemic transactions, explicitness is more highly valued (and required) the lower the stakes and the lower the status of the parties to the exchange.

On the basis of Simmel's diffuse discussions of the relationships between knowledge and money, nine analogies and two disanalogies can be identified. I enumerate and analyze them below. I accept all but the last analogy (i), while rejecting the two alleged disanalogies (j, k).

2.2.1. Knowledge's Likeness to Money

(a) *Mediation*: Both money and knowledge are things you need to have before you can get what you want. Both institutions arise indirectly, once diverse people attempting to achieve diverse ends find it in their own interest to go through a common means. Once enough people and ends are implicated, the pursuit of money (banking) and knowledge (science) become prestigious in their own right.

(b) *Objectivity*: In the long term, as power is indirectly accrued to bankers and scientists, the best functional explanation for the ends that individuals pursue is to maintain financial and epistemic institutions, which serves to give those institutions a sense of permanence and perhaps even transcendence.

(c) *Articulateness*: The money-based economy is based on interdependence among the widest variety of people possible, none of whom is indispensable in his or her function. In principle, everyone is replaceable at a price, which increases the scope of consumer choice but the uncertainty of producer profit. This is analogous to the dual virtue of theories as explicitly articulated knowledge structures. The explicitness that enables many different theories to stand for a given phenomenon is also responsible for the relative ease with which those theories can be tested and replaced.

(d) *Creditworthiness*: Prior to the introduction of uniform accounting procedures in the money-based economy, it was difficult to keep track of a person's creditworthiness. One would simply decide to trust a person (or not) on sight, which could lead to a false exchange of goods. Likewise, before evidence was taken to be independent of authoritative testimony, one would judge the epistemic merits of a claim on the basis of qualities of the person making them, which led to a greater focus on personal decorum than on data gathering (Hacking 1975, Grafton 1990).

(e) *Evaluability*: Labor can be evaluated more analytically (i.e., it is easier to determine a laborer's exact contribution to the manufacture of some product) once a price is put on it, even if the price turns out to be the Ricardian figure of the cost of replacing the laborer. Similarly, once the probability calculus was imported to epistemology, knowledge was effectively quantified, and the merits of competing theories could be formally compared (Hacking 1975). Not surprisingly, replaceability is an important criterion here as well. For example, the test of a theory's truth is the likelihood that the explained phenomenon would have appeared, if the theory were not true. If the likelihood is low, then the theory is indispensable (though it might also indirectly show the illusoriness of the phenomenon), whereas if the likelihood is high, then theory is dispensable (but the phenomenon itself is indirectly better grounded precisely because it affords alternative theoretical accounts: cf. Salmon 1967).

(f) *Control*: Money creates a sense of control over the value of a good by enabling a resolution of the good's price. Without money, if you brought a cow to market, you could not tell prior to the actual negotiation how much, or even whether you would get any, food in exchange for the cow. With money, however, the value of the cow can be more or less fixed, and the money you receive in exchange can be used to purchase whatever you want. The knowledge analogue here is the introduction of standardized methods that produce data domains that can be used by researchers operating from a variety of theoretical perspectives (Ackermann 1985). Indeed, scientists routinely use data generated by a laboratory operating from within an opposing theoretical framework.

(g) *Abstractness*: Explicitly represented mathematical and verbal knowledge have as their proximal objects of manipulation the actual pieces of paper inscribed with numbers and words. These offer their user little resistance. So, too, money invites speculative, long-term reasoning by enabling calculation without the "distal" objects of calculation—the purchasable goods and the referrable things—having to be present to the speculator.

(h) *Cool vs Hot*: In a McLuhanesque vein, it might be said that money and knowledge are both neutral in themselves ("cool") but controversial in their pursuit ("hot"). An important reason why the value of all goods can be determined by money and the validity of all beliefs can be determined by knowledge is that neither the money standard nor the knowledge standard is considered *a priori* biased toward any of the things it judges. It is precisely for that reason that all sides are drawn into competition to look good *a posteriori* by the standard. As I will suggest at the end of this paper, an important part of studying the proprietary grounds of knowledge is the construction and maintenance of such standards.

(i) *Invariance*: Simmel supposed that money and codified knowledge are similar in that their own value remains constant in relation to the things that they evaluate. In contrast, neither cows nor personal beliefs would make good evaluative standards because they change as they interact with other things (e.g., cows get sick, people change their minds). However, not only was Simmel clearly abstracting from the long-term effects of changes in the supply of money in circulation, but he also underestimated the degree to which codified knowledge is subject to unmonitored "semantic drift" as it is reproduced in increasingly diverse settings (cf. Fuller 1988, Part II), so that, say, the diffusion of a technical term such as "energy" in the 19th century—and arguably "gene" in the 20th century—served to devalue the information conveyed in the term, much as inflation devalues money. What is crucial here is that this shift in the standards of knowledge *appears* invariant either because no mechanisms are in place to check the drift or because mechanisms are in place to compensate after the fact, e.g., by exaggerating the difference between high and low culture appeals to "energy."

2.2.2. Knowledge's Unlikeness to Money

(j) *Scarcity*: Simmel claimed that the value of knowledge does not diminish in proportion to its distribution, whereas the value of money does. The idea is that to raise everyone to the same level of knowledge is neither to produce new knowledge, nor to destroy the old. Rather, it is simply to reproduce already existing knowledge in different places. By contrast, to raise everyone's level of income to equality is either to produce more money (and thereby devalue its purchasing power) or, if the money pie is fixed, to reallocate money from the rich to the poor. For Simmel, this boiled down to the fact that money is possessed individually (and hence egoistically), but knowledge only collectively (and hence charitably). But Simmel's alleged disanalogy does not take seriously enough the fact that the value of knowledge depends on its normally being in the hands of the few. The twin fears of "demonization" and "vulgarization" raised earlier respond to this point, namely, that knowledge has a representational or referential function only because judgments concerning correct usage, application, and extension of technical language and other knowledge products are in the hands of more or less well defined groups of experts. Indeed, if knowledge were more open to public evaluation, then, as suggested earlier, it would lose the special function that separates knowledge from other aspects of the material world.

(k) *Diminishing marginal utility*: In the late 19th century, economists had arrived at the principle of marginal utility as the basis for determining the value of goods: Specifically, assuming that the agent has been consuming certain units of a good, what is the value that she gains by consuming the next unit of that good? This provides a basis for contrasting money, which like all economic goods is subject to diminishing marginal utility, and knowledge, which is not (cf. Averch 1985, on similar assumptions made by "classical science policy" in the United States). In other words, whereas the $10 you get after having gotten $50 is worth more to you than the $10 more you get after having gotten $500, the information you gain after having engaged in an inquiry after a short period of time does not necessarily turn out to be of greater epistemic value to you than the information you gain later in the inquiry. After all, later information might overturn earlier judgments formed from a biased source. And while Simmel's disanalogy would have a point—a Popperian one at that— if the search for knowledge were itself a cost-free enterprise, it turns out that scientific inquiry is structured so that it is likely that, unit of knowledge gained per dollar spent, research at the later phase of a project will indeed add less than research at an earlier phase. The construction of expensive equipment, and the interests that turn out to hang on its use, ensure that most prior research will be insulated from the outcomes of that research. The possibility that science might exhibit diminishing marginal returns on investment has led the German "finalizationist" school of philosophy of science to argue that mature sciences need to be diverted from their natural research trajectories and applied, instead, to projects of general social import (Schaefer 1984).

Here I have attended to the economic character of knowledge without introducing its normative dimension. This dimension typically involves what Kuhn (1970) would regard as a "revolutionary" posture toward the scientific orthodoxy. As was especially clear in the discussion of diminishing marginal utility, I have been focusing exclusively on normal science. Yet, from an economic standpoint, the hallmark of the revolutionary posture is its basis on a theory whose production requires relatively slight material resources (cf. Latour 1988), but whose consumption entails that much of what had been previously produced and consumed by the scientific community is not merely obsolescent but outright *waste* (Thompson 1979). After the shift to the new paradigm, the old theories and techniques appear not simply to have been superseded in their knowledge producing efficiency, but rather to have produced knowledge in the past only because they were deployed so *in*efficiently— that is, they were allowed to range fortuitously and uncritically over a vast domain of phenomena that can now be understood in a more disciplined manner (cf. Hardin 1959, Chapter 13). From a materialist standpoint, then, a study of resistance to conceptual change would focus on the difficulties that people have had in shifting their view of their intellectual heritage from property to waste (cf. Rudmin 1990).

3. INTELLECTUAL PROPERTY AS THE NEXUS OF EPISTEMIC VALIDITY AND ECONOMIC VALUE

Economists have been just as reluctant as epistemologists to embrace the knowledge–power equation for reasons that become clear once we recall the standard definitions of power and knowledge proposed by political economists. Accordingly, *power is divisible* (Head 1962; Monk 1989, pp. 49ff). Even if a pie is divided into pieces of equal size, the piece I get is withheld from you. This point can also be extended counterfactually: I exert power over you only if I can get you to do something that you would not have done in my absence. In other words, when I have power over you, it is not your resistance, but only my self-restraint, that prevents you from doing what I want. In contrast, *knowledge is indivisible*: Knowledge is not supposed to be a scarce resource that remains asymmetrically allocated among relevant parties, unless a theory of distributive justice is drawn up. Rather, any knowledge that I have must be accessible to you, if it is to count as knowledge.

This double standard between the treatment of power and knowledge tracks the ambiguity between the distributive (cf. divisible) and collective (cf. indivisible) definitions of class terms that were seen in Chapter 1 to underwrite the elusive concept of public goods. The most striking consequence of knowledge's indivisibility is that epistemologists have ignored the diverse material containers (or vehicles; cf. Campbell 1988, Part 6) in which knowledge comes, since the same knowledge can supposedly be contained in, say, a book, a brain, a databank, or a communication network, in spite of the different costs involved in getting access to these different containers. In fact, rather than making this point a matter for empirical disputation, epistemologists usually presume that only that which can be conserved as it is conveyed through diverse containers—that is, "content"—can truly count as knowledge. At this point, we are back to Platonic propositions.

Intellectual property is founded on the idea that when knowledge is brought down to the level of concreteness in which human interaction is normally conducted and described, the seemingly indivisible character of knowledge is rendered divisible and its apparently discovered nature is rendered invented. We shall examine the implications of this point in more detail below by considering how a conception of intellectual property can be generated from a standard taxonomy of goods. First, consider some archetypal cases of goods (adapted from Croskery 1989):

(a) *divisible and discovered*: natural resources (coal, fish)

(b) *divisible and invented*: ordinary goods (match, car)

(c) *indivisible and discovered*: costless goods (law of nature, mathematical truth)

(d) *indivisible and invented*: copyable goods (rules of a game, business procedure)

My argument so far has suggested ways in which the idea of intellectual property might challenge the neatness of this scheme. Let us now consider the dual nature of this challenge a little more closely, both to *attributions of validity* in epistemology and *attributions of value* in economics.

3.1. The Challenges Posed by Dividing the Indivisible

3.1.1. The Challenge to Attributions of Validity.

Epistemologists have traditionally neglected what economists call the *process costs* of producing knowledge, i.e., the effects that an agent's pursuit of a particular line of inquiry *now* are likely to have on her (and her colleagues') ability and desire to pursue other lines of inquiry *later* (cf. Sowell 1987, Chapter 4). In philosophy, this issue normally appears under the general heading of *reflexivity*, in systems theory as *feedback*, and in sociology as *institutional memory* (Woolgar 1988b, Will 1988, Douglas 1987). To appreciate the difference that process costs can make to an epistemologist's sense of the value of knowledge, consider what separates Karl Popper's (1963) and Paul Feyerabend's (1975) vision of criticism in the growth of knowledge. Both place a premium on criticism, but only Feyerabend realizes the long-term difference that criticism would make to our attitudes toward science.

Popper (1970) exemplifies the philosopher's usual insensitivity to process costs when he calls for a "permanent revolution" in science through the relentless enforcement of the norm of criticizability, or "falsifiability." He fails to see that the social status of science is tied to the norm's selective enforcement. In contrast, Feyerabend's notorious lack of reverence for the methods and products of science is best seen as the result of calculating the process costs of engaging in Popper's strategy with the relentlessness Popper himself suggests. For if scientists believe that any hypothesis ought to, and probably will, be shown false, then it is reasonable to expect that scientists will develop a generally skeptical attitude toward the value of scientific inquiry itself.

Feyerabend's viewpoint is instructive because his sensitivity to process costs is divorced from an interest in *minimizing* these costs, as he believes that the activity of open and mutual criticism is worth pursuing for its own sake to the fullest extent, however institutionally destabilizing or personally discomforting the consequences may be. This reminds us that an "economistic" approach to knowledge production need not have conservative consequences, since, as a methodological doctrine, economism is committed only to calculating costs, not to minimizing them. Indeed, calculating costs for the purpose of *maximizing* them is a time-honored Marxist strategy for revolution, especially when Marxists distance their political agenda from that of social democrats by arguing that capitalism's fall—and, by implication, the revolutionary transformation of society—will be hastened by strategically refusing to enact welfare legislation designed to buffer a volatile economy's impact on the workforce.

Of course, process consequences may include *benefits* as well as costs, but these need to be calculated carefully. The ability to standardize an innovation into a routine is perhaps the most obvious business-oriented example. Its cognitive equivalent is the conversion of an explicit procedure into what has been variously called a "habit," "tacit knowledge," or simply a "reflex." Common to the pragmatist philosophical tradition and most knowledge management is the view that a potential process benefit of ordinary life experience is economy of thought, so that people need to engage in self-conscious reasoning only when they confront a new problem in the environment. This broadly "adaptive" view of the mind's workings has been recently dubbed "fast and frugal heuristics" by the experimental psychology research team at the Max Planck Institute in Berlin (Gigerenzer et al. 1999).

Yet, despite its Darwinian resonances, the word "adaptive" continues to worry philosophers because of its studied avoidance of meta-rationality, or *metacognition* more generally, as an explanation for how subjects achieve their goals under the time and resource constraints of realistic decision-making environments. Symptomatic of the problem, as well as a sense of the stakes, is provided by the discussion of the tradeoff between what Gigerenzer et al. (1999, 18) call "generality" and "specificity" of a particular heuristic's adaptiveness. They associate these two dimensions with, respectively, the coherence and correspondence theories of truth. At first approximation, heuristics "correspond" to the particular environments that a subject regularly encounters. But these environments cannot be so numerous and diverse that they create computational problems for the subjects; otherwise their adaptiveness would be undermined. In this context, "coherence" refers to the meta-level ability to economize over environments, such that some heuristics are applied in several environments whose first-order differences do not matter at a more abstract level of analysis. In short, people will continue using something that has worked, regardless of context, until it no longer works—*and not before then.*

However, philosophers do not regard correspondence and coherence as theories of truth in this way at all. Whereas correspondence is meant to provide a *definition* of truth, coherence offers a *criterion* of truth. The distinction is not trivial in the present context. A match between word (or thought) and deed (or fact) is not a sufficient mark of truth, since people may respond in a manner that is appropriate to their experience, yet their experience may provide only limited access to a larger reality. Consider Eichmann, the Nazi dispatcher who attempted to absolve himself of guilt for sending people to concentration camps by claiming he was simply doing the best he could to get the trains to their destinations. No doubt he operated with fast and frugal heuristics, but presumably something was missing at the meta-level. By regarding coherence as their criterion of truth, people are forced to consider whether they have adopted the right standpoint from which to make a decision. This Eichmann did not do.

Thus, when talking the language of "heuristics," one must always ask whether people have been allowed to alter their decision-making environments in ways that would give them a more comprehensive sense of the issues over which they must pronounce. After all, a decent model of rationality must account for the fact that any decision taken has consequences not only for the task at hand but also for a variety of other environments. One's rationality, then, should be judged, at least in part, by the ability to *anticipate* these environments. Nevertheless, Eichmann's refusal to question the background conditions that underwrote his decision-making environment would have received support from Gigerenzer's simplified approach.

Generally speaking, philosophers regard correspondence to reality as the ultimate goal of any cognitive activity, but coherence with a wide range of experience provides intermittent short-term checks on the pursuit of this goal. By regarding coherence–correspondence in such means–ends terms, philosophers aim to short-circuit the kind of locally adaptive responses that enabled Ptolemaic astronomy to flourish without serious questioning for 1500 years and the Nazi regime to endure for a dozen years. Philosophers assume that if a sufficiently broad range of decision-making environments are considered together, coherence will not be necessarily forthcoming; rather, a reorientation to reality may be needed to accord the divergent experiences associated with these environments the epistemic value they deserve. In contrast, Gigerenzer's group seems to regard coherence as simply facilitating correspondence to environments that subjects treat as given. Where is the space for deliberation over alternative goals against which one must trade off in the decision-making environments in which subjects find themselves? Where is the space for subjects to resist the stereotyped decision-making environments that have often led to the victimization of minority groups and, more generally, to an illusory sense that repeated media exposure about a kind of situation places one in an informed state about it?

Having said all that, Gigerenzer's group would find much support from the KM literature. Indeed, there is a strong anti-intellectualist current in the history of Western thought into which this line of thinking feeds. Championed in the modern era by Jean-Jacques Rousseau, it turns upside-down the conventional wisdom that says we are forced to think a lot (or expend resources on knowledge production) because we need to solve problems. Rather, we generate unnecessary problems by thinking too much! Much of the KM literature devoted to streamlining management levels and demonizing universities as "dumb organizations" seems to be conceived in this spirit. To be sure, there is an important strain of management thought that supports a more metacognitive perspective. It is epitomized by the expression "double feedback loop," which is precisely what a more philosophical study of rationality would urge against those enticed by the idea of fast and frugal heuristics (Argyris and Schon 1978).

3.1.2. The Challenge to Attributions of Value. Economists' lingering attachment to the classical conception of knowledge as indivisible is most apparent in their blindness to a particular species of process costs, namely, the costs incurred by agents trying to gain *access* to the knowledge production system (cf. Fuller 1988, Chapter 12). I have so far portrayed process costs as borne by the entire knowledge system. Thus, Feyerabend's relentlessly critical attitude has the long-term consequence of devaluing the scientific enterprise as a whole. However, process costs also affect the relative ability of agents to contribute to the system, for an agent cannot productively contribute to the knowledge system—say, by writing a book that moves its target audience—without first being in a position to consume the products that already circulate in the system. Each new text in circulation redistributes the balance of power, or burden of proof, among subsequent contributors. And so, even before setting pen to paper, an author has intuitions about the sorts of claims that will be easier or harder to defend, from which she will then decide on the burden of textual proof that she is ready to bear (cf. Fuller 1988, Chapters 2, 4). In other words, the author's paradigmatic moment of soul-searching is really a request to calculate access costs: How much more reading should I do before I start to write?

By contrast, when economists speak of the initial production of a public good (e.g., writing a book) incurring a much higher fixed cost than its subsequent reproduction (e.g., reading the book), they are catering to the classical epistemological intuition that, once revealed, knowledge is subject to free (or at least relatively inexpensive) access on the part of potential consumers. Yet, writing incurs such a significantly greater cost than reading only if it is presumed that the readers bring to the text the relevant background knowledge—which, as a matter of fact, often does not come cheap (e.g., advanced university degrees) or even well-marked in the text (e.g., obscure allusions and jargon). The situation of the text in this case may be likened to that of a mass-produced toy, which costs little to buy, but which then requires additional costs (or luck!) to be put together. In large measure, the economic mystique of knowledge rests on keeping such access costs hidden, at least from the production side of the economic equation. Thus, although mass-produced books appear incredibly efficient in empowering people to do things that they would otherwise not do, this is only because the cost of making these books usable to people ("user-friendly") is left to the distribution side of the equation.

The considerations in the last two paragraphs urge the conclusion that the degree of knowledge-likeness of a particular good is a function of the sharpness of line that is rhetorically drawn between the production and distribution of that good. In short: the sharper the line, and the more occluded the distribution side of the line, the more knowledge-like the good. The metaphysical model for this kind of thinking is the Platonic form, such as the essence of table (assuming, for the sake of argument, that tables have essences), of which particular tables are mere copies or reproductions that contain no more information (and hence no more value) than the prototype, and in fact may contain less, if the particular table turns out not to be very good. In a more psychological vein, we are prone to think that the "hard work" of invention or discovery comes with the original development of an idea, and that the subsequent work of transmitting the idea to others is negligible by comparison. Again, all the information is seen as packed into the initial conception, with transmission regarded as mere reproduction, whereby the initial conception is either preserved or lost, depending on the receptiveness of the targeted consumers.

Of course, neither philosopher nor economist officially denies that a complete story of knowledge reproduction would involve specifying distribution costs which have no obvious analogues in the original instance of knowledge production. In particular, access costs accrue both to the knowledge producer who must have the means of bringing the good into contact with the relevant consumers (into this category would fall the ability to write to a specific audience), and to the consumer who must have the means (including specialized training) by which to make the most use of the good. However, economists tend to neglect the costs of distribution in these contexts because they talk about knowledge *production* in terms of the material good embodying the knowledge (e.g., a book), whereas they talk about knowledge *consumption* in terms of the knowledge "contained" in the material good (e.g., the ideas). Given this asymmetrical treatment, it is not surprising that knowledge has often struck economists as an enigma, since it would seem to incur costs only to its producers but not to its consumers (Bates 1988). This puzzle merely reveals that economists have uncritically borrowed their analysis of knowledge from Plato-inspired philosophers. But the puzzle can be dissolved, and knowledge can start to look more like other goods, once the distribution of a knowledge good is included as part of the good's overall production costs. In that case, all knowledge is knowledge for *someone*.

Finally, for didactic purposes, let us reverse the course of our argument and consider what it would mean for cars to be treated as knowledge-like goods. The original prototype of the car would incur most of the total production costs, with each successive vehicle of this type incurring only distribution costs. The overall costs and benefits of cars to the economy would remain the same, of course, but they would be divided somewhat differently. To fully appreciate the shift in thinking involved here, imagine car production as a matter of transmitting the essence of a given make of vehicle to several places rather than as reproducing the vehicle several times. In the first case, the bulk of the consumer's cost would lie in getting access to a vehicle by being at one of the distribution points. Thus, obtaining a driver's license would absorb the expense that in the second case would be reserved for purchasing a car. The car would simply provide the opportunity for the consumer to manifest her driving skills, and thus would become a much less costly item. This situation would then start to resemble that of the physics book, in which the book itself is relatively inexpensive, but the cost of being able to make full use of its contents (i.e., the cost of a university education in physics) is much higher.

3.2. The Challenges Posed by Inventing the Discovered

3.2.1. The Challenge to Attributions of Validity. Here epistemologists typically ignore the *opportunity costs* that arise from the fact that my pursuing a line of inquiry *now* prevents me from deploying resources to pursue another line of inquiry *at the same time*. The occlusion of these costs is essential to robust discovery claims, which are made rhetorically possible by the closing off of certain paths of inquiry—or the systematic discounting of alternative constructions of the world—that had been opened up to that point. In that case, the discovery is made to appear as an inevitable consequence of nature revealing itself to the inquirer. However, opportunity costs can be recovered by engaging in counterfactual historical reasoning (Elster 1979): what would have happened had another course of inquiry

been followed, at the latest opportunity that it was still available? Paul Feyerabend addressed exactly this sort of question when he speculated about what was lost by relinquishing Aristotelian standards of cosmological integration for the predictive success and mathematical precision of Newtonian science (cf. Fuller 1988, 221–232). Moreover, social constructivists routinely court opportunity costs by framing their studies of science in terms of how hermeneutical closure was reached on how to make sense of what had been an open-ended research situation (Brannigan 1981; cf. Fuller 1993a, 167–175). Just as the process costs of pursuing a certain line of inquiry can be occluded—or "justified"—by what Jon Elster (1980) has called "precommitting" to the pursuit of knowledge for its own sake, or wherever reason may lead, opportunity costs can be occluded by appeal to "sour grapes" (Elster 1983b), whereby alternative research trajectories are downgraded by stipulating that it is unlikely that they would have advanced knowledge by as much as the trajectory actually taken (cf. Lynch 1989).

3.2.2. The Challenge to Attributions of Value. Even economists underestimate the susceptibility of consumer demand to producer control. This partly due to the ambiguous implications of *Say's Law*, that is, "Supply dictates its own demand" (Sowell 1972). Does this mean that producers have a special talent for spotting what people will buy? On this interpretation, production is cast as an art of discovery. However, the more usual way of reading Say's Law is as suggesting that any good placed on the open market will attract some customers, though, at first, ones who did not originally intend to buy the good. On this construal, demand for a good is created by its very availability.

Now, shift the scene from the marketplace to the laboratory. There are similarly two ways of thinking about the demonstration of an experimental result. Like the prescient producer, the scientist may be seen as having revealed part of the reality that all inquirers seek in common. Or, she may have simply created an effect that, once made readily available through standardized replications, opens up lines of inquiry that fellow scientists had previously not considered, perhaps because they were perceived as not being cost-effective or simply because such novel research trajectories had not crossed their minds. Yet however manufactured these mnemonic consequences may seem to be, it is important for the credibility of the experimental result that the scientific community take them to be a revelation of reality. In the remainder of this section, I take an economistic look at the ways in which the manufactured character of this revelation can be itself revealed and occluded.

Consider the neoclassical economic assumption that the value of a good is determined not by its intrinsic worth (which it would presumably have prior to its circulation in the economy), but rather by the range of its possible uses in the hands of consumers. Typically, this determination depends on the demand for the good in question. However, speculators in a given market may try to improve their position by anticipating the goods that are likely to be in highest demand, which, in turn, confers value on those goods even before they have been put to extensive consumer use. At this point, the economist wants to know the extent to which a speculator in this market can meaningfully distinguish the task of anticipating the goods that will be in highest demand from the task of anticipating the collective opinion of her fellow speculators about the goods that will be in highest demand. This question is motivated by empirical analyses of market behavior, which show that, in a significant number of cases, anticipations actually constitute the demand for a good. In other words, had collective speculative opinion not prejudged that a good would satisfy enough consumer wants to put it in high demand, the good probably would have turned out not to be in such high demand (cf. Keynes 1936, Chapter 12). In those cases, the speculator would be advised not to make the sort of distinction implied in the economist's question, but instead simply to try to anticipate the speculation patterns of her fellows. In these situations, goods are most likely to be regarded as knowledge-like.

Of course, the distinction implied in the economist's question applies in most cases, which explains why even the convergent opinion of stock market speculators may end up losing money for everyone concerned, since the goods in which these people invested may turn out not to be able to satisfy consumer wants. An advanced promotional campaign for a new line of cars may convince many investors to pour money into the car company's stock, but, once on the market, the cars may disappoint consumers in a variety of ways, causing the investors to lose at least part of the value of their initial investment. Notice that this loss in investment was made possible by the independent check on the value of the cars that consumer demand provides. To the economist this is an obvious point, but it has interesting implications when we contrast the situation of knowledge-like goods.

Does one need to know physics—even aerodynamics—to design a spacecraft? An economist might rephrase this somewhat contentious question as follows: Is there a demand for knowledge of physics among spacecraft designers? The answer is presumably "yes," but for exactly what reason? Is it because we know for a fact that knowledge of physics plays a crucial role in the design of spacecraft? Or rather, is it because we know that a study of physics is necessary for earning the credentials that enable one to design spacecraft? Clearly, it is for the latter reason—which is not necessarily to deny that knowledge of physics contributes to an ability to design spacecraft. Yet, it is curious that students of spacecraft design are not ordinarily allowed to decide for themselves whether (how much, which sort of) physics is crucial for their work. In other words, there is no check for consumer demand that is independent of the convergent opinion of those who have invested in the production of the good. In philosophical terms, this is what is meant by engineering being an "application of" or "conceptually dependent on" physical principles. When the spacecraft works, the designer's (perhaps implicit) knowledge of physical principles is held responsible. And if we later learn that the designer really knew very little physics, then she is declared lucky to have done something that corresponded well enough to physical principles.

Now imagine what it would be like for the car market to become knowledge-like, and thereby to start resembling the physics market. Suppose a cartel of investors was convinced of the value of a new line of cars, and potential consumers immediately took that as sufficient reason to buy the cars, without engaging in the usual comparative pricing and quality checks, which, in turn, served to discourage investment in more marginal makes of cars that might have gained support if consumers had a chance to make such independent checks. If the cartel were to have such monopolistic control over the car market, then cars would start taking on knowledge-like qualities. For example, the chosen line of cars would set the standard for appropriate car usage, regardless of the different reasons that consumers have had for wanting to use a car. A prerequisite to driving anywhere would be mastery of the car's technique. Since the chosen line would clearly excel in some features more than others, in a world without rival vehicles, certain traditional functions for cars (drag racing perhaps) would become deviant—if not prohibited—because the chosen line cannot perform those functions well. Consumer misuse or incompetence—and not the limitations of the vehicle—would account for the deviant cases. Moreover, cases in which consumers manage to perform the canonical car functions without using the chosen line (e.g., driving to work in an older make of car) would be increasingly seen as a matter of happy coincidence, reflecting the extent to which the non-authorized cars share the same features that have been more deliberately constructed into the chosen line. In short, the chosen line of car would assume a normative character by becoming a necessary way station through which consumers must pass to accomplish a wide variety of driving aims and against which their competence is evaluated in ways only indirectly related to those aims.

From the standpoint of this economic strategy, the interesting question to ask about the physics market is, when did physics investors start to dictate the consumption patterns of engineers? After all, physicists and engineers engage in quite different lines of work in quite different settings. Most strikingly, physicists perform controlled experiments in highly artificial environments, whereas engineers construct buildings and machines of a more broadly public nature. Indeed, this is a crucial part of the authority that physicists exercise over engineers—what Bruno Latour (e.g., 1987) has called "action at a distance." Engineering is said to be "conceptually dependent" on physics, which, in turn, "implicitly governs" successful engineering practice.

Both highlighted expressions suggest at the very least that the relation between physics and engineering is a subtle one which cannot be easily read off the behavioral patterns of either discipline: that is, the alleged dependence and governance is barely visible to the naked eye. One needs to observe the resemblances in the ways physicists and engineers justify the success of their practices. But ultimately, one needs to move beyond the workplaces of physicists and engineers to study the forging of the physics market. Such a move sets into motion the following series of inquiries: When did people start talking about the alleged dependence and governance, and did that happen before or after physics was required in the engineering curriculum? In what other ways have engineers been made to pass way stations monitored by physics gatekeepers (e.g., the modes of argumentation used to justify knowledge claims)? But perhaps the most interesting inquiry would be into what prevents the physics market from losing its knowledge-like qualities and becoming more like the car market.

To illustrate this last inquiry, consider now what it would be like for the physics market to become more like the car market. Engineers would start to take an interest—much as the social constructivists in science studies have—in examining their actual reliance on physics in the workplace. Which bits of physics turn out to be most useful to engineers? Which bits turn out to be useless and maybe even misleading? Are there certain aspects of engineering that get along perfectly well without any knowledge of physics? Are there aspects that would benefit from branches of physics that are normally opaque or unknown to engineers? If social constructivist findings are any indication, there are bound to be some surprising answers to these questions. For example, it may turn out that physics is most useful when engineers write up their research for the archives, which would reveal the status of physics as a lingua franca, but as not much more (Knorr-Cetina 1981). Once so revealed, the physics market may become destabilized, as engineers are encouraged to distinguish their own interests from those who invest in the future of physics ("physics futures," as the economist would say). At first, this may involve the emergence of new curricular suppliers aimed more specifically at engineering needs. However, if the possibility for alternative curricular suppliers that are radically different from physics seems far-fetched, that is only a reflection of the extent to which engineering demand has been molded by what physicists have been willing to supply. But in the long term, physics investors may come to realize that the authority of physics depends, in large measure, on engineers consuming their goods, and consequently they may alter their investment patterns so as to promote a physics that is more "engineering-friendly."

4. INTERLUDE: IS THE KNOWLEDGE MARKET SATURATED OR DEPRESSED?: DO WE KNOW TOO MUCH OR TOO LITTLE?

If the capitalist spirit is moved by a categorical imperative, it is to expand markets indefinitely. This imperative captures the capitalist belief that human wants are fundamentally insatiable and that the best way to increase everyone's wealth is by everyone trying to increase his or her own wealth. Thus, the idea that a market could have too many goods—a "glut"—would seem to be a conceptual impossibility. For this reason, economists have been intuitively attracted to Say's Law, as discussed in the previous section. Nevertheless, the fact remains that capitalism undergoes periodic depressions, the most obvious explanation for which is that *too many goods* are chasing too few buyers. Whereas defenders of Say's Law (e.g., David Ricardo and Karl Marx) have been forced to reinterpret the market contractions that appear to characterize depressed economies, opponents (e.g., Thomas Malthus and John Maynard Keynes) have taken the prima facie occurrence of depressions as refuting Say's Law. Yet, in either case, something needs to be done to repair the economy. What does the history of Say's Law have to do with knowledge management?

We ordinarily do not entertain the possibility that we already know *too much*. Of course, many have argued that not only the average citizen, but even the average member of the scientific community, increasingly faces an unmanageable glut of information (cf. Boehme and Stehr 1986). However, this state of affairs is not without its skeptics, and even those who concede the point typically treat it as symptomatic of a *lack* of knowledge—specifically, at the meta-level of how one's limited cognitive resources may be used most effectively as a selection mechanism; hence the need for "knowledge management." Generally speaking, we presume that something like Say's Law operates in terms of knowledge production. In other words, no knowledge is useless or unassimilable, though determining its use may require the generation of still more knowledge. However, by examining the historical detractors of Say's Law, we may come to see an alternative economic vision that provides a model for imagining a world with "too much" knowledge.

In one of the original defenses of Say's Law, David Ricardo argued that what economists call "depressions" are really depressed production levels, that is, the presence of too few goods. In Ricardo's diagnosis, large segments of the population are not producing the amount or kind of goods that can be exchanged in fair trade with goods currently on the market. Ricardo's answer, then, was to increase the production levels of the poor, which immediately led critics to charge that his thinking was more that of a "chrematist" (i.e., someone concerned only with increasing wealth, regardless of its other consequences) than of a proper economist. The critics, most notably Thomas Malthus, argued that given the periodic nature of depressions, Ricardo was only setting up the economy for a still bigger fall in the future. Instead, efforts should be taken to stabilize markets by containing their size. Malthus accepted the commonsensical view of depressions as resulting from an oversupply of goods, which suggested to him that the surplus ought to be sold off at reduced prices and production subsequently scaled down to reflect a more "human" level of consumer demand. Sowell (1972) notes the rival interests behind these two views in early 19th century Britain. Ricardo drew support from expansionist factory owners and proponents of Adam Smith's new "abstract" (i.e., universal) science of economics, whereas Malthus found support in aristocrats concerned with the depletion of agricultural resources and defenders of the traditional Aristotelian conception of economics as household management.

How do these policy recommendations bear on the possibility of an analogous "knowledge glut"? The epistemic analogue to an economic depression is *incommensurability*, whereby a plethora of specialized discourses is met with a paucity of channels for communicating across them (Fuller 1988, Chapters 5, 6). Consequently, bodies of knowledge accumulate in a form that is, for the most part, unbeknownst and unavailable to potential consumers. The Ricardian knowledge manager traces incommensurability to a lack of higher-order languages into which these jargons may be translated for the mutual benefit of all concerned. Thus, she recommends the positivist solution of employing philosophers (who, bereft of subject matter, would otherwise contribute nothing to the knowledge system) to produce schemes for effecting such translations.

By contrast, according to the Malthusian knowledge manager, this strategy is exactly the wrong one, since it fails to come to grips with the fact that incommensurability results from the unmonitored proliferation of discourses, which can only be alleviated by lowering the epistemic advantage gained by engaging in such self-driven language games. In turn, will follow the collapse of inconsequential distinctions and the reformulation of esoteric discourses in plainer terms. And so, just as the Malthusian economist takes it at face value that a depression results from the presence of too many unmarketable goods, her epistemological counterpart diagnoses incommensurability as proceeding from too much unusable knowledge. Rather than employ philosophers to generate still more knowledge of this sort, the Malthusian knowledge manager would focus several currently incommensurable discourses on articulating a common problem space of general public concern, which would thereby inhibit the further production of esoteric knowledge.

5. RECAPITULATION: FROM DISCIPLINES AND PROFESSIONS TO INTELLECTUAL PROPERTY LAW

A common strategy for casting aspersions on a knowledge claim is to argue that the claim's validity is tied to a particular embodiment, one which empowers some agents at the expense of others. The epistemologist's animus toward relativism is easily understood in this light, as relativism privileges singular expression over universal translatability. From Plato onward, *rhetoric* has been the chief source of power in this objectionable sense. The power of a rhetorically effective speech is said to lie in the speaker's ability to move her audience in ways it would not have been moved had someone else expressed the same points but in a somewhat different manner. An updated version of this problem is the attempt to demarcate science from the "pseudo-sciences" (usually religious and political movements) that simulate the powerlike qualities of knowledge by restricting access to those who carry the right credentials (cf. Fuller 1993b, Chapter 4). This is said to be in striking contrast to science, all of whose claims to knowledge are (at least in principle) translatable into the publicly scrutable terms afforded by, say, calculation, measurement, and debate.

Yet, such demarcations are easier to make in theory than in practice, since one needs to acquire skills in "public scrutiny," which can be done only in particular places, working with particular people. And as knowledge has migrated from human bodies to other material containers, lawyers have been faced with analogous problems surrounding the patentability of mathematical theorems whose proofs are derivable only by specially customized machines— not by humans or even readily available computers. The tendency here, too, has been to use the supposed indivisibility of knowledge as a backhanded argument for classifying those theorems not as knowledge *per se*, but as the sort of technical inventions for which patents are routinely sought and given (cf. Weil and Snapper 1989, pp. 141–192; Andrews 1989).

The sociologist Andrew Abbott (1988) has usefully distinguished between *disciplined* and *professional* bodies of knowledge in terms of their sources of power. Disciplines stress control over the means of knowledge production, which is sharply separated from applications of the discipline's knowledge. A Kuhnian "paradigm" exemplifies this orientation toward knowledge. In contrast, professionals display a greater interest in "colonizing" everyday life, and hence open themselves to more heterogeneous standards of evaluation, including the effects of their knowledge on lay people who expect to benefit from their goods and services. Thus, each time a patient relapses following medical treatment, the medical profession's epistemic status may suffer, but biology's usually remains intact.

Eligibility to produce "cutting-edge" disciplinary knowledge is restricted to those who have learned to embody knowledge in some canonical way. This may involve mastering the exact verbal or mathematical formulation of some theory or the cycle of routines that constitute a laboratory practice. By submission to such training, the knowledge producer has *de facto* agreed to have her subsequent actions judged in terms of whether they appropriately extend the canon. Moreover, the agencies that initially administer the canon— say, the curriculum committees of academic departments—are the same agencies that subsequently evaluate actions against the canon, say, in contexts of promotion or publication. The disciplinarian's commitment to a canonical embodiment of knowledge has the psychological consequence of making her more circumspect in extending the knowledge base than had she been taught to take seriously the fact that the same knowledge content can be embodied in any number of ways (cf. Wicklund 1989). For example, she is less likely to claim originality (at least over a large domain) for her own efforts, given that her credentials need to be examined and reaffirmed on a regular basis by keepers of the canon, with whom she is presumed to share a common body of knowledge. This helps explain the narrow stylistic range within which scientific findings are reported in research journals.

In contrast, the professional knowledge producer may be distinguished by her ability to derive power from presenting herself as an intermediary through whom others outside her profession must pass in order to achieve their ends. The paradigm case here is the need for a physician to provide a "clean bill of health." Thus, the professional will err on the side of popular overextension, whereas the disciplinarian will err on the side of academic involution. And whereas disciplines are never explicitly declared dead, but rather fade away as their student numbers dry up, professions have lost their jurisdictions in bitter turf wars, where rivals managed to persuade the public of their superior effectiveness in delivering functionally equivalent goods and services. Abbott's (1988, Chapter 10) chief example is the clergy's loss of authority in the realm of personal problems over the past century.

However, Abbott's neat discipline–profession distinction becomes complicated, once the orthodoxy of one discipline revolutionizes another discipline or even public policy through cross-disciplinary migrants, or "intellectual carpetbaggers" (cf. Hoch 1987). In that case, discipline-based knowledge is used to colonize part of the knowledge production process itself. Perhaps the most celebrated case in point is the establishment of psychology as an academic discipline, once some ambitious migrant physiologists transferred the technology used in experimental medicine into philosophy to address the mind–body problem (Collins and Ben-David 1966). Moreover, these "foreign imports" may retain currency in the new discipline, even after they have become defunct in their discipline of origin. Of course, the opposite move can occur, namely, when lay audiences, who are unqualified to challenge a body of knowledge on its own grounds, nevertheless revert to pre-professional "folk knowledge" once it fails to provide its advertised benefits. This is possible because public commitment to state-of-the-art science, technology, and medicine remains broad but superficial—that is, a commitment to the professional but not the disciplinary dimension of these bodies of knowledge.

6. THE LEGAL EPISTEMOLOGY OF INTELLECTUAL PROPERTY

If the original epistemological myth is to think that one can represent the world without intervening in its causal processes, the original economic myth is to think that knowledge has use value but no exchange value. In other words, for their part, economists have tended to regard the value of knowledge in the way that Adam Smith regarded the value of air: its value lay entirely in its utility to the consumer, not in its exchangeability with other goods, largely because air and knowledge did not seem to be scarce resources. Yet, just like air in our polluted times, knowledge is now increasingly seen by economists as a good that some have only at the expense of others. As we have seen, however, both philosophers and economists try to salvage the original, uncontaminated view of knowledge by shifting the emphasis from the *immaterial* to the *multimaterial* character of knowledge. In particular, economists have minimized the extent to which knowledge's material container contributes to its value by distinguishing the "high fixed cost" that a piece of knowledge has for its initial production (i.e., the original formulation—be it discovery or invention) and its "low variable cost" for each additional unit of production (i.e., its reproduction). Indeed, this is what makes knowledge an "ethereal good" in the terms of Chapter 1.

For example, it may have taken Darwin 20 years of toil to construct the theory of evolution, but since its publication and subsequent refinement by biology researchers and teachers, if a student nowadays takes even a third of the original time to master a more advanced version of Darwin's theory, it is regarded as a sign, not of the theory's profundity, but of the student's incompetence. This example suggests an epistemological analogue to the economic strategy of lowering the variable cost of mass production. It may be seen in the disproportionate epistemic value credited to the products of research on the "cutting edge," which are accessible only to a few knowledge consumers, over products whose chief source of value is their role in education and other forms of knowledge diffusion. Consider, for instance, the minimal epistemic value added to evolutionary theory by each new biology student who learns it. Indeed, learnability is already built into the value of an accepted scientific theory to such an extent that it would be more to the point to say that evolutionary theory would *lose* epistemic value if it proved too difficult to teach and learn. But it does not follow that the theory *adds* value by virtue of its learnability.

The associations implied here between initial inaccessibility, originality, and epistemic value were forged when intellectual property first became a matter of personal ownership in 18th-century Prussia (Woodmansee 1984). Before 1750, it was common to regard the author as someone who derived her "authority" from a craftlike ability to recombine timeless ideas into a timely text. Whenever this process was personified, the author was said to be a "vehicle" of the Muses. But from an economic standpoint, the author provided only one part of the labor needed for producing a book. Just as the book's typesetter could be replaced by someone else, so, too, could the author, since essentially the same ideas could be embodied in a variety of ways by a variety of people. However, the situation changed with an increase in the number of people earning a living from the sales of their writings. Yet, this alone would not have necessarily encouraged an author to regard herself as creating high-quality, highly desirable, yet also highly unique products. After all, rather than staking out her own niche in the market, an author might have argued that she can serve the same market as a host of other authors, but less expensively by offering clearer prose, shorter texts, and the like. Had the history of intellectual property taken this alternative route, the greatest epistemic value (as well as financial profit) would accrue, not to difficult works that represent "first passes" at new areas of research, but to widely accessible works that can displace the more arcane works on the cutting edge.

What prevented the alternative route from being taken, however, was the pirating of popular books that were then sold at the lowest possible price. Given that situation, both authors and publishers were best served by arguing that every book, perhaps especially the most esoteric ones, conveyed a unique form of knowledge that merited their high price. Of course, this marriage of convenience between publishers and authors did not prevent the two parties from contesting ownership rights among themselves. In particular, publishers strategically held on to the Platonic view that ideas can neither be created nor destroyed, only their embodiments can, which implied that the lion's share of the profits ought to go to the producer of the physical object, the book. The idealist philosopher Fichte reversed this opinion in the late 18th century, thereby laying the philosophical foundations for copyright, by countering that the author deserves credit for informing an audience of ideas that had previously enjoyed only a transcendent existence. When we talk about the instantiation of ideas in the material world, we automatically shift ontological gears from timeless forms to timely texts. In that case, priority of expression, or "originality," becomes a legitimate ground for ownership claims.

The ambivalence philosophers and economists have about treating knowledge as something fully embodied in the world is routinely resolved in the context of legal judgments and prescriptions about the sorts of social relations into which things can enter. A judge or legislator does not have the philosopher's (or even the economist's) luxury of suspending the products and processes of knowledge in ontological limbo. But that does not mean that intellectual property law is any less subtle an exercise in social epistemology, especially once we take seriously the idea that knowledge products have determinate consequences in the world by decisively contributing to—or inhibiting—public welfare. In that case, the knowledge producer will need to be regarded as having a less determinate identity, that is, as one of a number of people who could have caused the same effects. Thus, the more efficacious the telephone became in a variety of disparate settings, the more accidental it seemed (at least from a legal standpoint) that Alexander Graham Bell was its inventor. By ceding most of her claim to cognitive uniqueness, the individual producer becomes a morally tolerable member of her community. The crucial presupposition for this argument is that social life is facilitated by agents presuming that they are not in complete control of their fates (e.g., the telephone would have been invented around the time it actually was, even if Bell had not existed), and hence can only be held responsible for a limited range of consequences of their actions.

Generally speaking, two features of the classical conception of knowledge must be transformed before the courts consider it to be a proper object of regulation: First, knowledge must be depicted less like the open air (at least circa 1776, when Adam Smith deemed it to have only "use value" but no "exchange value") and more like any ordinary economic good in terms of its scarcity and divisibility. Secondly, the power of knowledge must be held to lie, not in the mere presence of certain universal laws of nature, but in the embodiment of such laws in a concrete human invention (cf. Croskery 1989). The *legal problem of knowledge* is that any new knowledge product has the potential for empowering many more people than it initially does, yet the nature of the power imparted could well change as more of those people come to use the knowledge in promoting their diverse ends. In this formulation, the classical account of knowledge as distinctly *universal* and *autonomous* is translated into a concern for, respectively, the *ubiquity* and the *unpredictability* of the consequences that knowledge products have when made generally available. Patents, trademarks, and copyrights are the means at the court's disposal to resolve this problem in specific cases.

Whereas philosophers consider it a virtue that the same knowledge content can come in a variety of material containers, and economists portray the producer of ethereal goods as striving for ever more efficient ways of conveying functionally equivalent pieces of information, the judge sees only the potential for lawsuits in these situations,

as rival knowledge producers claim priority, uniqueness, or originality for their knowledge products. According to the materialist perspective of the legal epistemologist, no knowledge producer will want
to deem her products as "essentially the same" as those of another
producer, unless the latter producer's products have consequences
(e.g., yield fame, fortune, influence) that the former producer thinks
her own products ought to have had. Therefore, the judge presumes
that knowledge products are different unless litigation proves otherwise. Insofar as intellectual property law is designed to handle
cases where distinctions matter but are routinely ignored, it serves
to legitimate the spontaneous bourgeois imperative, "To be is to be
different" (Bourdieu 1984).

However, the more socially significant a product's impact is alleged
to be, the more the burden of proof is shifted, as extensive inquiry is
required to assess the exact difference between that product and the
one of the allegedly (or potentially) slighted knowledge producer.
Thus, since inventions—defined as the application of principles that
already have some epistemic currency—are generally seen as having a
greater impact on society than the free expressions of the mind, which
include most textualized materials, the novelty of a patent turns out
to be more difficult to establish than the originality of a copyright.

The quick and dirty way of distinguishing copyrights and patents
is by noting that copyrights typically cover written works, while
patents cover inventions. However, the epistemologically salient
feature of this distinction lies in the sort of credit that legal theorists
have deemed appropriate for producers of materials covered under
the types of intellectual property. Copyrights essentially offer backward-looking protection to a knowledge producer by acknowledging
her as the independent originator of a particular product. But the
protection offered is minimal, as it implies no judgment about the
genuine novelty of the product in question. Anything short of plagiarism is copyrightable. Thus, copyright law arose from publishers'
concerns with maintaining a monopoly over the products of their
presses. It was only later that authors separated their own interests
in copyright from those of their publishers (Woodmansee 1984).

In contrast, applications for patents typically require substantial
investigations into the novelty of the product in question. For the
outcome of such an investigation to favor the patent applicant, she
must demonstrate the uniqueness of her invention, at the same time
establishing its relevance to whatever subsequent research is done in

the area served by the invention. The distinction between "backward-looking" (copyrights) and "forward-looking" (patents) legal protection of intellectual property parallels Rawls' (1955) distinction in the types of justice, in which a backward-looking sense of justice is retributive and underwritten by a Kantian ethic of strict rule following, whereas a forward-looking sense of justice follows the utilitarian ethic of aiming for the overall best consequences for society. This helps explain why copyright cases focus on redressing damage to individual knowledge producers, whereas patent cases typically take a more holistic view of the likely effect of any ruling on the knowledge-producing environment.

Not surprisingly, then, patent cases turn out to be quite subtle affairs, involving counterfactual historical reasoning, to determine the inventor's dispensability to her invention. In order to stake a strong claim to ownership, an inventor will focus on the most intuitively apparent features of her invention, which also happen to be its most divisible ones, namely, the features that point to the invention's material uniqueness. At the same time, the inventor will downplay the invention's less tangible and indivisible features, namely, the combination of generally available procedures and principles that explain how and why it works. The claim to ownership would be weakest if a putative invention came to be regarded as nothing more than an occasion for universal physical principles to play themselves out.

However, the law typically burdens any claim to ownership with a "fair use" requirement, which forces the inventor to say why her invention should *not* be made generally available at a nominal cost to other interested parties. At first, this may seem to be a case in which the law acts in the public interest at the expense of individual creativity. But on closer inspection, the law serves the creative individual as well. For, if the inventor deserved all the profits that accrued from those who use her invention to their benefit, then, by parity of reasoning, she would also deserve to suffer all the liabilities incurred by those who use her invention to their detriment. What the law supposes here is a symmetry principle for the efficacy of personal agency. In other words, my power to do good can only be as great as my power to do harm. And so, in order to make bearable my responsibility for the consequences of introducing a new knowledge product into the world, the law must portray me as interchangeable with some other people who could have just as easily introduced the same product.

American textbooks on intellectual property law (e.g., Miller and Davis 1983) routinely confess to the "arbitrariness" with which considerations of patents, trademarks, and copyrights are lumped together in one course. However, this judgment may shortchange the implicit coherence of the law's epistemology. True, rather separate issues are raised by patents (is there a precursor to this invention?), trademarks (does this symbol already mean something in the marketplace?), and copyrights (is this text the author's own work?), but they all share an interest in establishing and protecting the distinctiveness of the knowledge product, in each case against a different background of products with which it could be easily identified or confused. These background products differ according to the historical horizon that the law deems relevant for defining the nature of the knowledge product in question. Thus, patents are identified against the backdrop of the nation's entire history, whereas the historical horizons of copyrights and trademarks are successively more limited. A copyright is given on the basis of the author's personal history, even if the ideas he expresses resemble those of another author, whereas a trademark is granted if the symbol does not have current market use, even if it did so in the past.

The evolution of intellectual property law in liberal Anglo-American societies reveals, for all three types of intellectual property, an increased restriction on the power that the knowledge producer can exert in society, without, in the process, completely inhibiting the knowledge enterprise. And so, originally, patents covered the inventiveness of the artisan, which enabled him to monopolize and mystify his expertise. But once patents were extended to inventions, the locus of legal investigation shifted from the credentials of the inventor to the efficacy of the invention itself. Similarly, as the secular replacements of ecclesiastical censorship, copyrights initially empowered book publishers to distribute the texts they produced as they saw fit. However, once the interests of authors became clearly separated from those of the publishers, "fair use" doctrines started to distance copyright law from its liberating origins. So, too, with trademark law: It was at first designed to protect a producer's control over the manufacture of his product, yet cases nowadays tend to emphasize the importance of trademarks in enabling consumers to distinguish between otherwise similar products. Thus, trademarks have evolved as signals from warnings to attractors. Indeed, some economists would reduce all knowledge transactions to the communication of such signals, which include not only trademarks but also credentials and jargon (Spence 1974). This would suggest that from a KM standpoint, trademarks should be foremost in intellectual property regulation, since under ideal conditions they convey crucial information by minimal means.

6.1. Two Strategies for Studying the Proprietary Grounds of Knowledge

The first strategy for studying the proprietary grounds of knowledge takes largely preventive measures, namely, to avoid emulating those aspects of economics that are themselves modeled on the classical conception of knowledge. This implies avoiding idealized markets, ethereal goods, perfect information flow, abstract outcomes, and costless transactions. Luckily, it is now easy to find extended discussions of the conceptual changes that are wrought by regarding economic goods as truly material, and hence embedded in the world where they are bought and sold (e.g., Block 1990, Swedberg 1990). A couple of points emerge from this literature—much in the spirit of removing the boundaries that separate economics from the rest of the social sciences—that are relevant to exploring what I have called the "interpenetration" of science and society (Fuller 1993b, Chapter 2). First, most of the relevant information about a (knowledge) product is to be found not in qualities of the product *per se* but in information about its relations to other products and producers. Second, no (knowledge) product is ever pursued in isolation of other ends, and so rarely do (cognitive) agents ever pursue a pure strategy or even desire to possess the (knowledge) product unconditionally.

The second strategy is to consider the ways in which knowledge may be embodied so as to become intellectual property. The general strategy here is to look for how *standards* develop, that is, a public thing (i.e., *res publica*) in terms of which other things are evaluated, and which may itself periodically be evaluated. Let us briefly consider the construction of three sorts of standards: (i) a behavioral norm (e.g., an exemplary person), (ii) a unit of measurement (e.g., a prototypical case), and (iii) a canonical body of writing (e.g., a paradigmatic text):

(i) This standard can be studied in small group experiments by watching the emergence and transmission of norms in problem-solving tasks (Paulus 1989, Fuller 1992b). How do people, especially professional knowledge producers, display their disciplined training and thereby reveal that their behavior is "informed" by the appropriate forms of knowledge?

(ii) This standard can be studied by examining the construction and maintenance of such things as pure samples and ideal cases. Perhaps the most concrete study of standards in this sense can be made of the role reversal recently accomplished by computer and human reasoners. Whereas computers used to perform "artificial" intelligence, nowadays humans are increasingly seen as "noisy" computers (cf. Fuller 1993a, Collins 1990). Which is known sufficiently well so as to serve as the model for understanding and evaluating the other?

(iii) This standard may be best approached historically by following the vicissitudes that have accompanied the production, distribution, and consumption of, say, Newton's book *Principia Mathematica*, which would be both more and less than an intellectual biography of Sir Isaac. It would be more in that it would also involve discussing many lesser figures whose labor contributed to Newton's book becoming the medium through which a wide range of narrowly scientific and other social interests could be articulated (cf. Latour 1987). But it would be less in that no effort would be made to render Newton himself a coherent agent for whom the *Principia* represented the crowning achievement of his cosmological vision. Instead, the final result would be a history of science that looks more like the diffusion of a technological innovation than the logical development of an idea (cf. Elster 1983a). The relevant counterfactual question to ask of this historical analysis would be *not* whether someone else could have arrived at the content of Newton's *Principia*, but rather whether someone (and her allies) could have mobilized sufficient resources so that her text became the central node in a network that had the same impact as the Newtonian network.

7. EPILOGUE: ALIENATING KNOWLEDGE FROM THE KNOWER AND THE COMMODIFICATION OF EXPERTISE

One way to understand what is really meant by "knowledge" in the ubiquitous expression "knowledge society" is by examining the other words that inhabit the same semantic universe: "expertise," "credentials," "intellectual property" are the sorts of things that denizens of the knowledge society either possess or acquire. These three words have been listed in order of increasing *alienability*. By degree of "alienability" I mean the extent to which what one knows can be distinguished from who one is. From that standpoint, of the three highlighted words, "expertise" refers to the least alienated form of knowledge, since the knowledge embodied in my expertise inheres to me in ways that are not clearly distinguishable from other aspects of my personality.

There are two ways of thinking about what happens as knowledge is increasingly alienated from the person of the knower. The first way reflects the intuitions of philosophers and economists who are influenced by classical epistemology. The idea is that the objective content of expert knowledge comes to be abstracted from its various subjective expert containers. The social processes behind this abstraction typically include the codification of the supposedly tacit elements of expertise, which then enables the flow of knowledge to be regulated in ways that can either maintain the status of knowledge as a "public good" or reduce it to just another commodity traded as "intellectual capital" (Stewart 1997). There are several grains of truth in this way of seeing things, which suggests that knowledge production may be capitalism's final frontier (Fuller 1997, Chapter 4; Fuller 2000a). However, the image obscures as much as it illuminates. The second way captures what is so obscured, namely, that many features of the emerging knowledge society, especially those surrounding intellectual property and knowledge management more generally, display elements of pre-capitalist, even feudal modes of production (Drahos 1995).

According to this second way, the successive processes of alienation pertain mainly to the *context*, not the content, of knowledge. In other words, expertise is seen ultimately as being constituted by a form of social relations that normally centers on a human expert, but could just as easily center on an expert system or even a mere image or formula (presumably, as a fetishized tool). Instead of intellectual capital, the operative term here is *social capital*, which has been used by political scientists and economic sociologists to explain the difference in the efficacy of similar items promoted by different people moving in different social worlds. If intellectual capital captures the knowledge *embodied* in an individual, social capital captures that which is *embedded* in a network of associations (Coleman 1990, Chapter 12). Robert Merton (1973, 439–59) had an eye for social capital when he identified a principle of "cumulative advantage" in science, which enabled those with elite backgrounds and ensconced in the most far-flung networks to get the most out of the ideas they peddled. Indeed, Merton was so struck by the importance of social capital in science that he argued that the optimal overall strategy for promoting knowledge growth would have low-status scientists donate their best ideas to high-status scientists with the social capital to make something out of them. (Merton never seemed to consider that the unregulated accumulation of social capital does more harm than good to science—but that is another matter: see Fuller 2000a, Chapter 1.)

Social capital appeals to a peculiar character of the knowledge embodied in the expert: namely, that the same act may be counted as adept or incompetent, depending on the history that is presumed to have led up to the act; specifically whether the agent is presumed to have acquired the relevant knowledge by the appropriate means, typically "credentials" (but also sometimes "experience"). Consequently, what may count as an error when performed by a novice or a charlatan may pass as a bold initiative or a gnomic pronouncement when uttered by a recognized expert. This difference is manifested in the range of responses available to those exposed to the act: One adapts to the pronouncement of an expert, whereas one corrects the mistake of an incompetent and ignores the ramblings of a charlatan. This point was promoted to a metaphysical conundrum at the dawn of the knowledge society in the form of the *Turing Test*, Alan Turing's thought experiment that almost single-handedly launched the search for "artificial intelligence" in the 1950s. In terms of the present discussion, Turing may be understood as having hypothesized that without the markers of social capital, it would be impossible to tell whether an expert human or a mindless machine is behind a suitably wide repertoire of verbal behavior. The mere belief that a given sentence was uttered by a *bona fide* human rather than an artificially intelligent machine may be all that licenses one to confer virtually limitless semantic depth on the former utterance, while reducing the latter utterance to a superficial, programmed response.

Social capital offers an attractive explanation for the increasing alienation of knowledge from knowers, since the concept does not presuppose any controversial views about the convertibility of tacit to formal knowledge. Specifically, if computer and human performance are indistinguishable, does that mean that the computer is "artificially" programmed with something that the human "naturally" possesses? By all counts, any answer to this question would be very difficult to demonstrate. However, social capital itself seems to presuppose that irreducibly magical dimension in social life that Max Weber originally called "charisma," which ties the legitimacy of an act to the agent's entitlement to perform it rather than anything terribly specific about the act itself (Turner 1998). From that standpoint, the recent turn to intellectual property may be seen as an attempt to *commodify*—as opposed to *rationalize*—these charismatic entitlements. Thus, in defining the scope of a patent, the courts have increasingly circumscribed a range of protected items in terms of a common set of responses that their users are entitled to make, rather than any substantive properties shared by those items. In Fuller (1996), I coined the term "phlogistemic," named after that phantom remnant of the ancient fire element, "phlogiston," to capture this emergent tendency to treat knowledge as a magical placeholder for entitlements.

Consider the recent landmark U.S. appeals court case *State Street Bank v. Signature Financial Group* (1998). The bone of contention here was a computer-based procedure, patented by Signature, for pooling mutual funds from several different sources into a common investment portfolio. Once State Street failed to negotiate a license from Signature for using this procedure, which was vital to its own financial services, it sought to show that Signature's patent was legally invalid and unenforceable. When this case was first tried in 1996, the Massachusetts federal court had ruled in favor of State Street, drawing the traditionally sharp distinction between a scientific or mathematical formula and its patentable applications. In this case, the procedure executed a series of well-known algorithms that enabled financial advisors to calculate and record share prices at a given point in time. Thus, the "application" in question amounted to little more than the implementation of these algorithms in a computer, the numerical outputs of which could then be given financially relevant interpretations.

However, since the 1980 Supreme Court case *Diamond v. Chakrabarty*, U.S. courts have become increasingly liberal in what they count as a patentable application. Specifically, binaries such as nature/artifice and idea/use, traditional benchmarks for circumscribing intellectual property rights, are no longer seen as capturing mutually exclusive domains that roughly correspond to a public/private goods distinction. A sign of the times is the allowance of patents on machines that translate a generally available idea or a naturally occurring phenomenon from one medium to another, such as an electrocardiograph's waveform representation of a patient's heartbeat. In these cases, the courts typically preface their rulings by observing that because *all* human endeavor involves abstract ideas and natural phenomena, the mere presence of such things cannot count *against* the granting of intellectual property rights.

Had these rulings been made two centuries earlier, in the heyday of the Enlightenment, the court's observation would have probably issued in the opposite verdict—as grounds for *denying* said rights. The judge would have reasoned that since these ideas and phenomena are already in reach of all rational beings, the best institutional setting for bringing them into the public domain is provided by the *contest*, whereby a one-shot prize is given to the person who first arrives at the invention, but the invention itself is then made freely available. In other words, befitting the elusive period of "civic republican virtue" that transpired between the twilight of feudalism and the dawn of liberalism, the competitive spirit would be promoted quite independently of the acquisitive impulse, so that individuals could satisfy their own interests without sacrificing those of society (Hirschman 1976).

When those heirs to the Enlightenment, the U.S. Founding Fathers, installed the intellectual property provision in the heart of the Constitution, they were well aware that the pursuit of innovation is not necessarily the most efficient means to foster one's self-interest: the obstruction of innovation might do the trick with much less effort. But their main concern was the transmutation of private vices into public virtue. Thus, a patent's promise of a temporary monopoly on the uses put to an invention was designed as a vehicle of economic liberalization that would encourage people to use their wits to destabilize existing markets and thereby increase the overall wealth and knowledge in society. However, as the Founding Fathers originally conceived it, an "invention" had to be more than simply a symbolic representation that licenses a pattern of action on a regular basis; it also had to be a novel application of abstract principles. They failed to anticipate that patents would be eventually granted for things already in existence, such as the genetic code of particular life forms, simply because they had not yet been codified—and more to the point, commodified.

In short, the legal promise of intellectual property has served as an open invitation to privatize public goods or, more evocatively, to convert the marketplace of ideas to a feudal regime of "virtual real estate." An especially extreme case in point concerns *bioprospecting*, whereby rare genetic sequences possessed by relatively inbred indigenous populations are codified and patented by transnational pharmaceutical firms. (Croskery 1989 was one of the first to locate bioprospecting in the conceptual universe of intellectual property.) Marginal differences in, say, the Papuan, Maori, or Icelandic genome are widely held responsible for protecting their possessors from ills that afflict the rest of *Homo sapiens*. Consequently, a financial incentive exists to manufacture drugs that enable these peoples' biochemical advantages to be made more generally available—albeit at a price.

A striking feature of the philosophical discourse surrounding bioprospecting is that, despite its grounding in utilitarian and broadly economic perspectives, it generally fails to acknowledge that bioprospecting is, first and foremost, a profit-oriented enterprise that attempts to secure private gain from contingent outcomes of the genetic lottery. Although the ultimate effect of the enterprise is to redistribute any genetic advantages held by particular groups, it would be mistaken to regard bioprospectors as operants of distributive justice in a welfare-state regime. Indeed, as the 1999 United Nations Human Development Report has made clear, bioprospecting largely exploits the absence of global intellectual property regulation that would otherwise force firms to confront the demands of distributive justice more directly. Philosophers simplify the life of bioprospectors considerably by assuming that the treatment of economic and biological "inheritance" can be guided by the same moral intuitions, such that the genetically wealthy Maoris should be levied the moral equivalent of a "tax" on their inheritance, just like an heir to a large fortune (Steiner 1998).

Lurking behind this analogy is the belief that an inheritance, be it economic or biological, is always unearned and hence best treated as something its possessor does not fully deserve. This belief is bolstered by the lottery-like character of genetic variation combined with the tendency of economically vulnerable yet genetically wealthy groups to respond to bioprospectors in much the same way as many 18th- and 19th-century *rentiers* did to developers who wanted to build factories on their land. As a result, indigenous peoples appear in an especially unsympathetic light: They do not merely resist "progress," which by itself could be easily understood as a Western hegemonic project; but more significantly, they seem to be blocking a specific strategy for benefiting the bulk of humanity. The most obvious lesson to be drawn from this episode is that economistic conceptions of value are bound to support pernicious policies, if they are disembedded from the actual political economies to which they are meant to apply.

One way around this emerging public-relations problem would be for indigenous peoples to argue that the value contained in their genetic material should be interpreted as *labor*, not property. In other words, their genetic uniqueness should not be seen as akin to inherited wealth to which the current generation contributed nothing, but rather to the ongoing work it takes to keep a population relatively inbred. In the current geopolitical scene, such labor requires upholding the value of cultural purity and continuity, in the face of capitalism's global tendency to hybridize or homogenize the differences between people. Moreover, a labor-based approach highlights the *risk* a community assumes in cultivating a distinctive genetic profile. After all, inbreeding is just as likely to result in harm to the inbred individuals as good to members of other populations who receive treatments synthesized from the products of their inbreeding.

If bioprospecting appears to send our moral compass spinning, that is because it undermines the privileged status of *Homo sapiens* as a source of value, an assumption that unites Marxists and others (such as Hayek's Austrian School) who closely adhere to Adam Smith in regarding political economy as the ultimate *human* science. To be sure, major differences separate the followers of Marx and Smith. Marxists regard humans as unique contributors to the means of production (a.k.a. "labor"), whereas Smithians subsume human activity under the general category of property: i.e., if each person owns his body, then each person can dispose of it as he sees fit (if at all). But bioprospecting opens up the third possibility that human bodies are just obstacles to expediting the rate of wealth production *as such*, the human component of which ultimately must be mastered and superseded by less costly means. In such a regime, claims to the uniqueness or inviolability of human beings no longer carry merit. In terms introduced in the previous chapter, bioprospecting's challenge rests on its *profit* orientation toward human knowledge bearers, in contrast to the *rent* orientation of the Smithians and the *labor* orientation of the Marxists.

Consider, once again, the plight of our time-traveling Enlightenment judge. After bemoaning humanity's regression since his day, he would probably recommend that we resort to the standard 18th-century tactic of fighting property claim with property claim: specifically, to assign *copyright* at birth to each individual for his or her unique genetic sequence. In that case, any attempt to patent such sequences as an innovative application of natural laws would automatically come into conflict with copyright claims on behalf of each individual as an original genetic product, thereby placing the prospector and prospected of biological capital on a more equal legal footing for further negotiations as to the terms under which a "copy" of an individual's genetic sequence may be taken. Of course, this strategy would leave unanswered questions about who exactly would hold the copyright at the time of birth: the child or the parents? If the parents are the holders, would the copyright then transfer to the child after a certain point? And what if the parents are unknown, perhaps because they abandoned the child? Whatever answers are given to these questions, taking them seriously would amount to yet another moment in the devolution of the welfare state, as individuals come to be seen as born stewards of their biological estate.

Of course, the idea of tying knowledge, in either its alienated or unalienated forms, to property is hardly new. Civic republicanism (more about which in Chapter 4) typically required that men own property before they were empowered to vote. The sense of stewardship associated with maintaining a piece of land implied a measure of social responsibility that would be otherwise difficult to gauge, given the diverse and relatively hidden character of life experiences. This criterion was superseded only in the late 19th century by the state's commitment to universal primary education, some version of which has come to underwrite the right to vote. John Stuart Mill's 1859 essay *On Liberty* was a controversial but ultimately influential defense of this transition. Today it is easy to miss the disciplinary intent of Mill's proposal, especially if one presumes that his famed defense of "minorities" was made on behalf of the powerless. On the contrary, for Mill, education would enable the masses to recognize and heed *their betters*, thereby providing a sort of uncoerced, self-applied form of social control in a democratic setting. Since Mill's day, a highly differentiated system of academic requirements beyond basic schooling has rendered today's knowledge society as stratified as any class-, caste-, or estate-based system of the past.

Sometimes this point is lost because the knowledge society is supposed to be organized "horizontally," not "vertically," on the basis of "networks" rather than "hierarchies" (Castells 1996). Yet, even cultures with little social mobility have admitted the mutual dependence of their various castes or estates. Nevertheless, these "horizontal" appreciations of a common fate have not prevented agreement on which strata are "higher" and "lower" in the societal pecking order. Perhaps, then, the knowledge society is distinctive in allowing individuals to move more easily between the higher and lower strata than past principles of social reproduction (Ringer 1979). However, the evidence is disconcertingly mixed. Although the proportion of professionals in the workforce of most countries has increased in recent years, there is also evidence of restrictions on the amount of movement across classes that the possession of credentials enables people to make over, say, one generation. Moreover, those who promote the increasing socioeconomic importance of credentials typically ignore their *positional* character (Hirsch 1977). In other words, credentials are a source of real advantage only if not too many people possess them. The drive toward greater professionalization may simply reflect a desperate attempt to gain some temporary marginal advantage in a system that continually erases advantage in its very encouragement of the pursuit of credentials.

At most, then, credentials are necessary, certainly not sufficient, to gainful employment. Thus, from being a principle of empowerment, credentials have now become indirect markers of exclusion. They have succeeded race and class as the premier mechanism for discriminating and stratifying a population, and have even begun to generate the sort of status-based resentments traditionally associated with those other markers, especially now that the relationship between academic training and job performance is increasingly called into question. As this feudal residue of credentials is revealed, private-sector vocational training centers emerge to undermine the monopoly enjoyed by universities, in large part by capitalizing on the close, albeit often temporary, connection between knowledge imparted and employment secured.

Compounding the problems caused by this credentials race is that the recent growth in intellectual property legislation has hastened the migration of the knowledge embodied in credentials from human to nonhuman containers, most notably expert-system computers. In that case, you may lose whatever advantage you gained from credentials, not by others also obtaining them, but by machines rendering your segment of the credentials race obsolete. The emergence of intellectual property as a form of "knowledge acquisition" (the phrase most closely associated with the design of expert systems) that supersedes credentials is noteworthy in the largely negative and defensive rhetoric surrounding the encouragement of its pursuit (Thurow 1997). Whereas you would acquire credentials, often at considerable expense, in order to increase your own sphere of action, you acquire intellectual property, in the first instance, to block other people's actions unless they first pay tribute to you. From an economic standpoint, what had been value added to labor is now converted into rent that others must pay in order for you, the intellectual property holder, to earn a profit. In that case, "knowledge" has become a euphemism for control over the means at an agent's disposal to realize his or her goals.

Let us call this conversion *Turing's Revenge*, after the Turing Test discussed above: If you cannot tell the difference between human and machine utterance unless you are told, then does the difference really matter? At the very least, this suspicion invites attempts to perform the ultimate act of alienation: to extract the formal character of credentials, package it as a new product, and sell it at a price that undercuts the original credential holders and ultimately forces them into specialty niches, if they are not driven out of the market completely. For example, even if a computer designed to diagnose illness lacks the bedside manner of a (very good!) physician, it is not clear that the human touch is worth the additional cost and hassle for most individuals and institutions. After all, the more physicians excel in qualities the computer cannot match, the more likely it is that their services will be in high demand and hence the higher the fees they can command. As with labor-saving technologies of the past, machines can *replace* humans without necessarily *reproducing* the actual labor they performed. In that case, the fact that a computerized expert system lacks something called "consciousness" or "cognitive complexity" that is supposedly unique to humans is by no means a hindrance in the marketplace. The next chapter explores the wide-ranging implications of this point.

3

INFORMATION TECHNOLOGY AS THE KEY TO THE KNOWLEDGE REVOLUTION

1. Introduction: From Epistemology to Information
   Technology   117
2. The Post-Industrial Dream: The Intellectualization of
   Information Technology   125
3. Society's Shifting Human-Computer Interface:
   An Historical Overview   137

4. From Expertise to Expert Systems 143
   4.1. A Brief Social History of Expertise 143
   4.2. How Knowledge Engineers Benefit from the Social
        Character of Expertise 145
   4.3. The Lessons of Expert Systems for the Sociology of
        Knowledge Systems 151
   4.4. Expert Systems and the Pseudo-Democratization of
        Expertise 154
   4.5. Recapitulation: Expertise as the Ultimate Subject of
        Intellectual Property 161
5. Why Even Scholars Don't Get a Free Lunch in Cyberspace 167
   5.1. A Tale of Two Technophilosophies: Cyberplatonism
        versus Cybermaterialism 169
   5.2. The Publishing Industry as the Cyberscapegoat 174
   5.3. Adding Some Resistance to the Frictionless Medium
        of Thought 178
   5.4. Why Paperlessness Is No Panacea 183
   5.5. Does Cyberspace "Deserve" Peer Review? 187
   5.6. Conclusion: Purifying Cyberplatonism's Motives 189
6. Postscript: Capitalized Education as the Ultimate
   Information Technology 191

1. INTRODUCTION: FROM EPISTEMOLOGY TO INFORMATION TECHNOLOGY

As we saw in the previous chapter, the philosophical discipline of *epistemology* has been traditionally concerned with knowledge as a disembodied set of propositions about reality that are true for all times, places, and people. The epistemologist then tries to determine the conditions under which one has access to these disembodied truths. The prime candidate for realizing those conditions usually turned out to be some form of mathematically based physical science. By focusing so exclusively on knowledge in this ideal and rarefied state, philosophers left it open to social scientists to explore all other forms of knowledge, especially the full range of religious and political doctrines that fall under the rubric of *ideology*. In explicit contrast to the philosopher's conception of science, social scientists portrayed the validity of an ideology as dependent on the people who believe it and the power they have to realize their beliefs in organized action.

This division of labor between philosophers and social scientists leaves no space for the concept of *information technology* (IT). Indeed, any sharp distinction between "science" and "ideology" is challenged once we introduce IT as a form of knowledge. To see what I mean here, consider the difference between *embodying* and *embedding* knowledge. Knowledge is embodied by being placed in a material container, whereas knowledge is embedded by being situated in a social context. Science, according to epistemologists, was both disembodied and disembedded. Ideology, according to sociologists of knowledge, was both embodied and embedded. But what about knowledge that is embodied but significantly disembedded? Or knowledge that is embedded but significantly disembodied? *Technology* answers to the first possibility; *information* the second. This expanded understanding of the forms of knowledge is represented in Figure 3.1.

Technologies are clearly embodiments of human knowledge, yet they cannot adapt nearly as well as their human creators to changing social environments. If a potential user does not understand the instructions for operating her computer, it is rather unlikely that the computer will be as capable as a neighboring human of assisting the user. In one very obvious sense, this proves that no technology can know more than its designer. However, the sheer possession of knowledge is not always a source of strength. For example, it is no exaggeration to say that Western science only started to make an impression on the rest of the world once non-Westerners wanted to figure out how Western technology worked (Fuller 1997, Chapters 5–7). Indeed, humans may be a little too flexible in adapting to the

IS KNOWLEDGE EMBODIED?	IS KNOWLEDGE EMBEDDED?	
	YES	NO
YES	Ideology (sociology of knowledge)	Technology (political economy)
NO	Information (cybernetics)	Science (epistemology)

Figure 3.1.
Forms of knowledge as embodied and embedded (and the corresponding disciplines)

social contexts in which their knowledge is required; hence the utility of the concept of "adaptive preference formation" (more about which below). In any case, under normal circumstances, humans are expected to do much more work than corresponding technologies to convey their knowledge in an unfamiliar social context.

Consider the case of a Chinese university that receives on the same day a sociology lecturer from Britain who plans to give a yearlong course in English and a computer imported from Britain installed with a software package whose instructions are written in English. Although the Chinese recipients may make do with both, they probably would have wished for a better fit from the human, not the computer. In this example, the Chinese have acknowledged (for better or worse) that the computer is a relatively disembedded entity, one whose function remains relatively unaffected by its social surrounding. It is equally important to realize that the natural tendency to treat technology (but not people) as disembedded has nothing to do with the inherent superiority of technology, but rather the different social expectations that are created when one is confronted with a person and a machine. Because technology is less flexible in its possible responses, once users are convinced that a piece of technology performs according to plan, they will adapt their behavior to fit its limitations. The large-scale result of this behavioral tendency has been the "standardization" of the world that sociologists have associated with the widespread adoption of virtually any technology.

However, technology is only half of what IT is about. There is also *information*, which can be conveyed in many different material containers, as long as the user already possesses the resources to access it. This is the sense in which a computer may be seen as "functionally equivalent" to a human being. Under the right conditions, we can get the same information out of both. Of course, the human being knows more than the machine, in large part because we do more than simply store and process information. Yet, our additional mental capacities may be irrelevant for a given user's purposes and even prove an obstacle to the user getting the information she needs. For example, it may be significantly more expensive to consult a human than a computer because the human is deemed an "expert" in her field and hence commands high consultancy fees. Also, the material containers in which people carry their information—their bodies— are not always very reliable. A person's state of physical and mental well-being can easily affect the quality of the information that others can extract from him or her.

Of course, humans and computers are not the only conveyors of information. Such pre-electronic media as books and journals perform virtually the same functions. The great virtue of the computer, however, lies in the potential for users to reliably access large amounts of information specifically relevant to their needs with minimal difficulty. Books, after all, are written only one way. If the book contains much relevant information, there is a good chance that it will impose a burden on the reader to know a lot of background material before being able to fully access its contents. Computers, in contrast, allow for multiple and equally reliable access routes to information and can even be customized to suit users' needs. Indeed, compared with books and humans, it is becoming increasingly difficult to characterize a computer as a self-contained material object. Rather, individual computers are better seen as nodes embedded in vast networks of information exchanges. A good semantic indicator of this disembodiment of information is that the more one can "access" information at will, the less one needs to "possess" it all the time.

A quarter-century ago, the sociology of knowledge started to break down the neat distinction between "science" and "ideology" with which we began this section (Bloor 1976). Nowadays, most sociologists would grant that science is no less embodied and embedded than political and religious ideologies. Indeed, some would go so far as to treat science exclusively in ideological terms. Upon turning to "information" and "technology," however, we find that the advance of computerization has done more to polarize than to erase the difference between these two concepts. Most popular renditions of IT lean on the liberating character of information, the newfound status of computer users as free-floating "net-surfers." Nevertheless, a more critical perspective on IT would stress the computer's technological character more heavily. However, this entails more than simply regarding the computer as a tool, since like all technologies, the computer equally has the ability to shape our modes of thought—including altering the status of "higher order" thought.

One traditional way of thinking about the value of technology is to observe that it relieves our lives of drudgery, those boring and exhausting activities that remind us all too much of our material natures, leaving little time and energy for the "higher" pursuits that have been summed up as "the life of the mind." But the spread of IT is gradually blurring this distinction and with it most of the traditional ways by which humans have distinguished themselves from machines and animals. In short, with the advent of mass computerization, formal ("logical") reasoning has itself come to be seen as a type of work that can be done more economically by replacing human with machine labor. A gross social indicator of this trend is that, in the last generation, most of the economically developed nations have come to experience unprecedented levels of *both* higher educational achievement and long-term unemployment. This seems to defy the conventional wisdom linking credentials and employability. Nevertheless, few social scientists have considered the larger significance of this tendency, especially the prospect that many of our culturally most valued skills are ones that could be more efficiently performed by machines.

The epitome of these developments is the *expert system*, a computer-based system capable of performing at levels comparable to those of human experts, but in less time and at lower cost. These automated services increasingly challenge the need to hire people for tasks traditionally performed by medical doctors, clinical psychologists, librarians, engineers, lawyers, and financial advisors. Arguably, sophisticated software packages for analyzing large amounts of social scientific data belong to this trend, insofar as they remove the need for researchers to hire assistants. Although controversy continues to rage over whether expert systems could ever reproduce the thought processes deployed by their human counterparts, economic imperatives render such speculations beside the point. For, even if we are never able to design computers capable of imitating the processes of human thought, machines already exist that can produce results that are at least as reliable as those of the humans they purport to replace.

In other words, a computer may be able to analyze a large sample of statistical data or diagnose a large number of mental patients more accurately than its human counterpart, not because it follows exactly the same steps in reasoning that the human would, but because it consistently applies a set of "inference rules" without falling afoul of the usual impediments to human performance in complex reasoning tasks, such as bias, fatigue, and sheer storage limitations (Faust 1985). These inference rules prescribe the significance (or "weighting") that is accorded to various bits of evidence in relation to various hypotheses that are of interest to the system's user, and then perform a calculation according to a programmed formula that takes into account typical exceptions to the formula. Often *simulation* is used to describe such an expert system because it manages to reproduce the results of the human expert (on a good day!) without reproducing the means by which the human would reach those results.

A useful precedent for thinking about the relationship between computerized expert systems and human experts is provided by the history of aviation. The word "aviation" derives from the Latin *avis*, bird, which nicely captures the fact that humanity's original interest in flight was triggered by a desire to reproduce mechanically the wing motions that allowed birds to fly simply by using their own physical resources. Leonardo da Vinci is only the most famous of the many people who tried to design such a machine. However, by the 19th century, this strategy came to be seen as unproductive, and would-be aviators shifted toward the more feasible but decidedly unbirdlike fixed-wing design that has become commonplace in modern aircraft technology. Although there are still many aspects of flying at which birds surpass airplanes (not least, esthetic ones), few complain of these shortcomings because planes manage to excel at humanly significant features of flight, especially those involving speed and convenience. Something similar may be said of computers replacing humans in various professional lines of work, since not everything that goes into professional training or practice is necessary for producing results that clients (or "users") find satisfactory to their needs. Indeed, there is every reason to suppose that computers could produce comparable, and perhaps even better, results by following rules of inference quite unlike those followed by humans. Moreover, provided the price is right, even the much-fabled "human touch" is traded off for machine efficiency. (Consider the trust that people nowadays invest in automated bank tellers.)

To be sure, we remain captive to a hoary philosophical dualism: *mind versus matter*. Whatever the exact relationship between computers and humans, it is still generally supposed that the two have radically different natures. In particular, no matter how powerful computers become, they are seen as lacking some essential mental qualities that make humans what they are. Whether computers represent a sophisticated control mechanism over the creative capacities of humans or they constitute an inherently neutral set of tools, in both cases computer nature is depicted as radically "other" to human nature (Dreyfus and Dreyfus 1986, Collins 1990). This dual sense of otherness can be found even within the same theorist, though in the more general context of comparing the free expression of thought epitomized by scientific inquiry and the communication and information technologies that we now associate with the "mass media." Thus, the founder of the sociology of knowledge, Karl Mannheim (1936), began his career in the decade following World War I by arguing that genuinely scientific thought escaped its original material containers. Whereas the strength of ideology rested with those in control of the media that conveyed it, science could demonstrate its validity without first persuading people that a certain view of the world was correct: One could simply perform an experiment or a chain of deductive reasoning, the results of which would be accepted by all rational beings.

However, by World War II, Mannheim (1940) had had a change of heart, especially in light of science's obvious role in magnifying the state's capacity for surveillance and destruction. He came to hold that, as science increased technological capabilities, humanity had made a decisive transition. Originally, technology freed humanity from nature's constraints through labor-saving devices, but now it enabled authoritarian regimes to perfect their policies of enslavement. Indeed, the word "totalitarian" was coined at the time to express the heretofore unthinkable prospect of a political regime becoming so powerful through its mastery of technology that it would be virtually impossible to overturn. These two rather polarized images of technology—as liberator and captivator—share a common feature: namely, that technology is treated exclusively as a tool used by humans on humans. Technology never acquires or replaces the characteristics of a human (or vice versa); rather, it simply serves in the realization of human goals, be they good or evil. Thus, computer technology would be specifically discussed, if at all, in contexts such as military intelligence operations, the administrative apparatus of the state, or as a factor (albeit an increasingly important one) in economic productivity. This view of technology only gradually changed in the postwar period, as social and political theorists came to appreciate the unintended consequences—especially the negative ones—of large-scale technologies of surveillance and administration, all of which came to be symbolized by the computer (Williams 1971).

The "unintended consequences" of social action can be conceptualized in a couple of ways. The simplest way is in terms of people coming to realize that their actions have led to a situation they did not set out to produce. This new situation may be better or worse than the one they aimed for, but at the very least they would admit that it was not part of their original plan. However, when social scientists (and social critics) speak of the unintended consequences of the large-scale technologies associated with computerization, they usually mean something a bit deeper. There is often the implication that computers have altered people's sense of what they want and what counts as satisfying those wants. Consequently, it is argued that an important unintended consequence of computerization is that people redefine their desires so that the new technology appears to satisfy them, and hence they fail to appreciate the major changes that computers have actually made in their lives. Interestingly, this has been a prominent theme in the science fiction literature devoted to the advent of mass information technologies. Good cases in point are Aldous Huxley's *Brave New World* and George Orwell's *1984*, both of which were written more than a quarter-century before computers became part of everyday life in the Western world. The jarring satire in these novels stems from characters routinely claiming that regimes which appear rather oppressive to the reader are in fact providing human happiness in ways unmatched by previous societies.

Computers have the potential to change people's fundamental sense of themselves and the societies in which they live precisely because computers engage with those aspects of our lives, the "mental" ones, that are most intimately tied to our sense of humanity. In this respect, the difference between computers and drugs is simply that people ingest the latter but not the former. In both cases, the sense of mental well-being one quickly receives from their use tends to obscure any concern for their long-term effects. This is part of a general phenomenon, *adaptive preference formation* (Festinger 1957). Social psychologists have observed that in order to maintain mental stability (or "reduce cognitive dissonance," in their jargon), people continually revise their beliefs and desires to allow them to act in a manner they deem rational. Thus, we aim for a "realistic" approach to the world. Often this takes the form of seeing good in what was previously deemed bad, once the "bad" state appears to be inevitable—and vice versa.

The political theorist Jon Elster (1983b) vividly expresses these possibilities as "sweet lemons" and "sour grapes," respectively. In the case of computers reorienting people's values, "sweet lemons" turns out to be the operative concept. Even those who were initially reluctant to rely on computers for composing and communicating their texts often end up wondering how they could have ever coped without incorporating these machines into their lives. They have effectively adapted their preferences to the new world they inhabit. Indeed, many activities that currently require direct contact with other people will probably come to be "virtualized" through human–computer interaction. A remarkably prescient analysis of this prospect was presented a half-century ago by the theologian-turned-sociologist Jacques Ellul (1965), who has been often cited as an inspiration to the countercultural movements of the 1960s. However, as we shall now see, the 1960s also marked the dawn of virtualization.

2. The Post-Industrial Dream: The Intellectualization of Information Technology

The American sociologist Daniel Bell had a dream, one that has captured the imaginations of knowledge producers and policy-makers for the better half of the past half-century. In the 1950s, Bell first dreamed that a new age of "intellectual technology" had dawned which would at once rationalize and depoliticize the complex divisions that had come to characterize American society. This was his famous "end of ideology" thesis (Bell 1960). At the helm of Bell's vision was the university, the leading manufacturer of new forms of human capital and capital goods, technical expertises, and their computer simulations. If class strife was born of industrial society, a newly differentiated and integrated workforce would issue from "post-industrial society."

But if *The Coming of Post-Industrial Society* was supposed to be, as the subtitle of Bell (1973) suggests, a "venture in social forecasting," then it must be deemed a failed venture. However, the nature of the failure is not easy to explain. It is certainly true that every sector of the economy has raised its academic requirements for employment, which would superficially suggest that work has become more "technical" and "specialized" over the years. The university itself is, of course, no exception to this trend. Moreover, computers and other computer-based products have become indispensable aids in the production of all kinds of knowledge. This, in turn, reflects the vast amounts of information that must now be routinely processed, stored, and retrieved before any action is taken. Yet, these developments have not added up to a harmonious social order supported by a benevolent technocracy.

To be sure, there are those who regarded Bell's dream as a nightmare from the start. Such anxieties were largely responsible for the widespread campus unrest in the late 1960s, a point Bell (1966) himself admitted in the report he did for Columbia University, *The Reforming of General Education*. Perhaps because many of these critics were trained in the humanities or the "softer" social sciences, there has been a tendency to caricature their objections as anti-scientific and Luddite. However, a perusal of a major manifesto of the period, Theodore Roszak's (1967) *The Dissenting Academy*, reveals a more nuanced concern. Roszak and his comrades feared that the post-industrial mentality sacrificed the critical mission of science—associated with the Enlightenment motto "Dare to know!"—in the name of increased productivity, which, in turn, strengthened the grip of the emerging "military–industrial complex" on American society. Technocracy for them was not science applied but science betrayed.

The disagreement here was more over interpretation than facts. The prophets of post-industrial society did not hide the fact that the university figured so prominently in their vision because embodied information—both human and machine—was quickly becoming the leading factor of production in the economy. The dispute between the prophets and their critics turned on the quality of the products—again, both human and machine—that this new economy was generating. In particular, the dissenters were worried about the kind of *people* that such an economy produced.

Although artificial intelligence (or AI) research was still very much in its infancy in the 1960s, it was already clear that even relatively unintelligent computerized systems could perform well in environments that simulated the complex problems facing a harried bureaucrat, manager, or field commander who cannot wait for perfect information before deciding on a course of action. The advertised virtue of these machines was, in large measure, a function of their very stupidity. Precisely because these machines could not capture the full range of factors that would influence a human decision-maker, they ended up saving time and resources by avoiding potentially irrelevant lines of thought.

The obvious but politically abrasive point in all this was that these machines could not effectively operate without a hospitable human environment. In other words, the attending humans had to be just as focused on the goals pursued by the computers as the computers themselves were. Any critical interrogation or creative reconfiguration of the software would defeat the purpose of "informatization." However, the prophets of post-industrial society realized that old human habits die hard, and so new forms of research and teaching entered academic life that soon made "simulation" seem like second nature. Business schools were in the vanguard of these developments, with Herbert Simon at Carnegie Mellon University playing a leading role.

In the past 30 years, computer simulations have been increasingly used as research tools in the natural and social sciences. Indeed, the ease with which scientists today confer on simulations the title of "experiments" speaks volumes about how "natural" the artificial has become. Simulations nowadays often replace costly laboratory experiments, which a couple of generations earlier would have themselves been regarded as lacking naturalness or "external validity." However, dissenters from the post-industrial dream were originally more concerned about the role of simulations in the classroom. Here I mean not the actual use of computers, but the attempt to get teachers and students to think more like computers.

These simulations often assumed such humanistic guises as "games" and "role-playing," but were in fact no different from what military and business strategists had begun to call "scenarios." The players of these games occupied positions in an artificially constructed situation calling for a decision. However, the abstract setting sufficiently resembled the "real world" to be of some pedagogical value. Each position came built with assumptions that constrained the player's deliberations. Adeptness at play came from making the best decision possible operating exclusively within those constraints. In fact, players would be faulted for "breaking frame" and introducing "extraneous information" that nevertheless would be pertinent in the real-world setting. Sometimes these faults would be diagnosed as "errors in formal reasoning," if not signs of outright "irrationality."

Regularity and reproducibility—the virtues that Bell had identified in the new intellectual technologies—appeared, in the eyes of his critics, as the latest trained incapacities of the learned classes. Classroom simulations favored those whose conception of accountability was limited to their assigned frame of reference. The implicit message of these exercises was that a complex decision should be taken at some distance removed from the issues—and perhaps even the very parties—potentially affected by the decision. So, whereas the fuzzy-minded would deal directly with the concrete lives at risk when deciding how to trade off productivity against safety in the workplace, the rigorous simulator would start by translating these people into more abstract units of analysis. From under the veil of the algorithm, then, post-industrial reasoners were to be insulated from the remote consequences of their decisions.

The discontent generated by the new intellectual technologies in the 1960s was epitomized in a word: *alienation*. However, this word was used in so many different ways that the post-industrial prophets and their critics ended up arguing at cross-purposes. The critics complained mainly about how the computerized environment disabled the skills classically associated with participatory democracy, especially critical deliberation in a public setting. Their fear was that, given the "proper training," people would come to lose any interest in collectively questioning the ends that their work serves. It would be enough for them to do the work as efficiently as possible. Bell and his defenders interpreted these complaints to be more about the character of post-industrial work itself—whether it retained enough "craft" elements to give aesthetic satisfaction to the people doing it.

At the most basic level, "alienation" refers to the process by which people come to lose what they regard as most human. But, of course, there are as many senses of "being human" as there are schools of philosophy. Addressing the alienation of Aristotle's *zoon politikon*—the concern of the dissenting academicians—is quite different from addressing the alienation of Marx's *homo faber*—the concern of the post-industrial prophets. However, in the confused heat of the debate, the latter concern came to dominate the former. In large part, this shift reflected a widespread belief that the social order projected by the post-industrial prophets was, indeed, an inevitability, and that the best one could do was to adapt one's sense of intellectual integrity to it. The call to craftsmanship was one such adaptation.

Bell's inspiration for introducing craft elements into technocratic work was the attractive picture of "normal science" presented by Thomas Kuhn (1970) in his blockbuster book *The Structure of Scientific Revolutions*. Instead of making all scientists look like such "countercultural" figures as Galileo and Darwin, Kuhn portrayed the average scientist as focused on technical puzzles that make sense only in the context of the "paradigm" under which she is laboring. As for "scientific revolutions," Kuhn said that scientists studiously avoid them until too many insoluble problems arise. But even then, a revolution should end as quickly as possible so that normal science can resume, now in a field that may be subdivided into two peacefully coexisting specialties. Despite restricting his own account to the natural sciences, Kuhn's tendency to identify a paradigm with a self-selecting, self-governing community of inquirers helped persuade many humanists and social scientists that they, too, could enjoy scientific status—or at least raise their standing in the university—by doing things that look like normal science (Fuller 2000b, Chapter 5). Thus, by the 1970s, the rhetoric of the dissenting academy had subtly shifted from claims that the sciences were allowing the military–industrial complex to colonize the university to claims that one's own field had the right to pursue its paradigm alongside the sciences.

The rhetoric of "If you can't beat 'em, join 'em" worked well in this time of plenty for the universities, when ideological enmities could be resolved by the creation of separate departments. However, the fiscal contractions of the post–Cold War period have forced somewhat different conclusions to be drawn from the normal science mode of inquiry. A paradigm in the arts and sciences not only marks its practitioners as disciplined and its practices as self-contained, but also increases the likelihood that both will be dispensable from the standpoint of general education and the public mission of the university. In the case of the professional schools, the conversion of their expertises to normal science renders them tractable to the class of intellectual technologies—*expert systems*—that similarly threaten the employment prospects of therapists, medical technicians, engineers, financial planners, legal advisors, and many more.

In Herbert Simon's (1981) terms, the post-industrial prophets managed to persuade academics to think about their work as constituting a "near-decomposable" system. A paradigm is essentially a module of knowledge production whose business can be conducted largely in isolation from other bodies of knowledge. The source of its autonomy—a limited domain and well-defined procedural rules of inquiry—is also the source of its replaceability, either by a successor paradigm, in the case of revolutionary science, or by an expert system, in the case of normal science. In both cases, however, the rest of the knowledge system can proceed as if nothing has happened.

In hindsight, the great irony of the debate between the post-industrial prophets and their critics was that both sides presumed that the worst that could happen to knowledge work was that it would become machinelike, and knowledge workers would suffer the intellectual equivalent of "deskilling." No one originally suspected that knowledge workers could themselves be replaced by machines. In other words, neither Bell nor Roszak took seriously enough the fact that intellectual technologies are primarily *technologies*, and hence likely to have the same effects on academic capital and labor as other technologies have had on other socioeconomic factors. Thus, from the standpoint of academics worrying about their job prospects, a Luddite response to the introduction of computerization in the 1960s would have been remarkably prescient.

However, the Luddite response was not forthcoming because academics allowed metaphysics and epistemology to do the work of economics and politics. Epitomizing this tendency is the philosophical debate over "the very idea of artificial intelligence," which has fascinated practitioners in many fields (Haugeland 1984). Indeed, AI research entered the world already accompanied by skeptics who have tried to come up with "tests" which only human intelligence can pass, not its machine simulations. Championing these skeptics for the past 30 years has been the Berkeley phenomenologist Hubert Dreyfus (1992), whose 1972 book, *What Computers Can't Do*, popularized the idea that computers cannot think unless they can *reproduce* human thought processes. Yet, from the 1950s onward, military, industrial, and ultimately academic interest in AI research has been motivated by the idea that machines can *replace* human thought processes in a variety of situations calling for quick and focused decisions. The advent of the automated workplace had demonstrated that machines could replace humans without necessarily reproducing exactly what the humans had been doing. Indeed, the economic lure of automation is precisely the prospect that machines can *avoid* certain endemic features of human performance—from fatigue to feelings—that limit productivity.

From an engineering perspective, human beings are built to do many things passably well but few things exceptionally well. A Swiss army knife comes to mind as the model of *Homo sapiens* implied in humanity's collective technological trajectory. The history of technology has been one long attempt to disentangle human capacities into separable skills with specific goals, each of which can then be simulated and refined to order. AI research is only the latest development along this trajectory. From that standpoint, Dreyfus's arguments against the possibility of AI sound a bit like the centuries-old complaint that humans will never be able to fly because we are physically incapable of doing what birds do. Such complaints are beside the point, once agreement is reached on which aspects of a bird's flight are worth simulating. Not all of them are of equal interest. Similarly, an expert system designed to diagnose mental illness may lack the subtlety and intuition of an experienced therapist, but if the goal is to classify large numbers of patients accurately and efficiently, then a calculator of symptoms might do *that particular job* better than the caring person (Faust 1985). What, then, should we make of Dreyfus's efforts at troubleshooting expert systems by asking the machines about the background conditions that make their expertise meaningful? Not surprisingly, machines fail to provide suitable answers, as they were not programmed to reflect upon the presuppositions of their claims to knowledge. The unspoken assumption here is that human experts would have done better. But would they?

With Bell and Kuhn as our guides, we can imagine that a human expert would refuse to answer Dreyfus's queries on the grounds that they violate the public trust and collegial authority that make expertise sociologically possible. Expertise, in the sense that makes "expert systems" even conceivable, requires a strong sense of who is "inside" and "outside" the body of expert knowledge. Colleagues question each other's judgments only within the approved parameters of the "peer-review" process. As lawyers and journalists have shown all too well, whenever experts agree not to limit the kinds of questions they answer, their expertise is soon eroded.

People seek out experts in the hope that the experts understand their problems better than they themselves do. Thus, a client is no more likely than a fellow expert to engage in acts of Dreyfusian impertinence. On the contrary, the client may well blame herself if expert advice fails. Perhaps she misunderstood what the expert had said or even misstated what her original problem was. Like the expert system, then, the human expert must control the frame of reference in terms of which questions are posed. Dreyfus comes across as much too eager to "break frame."

Despite being unwilling to test it in their daily practice, most people seem to agree with Dreyfus that there is something special about human experts that computerized versions could never fully replace. This is the "tacit dimension" of genuinely expert knowledge, the *je ne sais quoi* that supposedly distinguishes someone truly gifted in her field from one who is merely proficient at the rules. On this view, the plodding expert system has met its match in the inspired expert human. But how realistic is this distinction? And, to the extent that it does capture something real, how is it to be explained?

Experts flourish when they enjoy discretionary control over the domains in which they operate. Their ability to give good advice is matched only by their "meta-ability" to determine when they give advice at all. There are certain clients that smart therapists, lawyers, or accountants will not take—regardless of the promised remuneration—because, for whatever reason, the cases do not seem tractable to their expertise. Such rejections are considered signs of "wisdom" on the part of the expert human, yet when an expert system rejects the solicitations of a client, it is counted as a strike against the system.

For this very reason, the first stage in designing an expert system is figuring out how a human expert decides whether a case is relevant to her expertise. This typically involves extended interviews, in which the expert system designer, or "knowledge engineer," tries to map an expert's mindscape. To be sure, the assignment is far from simple, since, in large part, the tacit dimension of the expert's knowledge lies in her inability to articulate the principles that govern her practice. Thus, the knowledge engineer often needs some *je ne sais quoi* of her own—or at least methods that approach psychoanalysis in their indirectness—in order to retrieve expertise from its human container. This stage is followed by the construction of a computer interface that enables the expert system's prospective user to access that expertise as effortlessly as possible, presumably by building on what the user already knows and her interests in wanting such a system designed in the first place.

The two remarkable features of this process—that experts would grant interviews to knowledge engineers and that expert systems would be customized to user specifications—have begun to transform our conceptions of knowledge in ways that go beyond the original post-industrial prophecies. These developments parallel ones that have increasingly allowed the conversion of knowledge from embodied ideas to intellectual property. Together they challenge the assumption that knowledge is a "public good." Whatever else may be meant by this expression, it implies that once the good has been produced, no additional costs are incurred for additional people consuming the good. For example, an insight that originally took the genius of an Einstein or an Edison is eventually accessible to anyone who can read a physics textbook. If students today need to reproduce Einstein's original reasoning, they are probably proving a point about the psychology of scientists, not "earning" their knowledge of relativity theory. This idea plays to the classical notion that genuine knowledge is, at least in principle, equally accessible to all. In economic terms, the value of knowledge is not affected by its distribution.

However, the advent of expert systems challenges precisely this notion. In a slogan: *The multiplication of expert systems divides the value of expertise.* Like all slogans, it covers a complex of effects. The spread of expert systems in a given domain is likely to diminish not only the need for the corresponding human experts but also the value of the knowledge that each remaining expert has. However, these effects will have little to do with the ability of the expert systems to reproduce human expertise. Rather, they will result from people coming to realize that it is not worth paying the additional cost of consulting the human expert. The customized computer is likely to address the client's needs at minimal cost. In that case, professional consultations may go the way of hand-crafted furniture, the pursuit of a few artisans who eke out a modest living off the patronage of the rich.

Nevertheless, it would be a mistake to suppose that only the human expert experiences a depreciation in the value of her expertise. As more people have access to an expert system, the value which they can derive from its knowledge base will likewise decline. This is for two reasons. On the one hand, many people will be in a position to act on the basis of the same knowledge at roughly the same time, thereby diminishing whatever advantage that knowledge may have brought for its possessor in the past. On the other hand, the amount of knowledge that will be available to a given individual from the various expert systems at her disposal will make it increasingly difficult to locate what one needs to know in order to act decisively. Public ignorance thus ascends to the meta-level of not knowing the expert system in which the relevant expertise is contained.

If these emerging problems of knowledge seem strange, it is because they reveal that knowledge is less a public than a *positional* good (Hirsch 1977). In other words, the value of a piece of knowledge cannot be determined without knowing how many people have access to it, and how many other pieces of knowledge they have access to. Librarians and information scientists constitute one professional group that potentially stands to benefit from the positional character of knowledge. In recent years, their ranks have swelled with people originally trained in "proper disciplines" who were turned off by the hyperspecialization that is needed to succeed in modern academic life. Much of their time is spent tracing the contours of fields of knowledge and designing maps for inquirers to navigate in and around them. A hundred years ago, such work would have been done by philosophers proceeding with "systematic intent" in search of some fundamental principles for integrating knowledge. Today's information professionals continue this task by technological means, specifically by testing and selecting appropriate software for the storage and retrieval of large bodies of knowledge. At the moment, this work is accorded relatively low status in the academy. Moreover, the leadership potential of librarians and information scientists is inhibited in at least two ways.

First is the pervasive conception that library work is purely reactive to the current trends in scholarship. On this view, librarians can be only as helpful as the faculty who inform them of their research and teaching needs. However, if knowledge is a positional good, then its value is continually changing in ways that may not be apparent to the average researcher, who typically lacks an overview of the entire knowledge system. Instances of the sort of overview that information professionals can provide are regularly issued from the Institute for Scientific Information in Philadelphia, the publishers of the *Science Citation Index* and companion volumes in the humanities and social sciences. For example, tracking the citation patterns of journal articles has enabled information scientists to sketch the narrative that members of a discipline are collectively telling. Based on examining such patterns across disciplines, one may even be able to project subsequent turns in the collective tale.

All this suggests that information professionals should play a major role in any university planning policy. However, here a second obstacle emerges. Librarians have traditionally defined themselves as the guarantors of free access to information. Although hard to fault on its face, this mission often takes for granted that "free access" automatically means "equal access" and that "equal access" implies "quality access." Yet, just as we have no trouble spotting the errors in these conflations when "access" refers to democratic political processes, librarians must become sensitive to analogous differences that arise when "access" refers to knowledge bases. In short, information professionals must be more proactive than their self-image as facilitators would suggest. An apt metaphor may be that of a planner who issues zoning ordinances for accessing fields of knowledge in the virtual spaces traversed by the "information superhighway."

Economists of opposing ideological stripes have begun to speculate on the probable global effects of expert systems. Neoclassical economists paint a rosy picture of people doing complex jobs more efficiently because they need not rely on the whims of human experts. By simulating the tacit dimension of human expertise, knowledge engineers have supposedly eliminated a costly "middleman" from the labor process. In contrast, Marxist economists evoke a dire scenario whereby intellectual labor becomes generally deskilled and class differences widen. To replace tacit knowledge with computerized expertise is supposedly to enable people with less formal training to achieve comparable results. This, in turn, tilts the labor market toward the employment of lower skilled personnel who can be paid less and be more easily controlled by their employers.

Ironically, where Neoclassicist and Marxist most agree is probably where they are most wrong. Both presume that expert systems *eliminate* human expertise, when in fact it would be truer to say that they *displace* such expertise. At the same time computers replace humans in a given domain, they potentially empower people whose work complements that of the computers. Information professionals are an obvious case in point. But even at the academic department or unit level, there are people whose job it is either to maintain or to supersede the knowledge contained in expert systems. These are, respectively, the technical support personnel and the postdoctoral fellows. Yet, as long as the knowledge possessed by mainstream academics and professionals continues to set the standard of expertise, such complementary positions will suffer the indignity of low status and low pay. Nevertheless, these are precisely the positions that would be the most difficult for machines to replace.

Consider the case of a sophisticated expert system that has been installed in a science laboratory. This system is designed to judge the relative plausibility of competing hypotheses on the basis of experimental data that it is periodically fed. The system's knowledge base was constructed from interviews with leaders of rival research programs, which makes it—much more than any of the leaders themselves—capable of weighing how the same evidence affects a range of alternative research strategies one might pursue. Such systems are already used to identify and eliminate false leads, as well as to mix and match the remaining research strategies.

Even if knowledge engineers have designed this system with a specific set of users in mind, the actual implementation and administration of the system will vary across research sites. And no matter how clever knowledge engineers become, they will probably never be able to replace those jobs. The only question is whether the workers are paid according to the value of the service they render. To customize an expert system to a site is, at most, to make its knowledge accessible to a team of researchers who may differ significantly among themselves in their abilities and interests in dealing with the machine. The increasingly itinerant character of academic work also makes it unlikely that the research team itself will remain constant for the full life of the expert system.

The management of these local details is the job of support personnel whose expertise lies in knowing the flows of people and things in the space surrounding the expert system. They are often the ones who instruct the researchers on the system's operations and are able to anticipate and remedy problems that researchers have with the system. Although these support personnel may have some formal academic training, their expertise is primarily the result of carefully observing how members of the research site interact with each other and with machines. (For readers who have not yet encountered expert systems in their workplaces, consider the department secretary's management of some highly used technology, such as the fax or copy machine.)

The irreplaceability of postdoctoral fellows—or anyone at the cutting edge of research—reflects an equally mundane fact, namely, that an expert system is limited by the intellectual horizons at the time of its design. As radically different concepts and techniques emerge from the research frontier, the expert system starts to show its age. However, just as the support personnel's unique expertise does not extend beyond the place that houses the expert system, likewise the postdoctoral fellow's unique expertise expires once her knowledge has become incorporated into the "normal science" of her field and hence rendered into the stuff of which an expert system can be made.

To AI skeptics such as Dreyfus, these mutual limitations of human and machine expertise imply an essential barrier between the two that will always protect human intelligence from its machine simulations. However, if there is an essence to human intelligence, it is a peculiarly fugitive one. At the start of this century, scientific intelligence was marked by keen powers of observation, a trait readily found in the best astronomers, naturalists, and laboratory scientists. However, as increasingly arcane apparatus has come to mediate the scientist's sense organs, that mark has faded in favor of more strictly intellectual criteria that a scientist could still manifest—on her person, as it were—without instrumental accompaniment. Yet, as we have seen, there are now expert systems that can generate and evaluate hypotheses in ways that satisfy some of these intellectual criteria, at least as judged by the humans who take the advice given by such machines. Is it any surprise, then, that psychologists have been recently locating the seat of the scientific intellect in obscure parts of the brain traditionally devoted to artistic creativity?

But instead of marveling at the metaphysical peculiarities of human intelligence, we might do better to see these peculiarities in economic terms as indicative of a good that continually recovers its value by becoming scarce. In the past, elaborate credentialing rituals and collegial bonds ensured that most forms of knowledge remained in the hands of a few people designated as "experts." However, with the advent of artificial intelligence and the knowledge engineering business, the rituals are being circumvented and the bonds broken. Assuming that these developments continue unabated, I can imagine a time in the not too distant future when a significant part of academic life is devoted to selling one's expertise to a knowledge engineer before it is completely devalued by the proliferation of expert systems—which, of course, will have been the result of other humans having gotten to the knowledge engineer first. Is this yet another nightmare of capitalism unleashed? Or, is this the first time that academics have had a clear incentive to alter their lines of inquiry on a regular basis?

3. Society's Shifting Human–Computer Interface: An Historical Overview

All academics—natural scientists, social scientists, and humanists—have traditionally made a point of avoiding IT, either by minimizing its significance as a mere "tool" or by uncritically embracing its real and imagined benefits. This is because IT challenges fundamental assumptions about the social value accorded to organized human inquiry and even "higher order" thought. As computers are increasingly integrated into society, it is no longer clear whether they should be regarded primarily as tools for human beings to acquire knowledge or as themselves exemplary bearers of knowledge against which to judge human performance. This point strikes at the heart of the entire social science enterprise, which not only aims to produce knowledge but also takes knowledge production as itself an object of study. Daniel Bell is only a relatively recent example of sociological enthusiasm for technology, which stretches back to the origins of the discipline, when its French founders Count Saint-Simon and Auguste Comte (also the first knowledge management gurus) made lavish claims for industrial technology's abilities to restore the order that had been lost with the decline of the Church and the landed aristocracy.

However, one respect in which our situation differs from that of technology's 19th-century sociological promoters is that the new information technology poses deep problems at the level of what philosophers call *ontology*, the essential nature of things. At risk now is the very possibility of social science. Specifically, the idea of a "social science" presupposes that people possess something that is by nature lacking in other things. The possession of higher mental capacities has traditionally given human beings their unique nature, yet these capacities are precisely the ones that computers are designed to simulate. So, it would seem that if computers *literally* think, in the sense that airplanes literally fly, then social science has lost its *raison d'etre*. We would have to admit either that social science has no proper domain of inquiry (i.e., humanity has no essence) or that at least certain computers belong to that domain. Although either prospect seems drastic, both nowadays claim significant support.

On the one hand, Darwinian scruples have led biologists to doubt that certain traits (e.g., the possession of language) are exclusively the property of a single species, thereby subverting one historically important justification for a "science of man." Thus, social science may be ultimately subsumed under either a "sociobiology" or a still more inclusive "science of the artificial" (Simon 1981) that would distinguish, at the physical level, between carbon-based and silicon-based forms of intelligence (i.e., animals versus computers). On the other hand, the past few decades have witnessed the blurring of once-intuitive ontological distinctions among "human," "animal," and "machine." Heightened environmental awareness, combined with more powerful computers sporting user-friendly interfaces and the advent of computationally generated life forms, have not only expanded the circle of beings accorded social standing, but in some cases, have even made it difficult to distinguish from among such beings. The image of the "cyborg," a science-fictional creature melded of human, animal, and machine traits, symbolizes this perspective (Haraway 1991). It is the second horn of the dilemma, I believe, that most directly challenges the future of social science.

The ambiguous sociological status of information technology is epitomized in the contrasting definitions that British and American intellectual property law give to the word "computer." Whereas British law treats the word as metaphorically referring to a machine that enhances computational capacities that are seen as properly belonging to humans, American law regards the "computer" as a machine that literally performs computations, perhaps even ones that are beyond human capacities (Phillips and Firth 1995, 40–42). In British law computers are clearly treated as tools subservient to their human users, but in American law they are granted a more elevated status comparable to an agent or standard. This difference can be explored in depth with the help of a few distinctions, which are outlined in Figure 3.2.

Computers can either provide a means of attaining knowledge or be themselves exemplary bearers of knowledge. In sociological terms, they figure in relationships that exhibit, respectively, *functional* and *substantive* modes of rationality (Mannheim 1940). Such a technology can serve, on the one hand, as a *tool* for enhancing human performance or, on the other, as a *standard* for evaluating human

	MODE OF RATIONALITY	PRINTED WORD	ELECTRONIC WORD
STANDARD	Substantive	Sacred text	General problem solver
AGENT	Communicative	Expert opinion	Expert system
TOOL	Functional	Popular literature	Personal computers

Figure 3.2.
The social relationships of information technologies

performance. A rough-and-ready way of telling the difference between these two modes is to look at what happens when the user and the technology are mismatched. Where does one place the blame—on the technology's inadequacy to the user's needs (functional) or on the user's failure to grasp the technology's design (substantive)? But there is also an intermediate stage. Here the information technology may have been designed as a tool, but the resources invested in both its design and use may make its users reluctant to evaluate the tool's utility simply in terms of its ability to satisfy their immediate needs. Rather, the dissonance produced by the tool may be interpreted as much an opportunity for the users to reassess their own needs as to discard the tool. In that case, the user implicitly treats the information technology as an *agent* with which it participates in what, following Habermas (1984), might be called *communicative* rationality.

However, technology's shifting social status is not unique to our own information age but was decisive in the cultural transformation wrought by an information technology that predates the electronic medium by nearly half a millennium: *printing*. A glimpse at the shape of its history will help us understand the much more rapid changes associated with the computer.

Before the moveable type printing press, books were produced and interpreted under highly restricted conditions that required the mediation of monastic scribes whose work was licensed by the Church. These conditions enabled the texts to function much more as standards than mere tools. Indeed, the most widely transcribed book, the Bible, set the standard for both the conduct of the illiterate masses and the thought of the literate elite. However, moveable type changed all that by allowing for the large-scale production of relatively inexpensive texts that were often written, not in the Church tongue, Latin, but in the "vulgar" languages that readers could readily comprehend. Market forces soon overwhelmed the Church's efforts at regulating the contents of books, and the spread of literacy meant that books could be read silently to oneself rather than be read aloud by an ecclesiastical authority. Thus, every reader became a potential writer. The monastic middlemen had been eliminated. Moreover, the sheer proliferation of mutually contradictory texts—including several vulgar translations of the Bible itself—dissolved the pretense that one book contained all worthwhile knowledge (Eisenstein 1979). In the two centuries immediately following Gutenberg's invention, Europe was successively rocked by the recovery of ancient pagan authorities who challenged the scholasticism of the day (i.e., Renaissance Humanism) and the increased customization of Biblical interpretation to believers' needs (i.e., the Protestant Reformation).

However, the slide in the book's social status from standard to tool was accompanied by a crisis of authority: Lacking a universal church to determine whose word to believe, was each reader simply left to his or her own devices (Febvre and Martin 1976)? The most historically significant response to this problem has been the institutionalization of secular expert opinion in the form of scientific and professional communities, whose exclusive authority over a domain of knowledge is licensed by the state. Characteristic of this development are technical journals, access to which involves greater investments of time and money (in training) than simply consulting the relevant expert in person. Although the fallibility of expert opinion belies any hope of restoring a universal authority, the status of expert communities as "lay-clerical" mediators of public opinion and action has not escaped the notice of their critics.

The history of the electronic word retraces much of the plot of the printed word, but in one-tenth the time and with a twist in the last act (Perrolle 1987, 143–146). The first generation of computers in the 1950s—the ones that have been immortalized in science-fiction films of the period—occupied large rooms, though they contained less memory and processing power than today's average personal computer (PC). Back then computer programming was just as labor-intensive as manuscript transcription was before the printing press. But instead of securing cool, dry places for storing manuscript parchment and maintaining a ready supply of ink (not to mention steady eyes and hands), the programmers faced the continual challenge of cooling the vacuum tubes operating the computer and rewiring the computer's components whenever they wanted to change the program. Yet, it was also during this period that the most grandiose claims were made for "artificial intelligence" (AI) research producing an all-purpose machine, a "General Problem Solver" (GPS) that could resolve any real-world problem into a set of if–then procedures. But as the diffusion of semiconductor technology made successive generations of computers more efficient, the aims of computer design became increasingly customized. The ideal of a GPS located in one self-sufficient machine at the behest of the expert user yielded to vast interlocked networks of PCs, in principle accessible to anyone equipped with the requisite machinery. Even computer programming languages lost much of their forbidding mathematical character, thereby enabling many users to program their own machines.

In principle, the social space constituted by computerization is a free market for transacting information. In practice, however, the superabundance of information has made it increasingly difficult for users to find what they need in order to act decisively. This problem has two aspects, which shall be taken up sequentially in the rest of this chapter.

The first aspect of the problem is the radical prospect that computerization might commodify expertise, extending the processes of industrial automation from factory work to scientific and professional work. This would open the door to the legal subsumption of more abstract and general forms of knowledge under intellectual property, capitalism's last frontier. In short, post-industrial society may simply turn out to be the continuation of industrialism by other means. As we have already seen in the earlier sections of this chapter, the most direct route to this outcome is through the development of *expert systems*, computers whose design requires that the programmer "reverse engineer" human expertise and then repackage it in a format that is user-friendly, economical, and perhaps even more reliable than the simulated human expert. I shall consider this prospect in the next section.

The second aspect of the problem of mass computerization relates to the shift in computational ideals from the GPS to PCs whose "power" is measured, not in terms of the information they physically contain, but in terms of their ability to access remote information sources. The result has been to place computer users at the mercy of whoever controls the computer networks. Traditionally, the state has been at the helm, but as more people log on, the mounting costs of network maintenance are making privatization an increasingly attractive proposition. The prospect that the "information superhighway" will evolve into a toll road and the putatively paperless electronic medium will become "pay-per-view" means that the new information technology may end up reinforcing divisions that already exist between the "haves" and "have nots" in society at large. In Section 5, I address this issue at length, in relation to the specific case of professional researchers, for whom there is no "free lunch" in cyberspace.

4. FROM EXPERTISE TO EXPERT SYSTEMS

4.1. A Brief Social History of Expertise

"Expert," a contraction of the participle "experienced," first appeared as a noun in French at the start of the Third Republic (about 1870). The general idea was much the same as today, namely, someone whose specialized training enables him [sic!] to speak authoritatively on some matter. However, the original context of use was quite specific. The first experts were called as witnesses in trials to detect handwriting forgeries. These people were experienced in discriminating scripts that appeared indistinguishable to the ordinary observer. Thus, the etymological root of "expertise" in "experience" was carried over as the semantically heightened way in which the expert experienced the relevant environment. In contemporary parlance, the tasks that originally required the service of an expert principally involved "pattern recognition," except that the patterns recognized by the expert were identified in terms of an implicit explanatory framework, one typically fraught with value connotations, as in the case of identifying a script as a "forgery."

When evaluating the likelihood that a script was forged, experts were not expected to publicly exhibit their reasoning. They were not casuists who weighed the relative probability that various general principles applied to the case. Rather, it was on the basis of an expert's previous experience of having successfully identified forgeries that his judgment was now trusted. Of course, expert judgment could be contested, but only by another expert, a colleague. If no colleague came forward to testify against an expert's judgment, then the judgment would stand. The climate of collegiality that harbored the mystique of the expert led journalists of the Third Republic to distinguish experts from the "lay" public, thereby conjuring up a clerical image redolent of the secular religion that Auguste Comte's more zealous followers had been promoting under the rubric of *positivism* (Williams 1983, 129).

Moreover, experts were contrasted not only with the lay public but also with *intellectuals*. This point is important for understanding the source of what might be called the *epistemic power of expertise*. An intellectual takes the entire world as fair game for his judgments, but at the same time he opens himself to scrutiny from all quarters. Indeed, the intellectual's natural habitat is controversy, and often he seems to spend more time on defending and attacking positions than on developing and applying them. In contrast, the expert's judgments are restricted to his area of training. The credibility of those judgments are measured in terms of the freedom from contravention that his colleagues accord him. The mystique of expertise is created by the impression that an expert's colleagues are sufficiently scrupulous that, were it necessary, they would be able and inclined to redress any misuse or abuse of their expertise. The fact that they do not means that the expert must be doing something right.

Collegiality enables experts to exert what both Plato and Machiavelli would have recognized as an ideal form of power. In its ideal form, power thrives on a counterfactual condition that never needs to be realized—in less charitable terms, a persuasive bluff. If a prince's enemies believe that the prince could squash any uprising, the enemies will lie low, and the prince will seem invincible; however, if the enemies challenge the prince, and the prince defeats them only with great difficulty, then the air of princely invincibility will disappear, and the prince will need to prepare for redoubled efforts by his enemies in the future. Thus, ideal power is brought down to the level of brute force (Botwinick 1990, 133–180). Trial lawyers continue to exploit this point whenever they try to undermine the very possibility of expertise in a field by pitting particular experts against one another. The attorneys do not expect a definitive judgment to emerge from the crossfire; rather, they expect to show that no such judgment can be rendered.

Philosophers have traditionally shared the attorney's desire to dissipate the power of expertise, but without in the process undermining the possibility of knowledge. Be it embodied in machine or human, philosophers have looked askance at the epistemological status of expertise. For Karl Popper (1970), the expertise conferred on those trained in the special sciences serves to strategically contain critical inquiry, as the evaluation of a knowledge claim depends on the credentials of the claimant. The sociology of knowledge perennially incurs the wrath of philosophers because it seems to condone this tendency, which culminates in the formation of scientific guilds, or disciplines. These, in turn, divert inquiry away from questions of fundamental principles that go to the heart of disciplinary identity. Disciplines proliferate explanatory frameworks (jargons, if you will), whereas "science," in the philosophically honorific sense, unifies such frameworks. Not surprisingly, then, Popper regarded Kuhnian "normal science" as a "danger" to the advance of knowledge, if that advance is measured in terms of explanatory comprehensiveness, or the Newtonian virtue of explaining the most by the least.

Cognitive scientists display a similar disdain when they contrast the "knowledge-based" or "domain-specific" character of expert systems to more general-purpose problem-solving machines that utilize principles that cut across domains. What is often called the "orthodoxy" in cognitive science holds that an adequate theory of cognition is not to be found simply by compounding a number of distinct expert systems, just as an adequate theory of knowledge requires more than simply articulating the research conventions of all the special sciences (Haugeland 1984). The hope, in both cases, is that whatever principles govern the special cases are not unique to them.

4.2. How Knowledge Engineers Benefit from the Social Character of Expertise

To someone whose work is primarily in the design of expert systems, it may seem odd to juxtapose philosophical suspicions about human and machine expertise in the way I have. Perhaps this juxtaposition points to a residual positivist hankering that cognitive science and epistemology (or philosophy of science) share for the "unity of science." Without casting doubts on this diagnosis, I nevertheless want to stress some philosophically disturbing aspects of expertise that have yet to fully grip theorists in this area. As a first pass, these aspects turn on the following truism: *Expertise is a constitutively social phenomenon.* Indeed, expertise can be exhaustively analyzed as a social phenomenon. There are four distinct senses—presented below in descending order of intuitiveness—in which expertise is constitutively social:

1. The skills associated with an expertise are the product of specialized training. Expertise cannot be picked up casually or as the by-product of some other form of learning.
2. Both experts and the lay public recognize that expertise is relevant only on certain occasions. No expertise carries universal applicability.

3. The disposition of expertise is dependent on the collegial patterns of the relevant experts. Protracted internecine disputes over fundamentals typically erode expertise.
4. The cognitive significance of an expertise is affected by the availability of expert training and judgment, relative to the need for the expertise. Too many experts or too little need typically devalue the expertise in question.

So far, I have concentrated on sense 3, given its salience in the historical development of the expert as a social role distinct from that of the layperson, the intellectual, and, as we have just seen, even the scientist. However, all four senses echo the twin themes of *boundedness* and *compartmentalization* as essential to the definition of expertise. The cognitive science literature offers several ways of articulating these themes: Herbert Simon's heuristics, Marvin Minsky's frames, Roger Schank's scripts, Jerry Fodor's modules, and, most abstractly, Zenon Pylyshyn's cognitive impenetrability. Of course, these terms do not divide up the mind's labor in quite the same way. A similar proviso would have to be attached to sociological markers of expertise, such as "indexicality" and "functional differentiation" (cf. Cicourel 1968, Knorr-Cetina 1981). But for our purposes, the most striking comparison may be between, so to speak, the cognitive and political impenetrability of expertise, the so-called autonomy of the professions (cf. Abbott 1988).

The analogy I wish to draw here is not particularly difficult to grasp, but doing so may alert us to the conceptual baggage that is unwittingly imported in the images we use to characterize expertise. The profession that has most jealously guarded its autonomy—scientists—has often struck a bargain to ensure that professionally produced knowledge remains both cognitively and politically impenetrable. From the charter of the Royal Society in 17th-century England to the guild right of *Lehrfreiheit* (freedom of inquiry) that German university professors enjoyed under Bismarck, the following two conditions have been met (cf. Proctor 1991). First, the state agrees not to interfere in the internal governance of the profession, on the condition that the profession does not interfere in the governance of the state. Second, the state agrees to protect the profession from others who might want to interfere with its governance (e.g., other professional, political, or business interests), on the condition that the state is given the first opportunity to appropriate the knowledge produced by the profession, which includes the right to prevent others from subsequently appropriating the knowledge (e.g., for reasons of national security).

Most theories of the mind in cognitive science are fairly explicit in distinguishing an executive central processor or general problem-solver from domain-specific modules that function in relative autonomy from this unit. Sometimes (as in Simon 1981, Minsky 1986) the political imagery of governance is quite strong. However, it is not just any old image of governance, but one that is characteristic of 20th-century thinking about the state, namely, *democratic pluralism* (cf. Held 1987, 186–220). The pluralist portrays the state as mediating competing factions in a large democratic society by enabling the factions to flourish without letting any of them override each other or the national interest. The learning process of big democracies consists of these factions settling into interest groups and, ultimately (and ideally), professionally governed associations whose interaction is founded on recognition and respect for each other's work as essential to the business of society. Gradually, then, the state's role as mediator recedes to that of chairman of a corporate board of directors. The only point I wish to make here is that this is not the only, nor necessarily the most desirable, image of democratic governance. It might repay the effort for cognitive scientists to examine alternative forms of governance as a source of new images for arranging the parts of the mind. In the next chapter, I shall undertake just such a task for knowledge management.

Let us now explore the social character of expertise implied in senses 1 and 2, by considering what might be called a *behaviorist* and a *cognitivist* account of how expertise develops (cf. De Mey 1982, 216):

Behaviorist: Expertise is shaped from repeated encounters with relevant environments, such that increased exposure smoothes out the rough edges in the expert's practice until it stabilizes at a normatively acceptable standard, which can then be applied, "off the shelf" as it were, in subsequent encounters.

Cognitivist: Expertise consists of a core set of skills that are elaborated in a variety of environments, most of which are unforeseen. These elaborations are stored and themselves elaborated upon in subsequent encounters, all of which serves to confer on expertise a sophistication that is evident to the observer but difficult to articulate.

Thus, whereas the behaviorist sees expertise becoming more *stereotyped* in practice, the cognitivist sees it becoming more *nuanced*. In the ongoing dispute between cognitivists and behaviorists, it is often asserted that the cognitivist won this round. But before the final verdict is delivered, I wish to offer support for the behaviorist by way of revealing the hidden social hand of expertise.

To hear cognitivists (not to mention phenomenologists) emote about the "nuanced" and "craftlike" character of expertise, one would think that an act of professional judgment was tantamount to a magic trick, one in which the audience has attended a little too closely to the magician's gestures and not enough to the circumstances under which the illusion transpires. A professional magician does not perform tricks on demand, say, by adapting his performance to play off the specific gullibilities of his audience. Of course, the magician adapts somewhat to his audience, but before he even agrees to display his expertise, the stage must be set just right, and the audience must already be in the right frame of mind to be receptive to the "magic moment." A magician who is too indiscriminate in his eagerness to please is bound to look bad very quickly. An instructive case in point is the odd magician who submits his performances to the strictures of the experimental method (Collins and Pinch 1982, on psychokinesis).

It is worth noting that, in these scientific performances, the magician fares no worse than the expert witnesses in medicine and psychiatry whose testimony is routinely heard—and believed—in court (Faust 1985). The reliability and validity of expert judgment in experimental settings are low all around (Arkes and Hammond 1986). Perhaps the most celebrated historical case of the hubris of overextended expertise was the rise and fall of the Sophists in Athens over the 5th and 4th centuries B.C. After some fair success as teachers of rhetoric and confidants of the ruling class, the Sophists began to offer their services in competition with more established forms of knowledge in virtually every domain. According to a recent historical study (De Romilly 1992), the Sophists were perceived as opportunistic colonizers of conventional practices who failed to cultivate the trust required for their own practices to succeed. Consequently, the

Sophists were soon ridiculed by the people we now regard as the founders of classical philosophy and drama—people with a greater surface respect for tradition than the Sophists had.

Proponents of the operant conditioning paradigm in behaviorism would recognize what is going on here. Successful experts realize that the secret to their success lies in noting the sorts of situations in which clients come away most satisfied with expert judgment (and hence reward the expert appropriately) and then maximizing the opportunities for situations of that sort to arise in the future. In short, the smart expert controls the contingencies by which her behavior is reinforced (cf. Haddock and Houts 1992). She does not easily submit to an experimental test of her expertise, over which she exerts little control.

The strategy for achieving the relevant sense of control involves several tactics:

(i) Preselecting clients before officially engaging in treatment, typically through an interview process, an important aspect of which is to gain the confidence of the prospective client.

(ii) Learning to refuse certain clients, no matter how lucrative their business might be, if it appears as though they will resist treatment or, in some way, be likely to make the expert look bad in the long run.

(iii) Persuading the prospective client that her avowed problem is really one that the expert has seen many times before. Often this is done by first showing the client that she has not conceptualized her problem correctly. Once the problem receives its proper formulation—which neatly coincides with what the expert is in the best position to treat—then treatment can begin.

(iv) Obscuring any discussion of the exact method of treatment by recasting the client's problem in the jargon of the expertise, which will presumably lead the client to infer that anything that must be described in such esoteric ways must be subject to a treatment that would be equally difficult to convey.

The most obvious result of these four tactics is to shape the prospective client's behavior so that her problem falls into one of the stereotyped patterns with which the expert is familiar. A less obvious but equally important result is that the expert can now exert *spin control* over how the client understands her situation after the treatment. If the client's problem is solved, the expert can confidently claim credit for the solution. No suspicions of "spontaneous remission" are likely to be raised, especially if the client has paid dearly for treatment. But perhaps more important, if the client's problem remains unsolved after the treatment, then the expert can claim, with only slightly less confidence, that other unforeseen factors intervened, including the client's own recalcitrance. Whatever happens, therefore, reinforces the expert's competence and integrity.

On the basis of these considerations, I conclude that the key to understanding the distinct character of expertise may lie less in its associated skills than in the discretionary control that the expert has in deploying those skills. (Philosophers of science and cognitive scientists who are uncomfortable with brute talk of "control" may substitute this piece of genteel intellectualism: Experts have heightened "metaknowledge" of the *ceteris paribus* clause, or relevance conditions, for applying their expertise.) Thus, if the above preselection strategy fails to mold the client into shape, the expert can then tell the client that the problem lies outside her expertise, which will probably cause the client to believe that her problem remains unsolved, not because the expert was incompetent, but because the client has yet to locate the right expert, which may itself reflect the client's own failure to understand the nature of her problem. The element of trust crucial for the maintenance of expertise may be seen in the willingness with which the client holds herself responsible for an expert's inability to come to grips with her problem (cf. Gambetta 1988).

From what I have said so far, it may seem that my thinking about the social dimension of expertise has been strongly based on psychiatric encounters, which have often been subject to unflattering depictions as confidence games. However, the same observations apply, perhaps with greater import, to experts operating in the arena of public policy, especially those trained in medicine, engineering, or economics. For, the biggest single problem facing the future of democracy may be *cognitive authoritarianism*, the tendency to cede an ever larger share of the realm of participatory politics to expert rule (Fuller 1988, 277–288). The conversion is accomplished as government officials become convinced that the public has ill-formed conceptions of its own needs, needs that are best shaped and addressed by the relevant experts. When government fails to act speedily on this conversion, and hence does not clear the political environment to enable the expert's stereotyped knowledge to take effect, the expert will often appear as a moral censor, appealing to his special knowledge—which would supposedly be efficacious if politicians secured the relevant background conditions—as a norm against which the state of society is criticized.

But can all this talk about the strategically discretionary character of expertise be applied to computerized expert systems? I do not see why not. Suppose a knowledge engineer has been asked to design an expert system that will offer advice on playing the stock market. After some time, the knowledge engineer returns with a product that she announces was constructed from in-depth interviews with four of the best stock analysts on Wall Street, making sure that respected spokespersons for all the relevant market perspectives—fundamentalists, chartists, insiders, and traders—were canvassed (cf. Smith 1981). The effect of this pedigree on the client will be similar to that of the diploma and license that hang on the wall of the human expert's office and invariably engage the client's peripheral vision during a consultation. If the knowledge engineer designs the interface with protocols that make interaction between client and expert appear stilted, then the client will probably interpret that to mean that the expert is concerned with getting to the heart of the client's problem without dragging in superfluous information. Likewise, if the expert seems to give the client advice that causes her to lose money in the market, then the client may wonder whether a human expert could really have done any better, or whether perhaps she did not input all the information that was relevant for the expert system to provide the right advice. Moreover, the client's inclination to assume responsibility for the bad advice increases with the amount of money that she had to originally spend to purchase the system. That an AI pioneer, Joseph Weizenbaum (1976), should appeal to *moral*, rather than technical, grounds for restricting the use of expert systems reflects the propensity of clients to invest the same level of trust in computers as in human beings.

4.3. The Lessons of Expert Systems for the Sociology of Knowledge Systems

In our earlier list of the four senses in which expertise is "constitutively social," senses 1, 2, and 3 are consistent with a *constructivist* sociological orientation (cf. Knorr-Cetina 1981). Constructivists typically minimize the attribution of intrinsic properties to cognitive agents. Instead, these properties are treated as relational ones, consisting of two mutually interpretive agents who jointly negotiate who will be credited with which properties. As we have seen, an adept expert can shift the burden of responsibility onto the client for the unpleasant consequences of following expert advice. But for the constructivist, there is no "fact of the matter" about whether the expert's incompetence or the client's recalcitrance is to blame, until the transaction has actually taken place. In discussions of cognitive science that acknowledge that society is more than a metaphor for the mind, constructivism is often presented as *the* sociological perspective. But I shall ultimately appeal to sense 4 of expertise's sociality in order to introduce a different, and more comprehensive, sociological perspective.

Constructivism is a more heterogeneous doctrine than it may first appear. Weizenbaum and others who oppose the cognitive authority of either computer or human experts on mainly moral grounds presuppose that such experts can, indeed, exercise all manner of authority, if they are not limited by social convention. However, a milder species of constructivism is represented by Daniel Dennett's (e.g., 1987) instrumentalist approach to what philosophers expansively call "intentionality," namely, the aspect of our thoughts that is directed to something that lies beyond them. Accordingly, one's cognitive status is dependent on another's interpretive stance. Dennett's constructivism is "asymmetrical," in that he does not grant the computer the same degree of agency as most humans in constructing their respective identities. In other words, the interpretive powers of humans vis-à-vis computers are presumed to be much greater than vice versa. By contrast, a more egalitarian stance characterizes the more radical constructivists, the ethnographers who can be increasingly found on the sites where knowledge engineering occurs (cf. Greenbaum and Kyng 1991). Here knowledge engineers, human and computer experts, clients, and other people and artifacts are portrayed as engaged in a mutually reinforcing cooperative venture. What are the limitations of this version of constructivism?

Drawing on the work of cultural anthropologists, especially Clifford Geertz (1983), ethnographic constructivism makes much of the "local" character of expert knowledge, which is brought out very clearly in the design of expert systems. The idiosyncrasy of locales is brought out in the knowledge engineer's interviews with both client and expert, followed by the process of adapting the expert system to the client's specific needs and abilities. These ethnographic accounts are meant to stand in striking contrast to the accounts typically given by the designers of AI systems in basic research settings, who often influence the way in which the applied researchers, the knowledge engineers, conceptualize their activities. Specifically, workers in AI tend to attribute properties to their programs (typically once embodied in a machine) that the ethnographers would prefer to regard as "boundary objects" in terms of which the identities (or cognitive capacities) of various agents are negotiated. For example, the degree of satisfaction that the client gets from using an expert system has implications for the amount of human expertise that is thought to have been transferred to the computer program. While this reinterpretation of expertise corrects the accounts given by AI researchers, it nevertheless shares the fatal flaw of its opponents. Ironically, the flaw is the tendency to universalize from a single case. Let me explain.

It is one thing to say that all knowledge is local. That is rather boring. It is another to say that all locales are significantly different from one another in cognitively relevant respects. That is more exciting. Ethnographers infer the exciting proposition from the boring one all the time. But what licenses this inference? Certainly, there have not been enough ethnographies of knowledge engineering to license the exciting proposition as an empirical generalization. Rather, the ethnographic appeal to locality presupposes a *conceptual cartography* whereby one imagines that the spatio-temporal distance between locales is seen to stand for conceptual distance. In that sense, "the local" presupposes "the global," an image of the whole. Admittedly, sometimes this image turns out to be right; but other times it doesn't. However, that is a matter for comparative empirical inquiry, which is not necessarily encouraged by the ethnographic brand of constructivism. For, to learn about the global properties of knowledge engineering, one needs to discover the pattern by which expertise is *distributed* across a representative sample of locales and the *aggregated* consequences of such a distribution for the knowledge system as a whole. Here I start to speak the language of *political economy*, and to signal the quest for statistical correlations among variables that are hypothesized to be salient for understanding how expertise works. In particular, one would look at changes in the correlations over time and the global flows of expertise they imply.

What sorts of people are the producers and consumers of expert knowledge? Provided with a serviceable answer, we can study the distribution of expertise by focusing on a cognitively relevant locus of scarcity: A client has only so much time and money to spend consulting an expert, be it human or computer. Under what circumstances does the client feel she has gotten what she has paid for? And, when she does not feel that way, how is the blame apportioned— who receives the lion's share of incompetence, the client or the expert? A key to understanding the distribution of expertise is to see how each side tries to convert its own sense of frustration into a perception of the other's liabilities. It would be fair to suppose that expert computers today receive far more attributions of incompetence than expert humans. A constructivist would diagnose this difference in terms of the client's lack of time, imagination, or interest in interpreting the computer as performing intelligently—perhaps because the client feels either that she has better things to do at this point, and the computer is in no position to prevent her from doing them, or that she would have to end up interpreting the computer as doing something other than she would have wanted (cf. Fuller 1993b, 179–185). However, as people become more accustomed to dealing with expert computers, this difference in attribution is likely to disappear. But before concluding that we are projecting a future in which experts of all sorts are engaged in mutually satisfying relationships with their clients, we need to consider the aggregated consequences of people increasingly turning to computers for advice.

4.4. Expert Systems and the Pseudo-Democratization of Expertise

The history of expertise teaches that the expert is not a universalizable social role. There are no "experts" in areas that are regarded as commonsense or part of general education or easy to acquire without specialized training. Consequently, knowledge engineers are in the curious position of potentially destroying expertise as they diligently codify it and make it available to more people in user-friendly packages. While this consequence is bound to elude any on-site description of the knowledge engineer's work (though it even seems to have eluded supposedly sophisticated social-theoretic accounts of expert systems: e.g., Giddens 1990), it is nevertheless felt by professional associations that believe that knowledge engineers are indirectly deskilling their members. For, even as the human expert retains discretionary control over when, where, and how she uses her expertise, she may be losing discretionary control at the *meta-level*, namely, over who—or what—else counts as an expert in her field. Librarians have so far been most vocal in their concerns (cf. Pfaffenberger 1990), but attempts by many doctors and lawyers to limit the scope of the interviews they give to knowledge engineers reflect similar worries. It would seem that knowledge engineering discourages the belief that expertise is valuable for its own sake. The guild-like autonomy associated with the pursuit of expert knowledge thus comes to be seen as a historical accident that is not required for the continued maintenance and dissemination of such knowledge (Krause 1996). Rather, the employment of a human expert is regarded as only one of several possible means for achieving the same end, in which case the human may not be the most efficient means, in terms of either cost or reliability. Under the circumstances, a customized expert system may appear an attractive alternative.

At first glance, it may seem that the proliferation of expert systems is the ideal vehicle for democratizing expertise, as it would seem to put expert knowledge within the reach of more people. Just because the knowledge engineer can extract elements of expertise from her interviews with experts, it does not follow that the expertise remains intact once it is programmed into a computer for a client. After all, if expertise is indeed constitutively social, then altering the context in which expert knowledge is deployed should alter the character of the knowledge itself.

Such change may be witnessed in the course of designing the interface that enables the client to interact with the expert system. Here the tendency has been to "go ergonomic" by designing interfaces that require the client to change his ordinary patterns of thought and behavior as little as possible (Downes 1987). Less charitably put, the ergonomic approach reinforces the client's cognitive biases and thereby minimizes the learning experience that he might derive from engaging with the expertise as a form of knowledge. A potentially "dialectical" exchange is thus rendered merely "instrumental" (cf. Adorno and Horkheimer 1972). The result is a spurious sense of autonomy, whereby the client's powers appear to be extended only because the environment in which he acts has been changed to his advantage (Fuller 1986). Thus, while the expert humans may lose some of their power as their clients increasingly rely on computerized systems, the clients themselves may not, in turn, become epistemically empowered. *Experts are deskilled without clients being reskilled.* Where has the original power of expertise gone? That power would seem to have dissipated somewhere in the knowledge engineering process, specifically when expertise was converted into a *tool* that exerted few of its own demands on the user (cf. Fields 1987).

This last point raises an important problem with the context in which expert systems are typically discussed in contemporary social theory, namely, in connection with the "reflexive modernization" thesis (Beck, Giddens, and Lash 1994). This literature is primarily concerned with explaining the array of phenomena and tendencies associated with the "postmodern condition" by revealing the often ironic and even subversive uses to which individuals and groups have put the supposedly inexorable forces of modernization. Thus, expert systems are discussed, not as the latest phase in the capitalist mediation of social relations, but rather as part of the vanguard of "lifestyle politics," which itself reflects the devolution of the state and the disorganization of capitalism (Lash and Urry 1987). Here the spread of market forces that have led to both the decline of state-protected professions and the rise of the knowledge engineering business is interpreted as ushering in a new era of "democratization," but one better attuned to neoliberals than to civic republicans.

Democracy has traditionally required spaces that enable forms of social exchange that serve to stretch the participants' horizons, in aid, one hopes, of constructing a sense of community, or at least common cause. However, the high value that reflexive modernization theorists place on user-friendliness and customization more generally as marks of democratization suggests a rather different orientation, one keen on consolidating existing biases into worldviews and ultimately "identities," even if this process does little to redistribute existing power relations. Hence, it is easy for these theorists to overlook the literal dissipation of expertise mentioned in the last paragraph, since people are, after all, getting more of what they want in ways they could not before.

A major source of the difference between this increasingly common social theoretic perspective on expert systems and my own is that the former treats matters of political economy from a *consumption* rather than a *production* standpoint. This consumptionist perspective stresses the phenomenological sense of freedom that comes from eliminating obstacles to the satisfaction of one's desires, while downplaying the relevant background material conditions, specifically the corporate suppliers of knowledge engineering services whose interests are served not merely by efficiently satisfying consumer demand, but more importantly by maintaining the shape of that demand so as to discourage any major reconfiguration of the market.

In other words, as consumers become better able to satisfy their desires, they become less inclined to want to change them. As Bauman (1993, 196ff) has critically observed, reflexive modernization theorists tend to presume that the mere presence of consumer choice—as in the case of multiple suppliers of expertise—constitutes a newfound sense of cognitive empowerment, when in fact it may be little more than another instance of the "repressive desublimation" that Herbert Marcuse (1964, 71–74) saw as characteristic of everyday life in liberal democratic societies that are underwritten by an advanced capitalist economy. Put in somewhat romantic terms, when the knowledge possessed by a human expert posed a definitive barrier to the pursuit of someone's interests, one faced a decision of some momentousness: Acquire the knowledge for oneself through schooling or employ the expert (often at great expense) in the hope that he will provide knowledge that will indeed turn out to be useful. Such a decision invariably forced the person to reflect on the exact nature of her interests that calls for the acquisition of expertise. But once expertise is commodified in computerized systems (or in some other way "offloaded to a smart environment": cf. Dennett 1996, 177–178), that deep existential moment fails to occur, as people can easily find alternative means of satisfying their desires as they are most immediately, and least reflectively, felt.

It is little more than a metaphysical conceit to claim either that computers cannot think or that their sheer use dehumanizes humans. But these excessive claims should not obscure the basic point that the increased reliance on expert systems has forced human experts to adapt their work patterns to the machines, or else risk, if not outright redundancy, a reduction in status to the intellectual equivalents of hand-crafted furniture makers in an age of mass production (Haug 1977; Krause 1996).

However, my pessimistic forecast needs to be qualified in two ways. First, expert systems are targeted to capture the knowledge base and reasoning patterns of a "normal practitioner" at a given point in time. Usually, it is not possible to model a normal practitioner unless a field is fairly established and subject to little doctrinal disagreement. This means that people who work in less established and more controversial fields are typically less susceptible to replacement by expert systems, even though these people may enjoy lower status than the normal practitioners. Second, not all professions feel the pressure of computerization equally, but the difference is due more to the moral suasion that a professional community exerts over its members (e.g., to reject interviews with knowledge engineers) and its mystique in the larger society than any inherent difficulty in computerizing the expert reasoning tasks. Thus, although knowledge engineers have amassed a record of designing expert systems in medicine and psychiatry just as creditable as in librarianship and engineering, computerization has made greater inroads in the latter pair of relatively weak professional fields (Perrolle 1987, 171).

The utopian vision of democratized expertise is foiled by the simple fact that expertise is a positional good whose value is directly tied to others not having it. In this context, the existence of positional goods is the dark secret of the welfare state (Hirsch 1977). According to welfare economics, capitalism can avert a Marxist revolution because lingering inequalities of wealth will be resolved once a level of productivity is reached that enables everyone to be supported at a minimally acceptable standard. At most, stabilizing this situation will require a modest redistribution of income through progressive taxation. Overlooked in this scenario is that, as more goods are made more generally available, the perceived value of the goods may decline as they no longer serve to discriminate people in socially relevant ways (Bourdieu 1984). Knowledge-intensive goods display such positionality effects. Higher education is perhaps the most obvious case in point: As it becomes easier for people to complete college, more postgraduate degrees are needed to acquire the same credentials. Should it become impossible either to stop the production of degree-holders or to set up additional barriers in the credentialing process, higher education will then no longer be seen as imparting an especially valued form of knowledge. Instead, it will take the place of bare literacy and the high school diploma as the minimum threshold for entry into the job market. Can anything be done to reverse such positionality effects, or is the value of knowledge-intensive goods—including human experts—doomed to continual deflation?

Moreover, the political scientist Yaron Ezrahi (1990) has argued that the scientific enterprise has come to consume so many resources and to produce so many questionable consequences that we may be reaching the end of the period (which began with the Enlightenment) when knowledge is *presumed* to be a public good. Ezrahi envisages that scientific forms of knowledge will gradually acquire the social character of art-forms: Their support will be privatized and their products customized to client tastes, which are presumed *not* to be universalizable. But even if expertise were to become entirely market-driven, the skills surrounding the expertise would still attract human practitioners as art continues to do, and for the same reasons. The skills would be detached from the fame, fortune, or power that had been previously tied to them. Most of the perverse consequences of positional goods rest on such coupling (Crouch 1983). For example, higher education is populated by a few people who are interested in the education process itself and many more who view it as a credentialing process, the surest route to a job. Decoupling those two groups might help restore the integrity of higher education.

The expansion of intellectual property law to cover more instances of "basic research" suggests that Ezrahi's prognosis is already taking shape. Given their own interest in customizing expertise for user demand, knowledge engineers clearly contribute to this overall trend toward privatization, which is by no means the same as democratization. Indeed, human experts may soon find the need to seek legal protection for their expertise, if only to earn royalties from the expert systems that are based on it. In that way, knowledge engineers would not benefit too much from what economic historians call the "Japan Effect," the process by which latecomers learn how to manufacture a product more efficiently than its originators as a result of having had the opportunity to observe the strengths and weaknesses of the product in use. This form of legal protection would, in turn, require a new category of intellectual property beyond the usual three of patent, copyright, and trademark. Knowledge engineers have a crucial role to play in the future disposition of expertise and knowledge more generally. Customized expert systems can hasten the demise of expertise and turn Ezrahi's image into a reality. However, the proliferation of such systems may also limit the client's potential for cognitive growth. A page from the history of manufacturing may prove instructive in resolving this dilemma.

Once the demand for manufactured products grew to a critical level, customization yielded to mass production (Beniger 1986, 291–343). This transition was accompanied by the design of quality control standards for the mass-produced goods. In the process of defining the minimum level of acceptability for a particular good, manufacturers effectively forced potential customers to adapt their behavior to the set dimensions of the good. Typically, these adaptations were dictated by the manufacturer's desire to cut costs, but knowledge engineers could collectively set guidelines for the design of expert systems, the successful use of which required clients to expand their cognitive repertoire. The sort of behavioral changes I envision here may be quite subtle. For example, an online library search system may discourage disciplinary provincialism by requiring the client to initiate searches by using protocols that are tied less to the jargon of specific disciplines and more to the exact topic or problem that client wishes to tackle. The system's database would, in turn, draw on the literatures of several disciplines so as not simply to confirm the course of inquiry that the client would be naturally inclined to follow (Cronin and Davenport 1988, 316–327).

It remains an open question whether the power of knowledge is tied more to its sheer practice or to its status as a positional good. Those keen on retaining the ethereal quality of knowledge may no doubt want to make a strong distinction between "genuine knowledge" and "mere expertise" (cf. Ford and Agnew 1992). They will object to my apparent conflation of these two concepts. Whereas expertise may ultimately reduce to matters of status and trust, the objector may argue, the test of knowledge is precisely that it does not lose its force as its availability increases. In response, let me grant the objector's distinction as the basis for an empirical hypothesis. If there are indeed types of "information" or "skills" whose power does not diminish with their increased availability, then I will gladly call them "genuine knowledge."

However, there are limits to the optimal distribution of these cognitive products. Consider the following homely observations:

(a) Everyone in a town may know the location of a particular store and the time it opens for business. However, if many of these people decide to act on that knowledge at roughly the same time to purchase the same goods, then a larger percentage of them will probably return home empty-handed than if fewer of them knew about the store in the first place. *Here knowledge lacks efficacy because the knowledgeable get in each other's way.* (A more realistic version of this situation is one in which everyone decides to take the same expert's advice on which stock to purchase.)

(b) It is often assumed that information freely exchanged among a large network of peers breeds the sort of critical inquiry that is necessary for genuine epistemic progress: the larger and freer the network, the more critical the inquiry. Unfortunately, this assumption presumes, contrary to fact, that inquirers have an inexhaustible ability and inclination to attend to each other's work. Yet, by the time the network of inquiry attains the dimensions of "Big Science," inquirers become more concerned with finding allies than opponents, and hence are likely to simply ignore work that cannot be immediately used for their own purposes. *Here knowledge lacks efficacy because more of it is available than can be assimilated.*

Knowledge was undermined in (a) because too many people possessed the same information, whereas in (b) it was because each person possessed too much information. In neither case did these skewed distributions actually convert a truth into a falsehood, but from a pragmatic standpoint, they might as well have. In other words, attention to the socially distributed character of knowledge may help explain the intuitions that have traditionally led philosophers to posit a conception of knowledge that "transcends" constitutively social character expertise.

4.5. Recapitulation: Expertise as the Ultimate Subject of Intellectual Property

One possible solution to the overall erosion of expertise that I anticipate is for human experts to seek legal protection, if only to earn royalties from the expert systems that draw on their expertise. As it stands, knowledge engineers seem to benefit from what economic historians call the "Japan Effect," in that the knowledge engineer's initial interviews with clients and experts enable her to design machines that operate "more efficiently" than the original experts themselves. However, the legal protection of expertise is easier said than done, for reasons related to the conceptual basis of intellectual property law. On the one hand, the products of knowledge engineering—the expert systems—are clearly subject to legal protection, though the exact coverage afforded by the law is a point that we shall have to look at more closely. On the other hand, the "raw material" out of which these products are made—the human expertise—cannot be so covered. The basic reason is that property rights extend only to things which, if not invented, are "divisible," that is, characterized by someone's gain always being someone else's loss (Croskery 1989). Traditionally, knowledge does not satisfy this criterion because, as we saw in Chapter 1, of its traditional status as a good that is "ethereal," "collective," or in any case, "public."

When thinking about the relationship between human expertise and expert systems, an interesting point of comparison is the distinction between natural resources and the goods made from them. Until the 19th century, it was common to regard nature as superabundant and hence not subject to the laws of the marketplace. As Adam Smith famously put it in *The Wealth of Nations* in 1776, nature had "use value" but not "exchange value." However, once the commercial exploitation of natural resources exceeded the rate at which nature could restore itself, two legal trends emerged, one reflecting the newfound divisibility of nature and the other the prospect that human inventiveness may simulate, extend, and perhaps even replace nature. The former led to environmental protection codes, the latter to intellectual property codes. From a legal standpoint, in recent years, human expertise has become the new "nature." Consider the problem of nature's failure to replenish itself in the face of commercial exploitation. The analogous problem faced by human experts is that expert systems can be designed to user specifications faster than the knowledge base of the relevant expertise undergoes fundamental change. In other words, once knowledge engineering has gained a foothold in a field formally dominated by human experts, computers are more likely render humans redundant than vice versa. Does this mean that human expertise should be protected in the sense one might protect an endangered species, especially in terms of restricting access to commercial interests?

For better or worse, the law has generally given a negative answer to this last question. Perhaps a more relevant model for understanding the law's generally laissez-faire attitude toward knowledge engineering is provided by the idea of *bioprospecting*, raised in the previous chapter. Here the idea is that nature—including human biology—possesses properties whose extraction and distribution can advance human welfare in ways that are presumably unknown to their natural possessors, yet do not require disruption of the possessors' normal lives. Bioprospecting is usually discussed in the context of genes possessed by certain relatively isolated ethnic groups. But it could also be argued that in virtue of the relative isolation (or "autonomy") of their training and practice, human experts possess certain properties that could enhance the human condition, were they made more widely available. As in bioprospecting, extracting those properties would require the services of an anthropologist or ethnographer. A synthetic process that increases the accessibility of these properties would then be patentable as an "invention" under intellectual property law. Just as a biotechnologist may patent a process that enables synthesized genetic material to prevent the occurrence of certain diseases in humans, so, too, a knowledge engineer may patent a computer program that simulates the expertise needed for reliable solutions to recurrent problems. That human experts regularly claim that their expertise is "tacit," and hence uncodifiable, is simply regarded as a "folk myth" by the knowledge engineers who make it their business to divine the nature of that expertise and to claim its discovery as their own.

Knowledge engineering can be plausibly subsumed under intellectual property codes only if expertise can be extracted and distributed without in the process diminishing it or its natural possessors, the human experts. However, in this chapter, we have suggested that such a diminution will be difficult to avoid, since knowledge is a positional good whose value lies not in its intrinsic qualities but its ability to discriminate between people's capacities for thought and action.

Here it is worth recalling that the paradigm case of a positional good is a university degree, in that its ability to secure employment for its possessors clearly declines as more people possess it, even though the content of the degree itself may not change. Hirsch's (1977) original point was made in the context of arguing that the tendency to regard goods as divisible requires a deeper explanation than the sheer presence of material scarcity, since divisibility persists in high-growth, welfare-oriented capitalist societies. Rather, he saw the tendency as ultimately related to the human need for recognition, that is, to be someone who has something that others do not. (The social implications of this phenomenon are explored in Fuller 1994b.) From a sociological standpoint, forms of knowledge that are regarded as especially profound or powerful are rarely within easy reach of the many. For example, automated laboratory technology has done much to devalue the "keen powers of observation" that at the start of this century had been thought to distinguish the scientific mind. Expert systems may be seen as following in this lineage, only now eroding the positional advantage of certain higher-order mental functions, such as diagnosis, causal modeling, and hypothesis testing. Not surprisingly, Turkle (1984) and others have found that people are shifting their sense of human uniqueness to "creative" qualities that are currently just beyond the reach of computer simulation.

Legal theorists and legislators of intellectual property from the 18th century onward have increasingly acknowledged the positional character of knowledge in their attempts to regulate its production through schemes designed to distribute equitably the costs and benefits of knowledge products across society. The basic problem is that any new knowledge product has the potential for empowering many more people than it initially does, yet the nature of the power imparts changes as these people come to use the knowledge in promoting their own diverse ends. In Anglo-American law, the historical tendency has been toward restricting the power that the original knowledge producer can exert in society, without, in the process, completely inhibiting the production of new knowledge. Thus, at first patents covered the *inventiveness* of artisans, which enabled them to monopolize and mystify their expertise, but once patents were limited to *inventions*, the locus of legal investigation shifted from the character of the inventor to the efficacy of the invention itself, and then the very scope and duration of the legal protection given to the invention began to shrink. In this way, inventors became morally tolerable agents whose activities no longer impeded the interests of other agents.

However, this delicate balance may well be upset in the near future. As all business and industry are increasingly computerized and the manufacture of computers and computer-based technologies is increasingly concentrated in a few transnational corporations, states are being pressured to extend the legal protection granted to intellectual property already in corporate possession. But as Drahos (1995) has observed, this is to take intellectual property too literally as landed property, the long-term result of which may be that we live in *information feudalism*. Under such a regime, corporations would have permanent and exclusive right to domains of knowledge, access to which would require payment of a toll or rent. For a conceptual appreciation of how this turn of events may take place, we need to see it in terms of one of three major ways of completing the account of the social history of information technology told in this chapter. The chart in Figure 3.3 will provide an aid in what follows.

Intellectual property law is *not* normally seen as the extension of property law to the intellectual realm. This is because the potential effects of knowledge products such as expert systems are less clearly bounded in space and time than, say, a tract of farmland. An unconditional right of property is typically granted only when the state is confident that the right will not unjustly interfere with the livelihoods of others. In contrast, the "property right" embodied in a patent is granted more in the spirit of retroactive compensation for labor that the state did not originally commission but from which its citizens may now benefit. Since the inventor took time from other activities to produce the invention, it is only fair that she enjoy the fruits of her own labor, specifically as a temporary advantage over potential competitors. Intellectual property law has struggled hard to maintain this middle ground against the contrary pulls of *libertarian* and *totalitarian* legal sensibilities. This distinction is elaborated in Figure 3.3.

A libertarian approach to intellectual property would essentially do away with legal protection for knowledge products and throw the whole process open to the marketplace. On this view, the state does not need to provide any incentives to invent, as the prospect of profits is sufficient to motivate people to try to satisfy consumer needs as efficiently as possible. At the same time, however, there are no guarantees that an inventor will reap all the profits of a successful invention, as competitors quickly step in to reverse-engineer the invention in the hope of providing a still more efficient product. This is roughly

	ECONOMIC LOGIC	MODEL OF VALUE	LEGAL PRIVILEGE	JUSTIFI-CATION
STANDARD (Totalitarian)	Monopoly	Rent on property	Permanent	Effort involved risk
AGENT	Exchange	Wage for labor	Temporary	Required original effort
TOOL (Libertarian)	Competition	Profit from sales	None	Effort was voluntary

Figure 3.3.
Alternative legal–economic models of IT's social relations

the situation that prevails in the efforts of knowledge engineers to design expert systems that replace human experts, especially in socially weak professions. Under such a regime, it would be difficult to stabilize bodies of knowledge that are valid for a wide range of domains and activities, as inventors would always be driven to customize their products to user needs, regarding the information embodied in their inventions as mere means.

A totalitarian approach to intellectual property represents the view of the transnational corporations discussed above. It gains initial plausibility from the idea that the inventor—or more realistically, the corporation that houses the inventor—bore all the risk in developing the invention, and so now deserves to reap what benefits it can in perpetuity. Yet, in effect, the corporation is also agreeing to assume more risk, as its unconditional right over the invention means that it must decide who will be able to use it, for what purposes, and at what costs. Of course, such a right discourages reverse engineering, if not makes it impossible. In the case of knowledge engineering, one consequence may be that all the expert systems designed to solve certain types of problems are written in the same private programming language, which would constitute a map of what has become, legally speaking, a literal "domain" of knowledge. At least, one would be able to draw once again—as one could in medieval times— a clear distinction between the stable body of knowledge constituted by the secret program (a.k.a. "reality") and the multiple user-friendly interfaces (a.k.a. "appearance") that the customers for the corporation's expert systems will confront.

In summary, in the first age of information technology—that of the printed word—state-licensed expert communities helped restore some sense of authoritative knowledge to the relatively free and chaotic world of published opinion. However, in the relatively free market that dominates the second age of information technology— that of computers—knowledge engineers have forced human experts to compete with expert systems to satisfy consumer needs. In several fields, this has reduced the social role of expertise from standard or agent to mere tool—and a relatively inefficient one at that, which has led to expert redundancies. But there is also a reverse tendency, as knowledge engineering becomes subsumed by larger trends in transnational capitalism. In that case, entire domains of knowledge may be effectively owned by companies whose intellectual property rights are so strong that they are the sole providers of the systems capable of satisfying consumer needs in those domains. Should we reach such a state of information feudalism, we would have come full circle to the idea of information technology as a standard of human performance, except that it would be a standard that would remain a mystery to all but the most elite corporate computer programmers. Since that would surely put us back in the Dark Ages, it is perhaps time to revisit the idea that human expertise is a scarce natural resource.

5. WHY EVEN SCHOLARS DON'T GET A FREE LUNCH IN CYBERSPACE

Inveterate "netsurfers" typically believe that electronic communication has removed all the material obstacles that have traditionally prevented scholarship from enjoying universal access and immediate impact. If you are one of these people, the odds are that your computer is connected to a university or corporate mainframe, which means that you are not directly charged any user's fees and you rarely suffer from delays in transmission. However, if you log on through a modem connected to your telephone, then the "information superhighway" fast loses its reputation for being a frictionless medium of thought. Depending on your location, telephone access fees can mount up very quickly, and the rate structure of commercial electronic carriers may force you into a suboptimal service that frequently suspends your messages in limbo while those of premium customers zip back and forth. Finally, if you are a technophobic scholar lacking connections to a major institution, the Internet merely widens the gap between you and the rest of the intellectual world.

These homely observations reveal that as the electronic medium revolutionizes academic communications, there is the inevitable tendency to hope that it will relieve scholars of the burdens of previous media without imposing any of its own. I shall dub prophets of the new medium who adopt this sociologically blinkered posture *tunnel-visionaries*. They have so far received the most media coverage in their attempt to shape the future of scholarship on the Internet (Kling and Lamb 1996). One imagines them also to be among the inveterate netsurfers. As they see it, scholars have a clear sense of what they want and sufficient resources to make it happen, even though a full transition to the electronic medium may incur some short-term institutional costs. The tunnel-visionaries envisage business-as-usual in academia becoming increasingly efficient, as scholars can access materials and audiences more easily, produce more text, and receive quicker feedback. They never consider the congestion problems that will arise as more scholars log on, nor do they worry much about assigning intellectual property rights to tracts in cyberspace. In fact, the tunnel-visionaries tend to blame the publishing industry for anything that reminds academics that their work has an economic dimension. Perhaps the most visible and imaginative of the Internet's tunnel-visionaries is Stevan Harnad, best known as the founding editor of the most successful open peer commentary journal in the social sciences (*Behavior and Brain Sciences*) and of the first peer-reviewed electronic journal to be supported by a major academic professional society (*Psycoloquy*, which is partly subsidized by the American Psychological Association).

I enter the debate, also as the founder of an open peer commentary journal (*Social Epistemology*), as well as someone who sits on the editorial boards of *Psycoloquy*, and the British Sociological Association's electronic journal initiative, *Sociological Research Online*. Although enthusiastic about the potentially transformative powers of the electronic medium, I diverge from Harnad over exactly what those powers are, their costs and benefits, and how these matters are likely to be resolved. Our disagreement is more profound when it comes to the desirability of peer review as a scholarly regulator (as opposed to "open peer commentary," which publishes alongside the original article criticisms that might constitute grounds for revision or rejection were they voiced as part of the peer-review process). Harnad is much more satisfied than I with the normative sensibilities that the peer-review process perpetuates (e.g., Harnad 1998). But this does not mean that I oppose all regulation. (My own views on peer review appear in the Appendix.) On the contrary, I believe that the increasingly specialized academic order extolled by Harnad— what he sees as its tendency toward "esoterism"—is precisely what needs to be kept in check by countervailing forces, including *both* publishers and the Internet. As befits the topic, I first voiced my sentiments on an electronic mailing list devoted to Science and Technology Studies in early 1995, shortly after Harnad had bombarded *Psycoloquy*'s editors with manifestos about the "Post-Gutenberg Galaxy" toward which scholarship was allegedly heading. A reporter who had been lurking on the STS "listserv" asked Harnad and me to debate the matter on the pages of the *Times Higher Education*

Supplement. The result was the 12 May 1995 centerfold in which Harnad and I literally faced each other, 2000 words apiece. On that basis, Rob Kling, newly appointed editor of *The Information Society*, asked both of us to expand our pieces to full-fledged articles and to respond to each other's criticisms. This then became the centerpiece of Kling (1995).

My strategy in dealing with Harnad stems from my work in *social epistemology*, a theory of knowledge policy that synthesizes work in philosophy of science, historical sociology of knowledge, social psychology, and political economy—all with an eye to promoting the democratization of knowledge production (Fuller 1988, 1993a, 1993b). Social epistemology counters theories that define knowledge, or aspects of knowledge production, without first taking into account its empirical character. Although Descartes has few followers today, nevertheless it is still common to define knowledge-related activities in Cartesian terms, on the basis of first principles, and then to deduce from them consequences for action. Unfortunately, this only creates a serious strategic gap between the notional world in which the definition and its deduced consequences exist and the empirical world which already carries its own implicit definitions of knowledge and its own possibilities for action. Basically, the social epistemologist starts with the empirical world of knowledge production and then tries to move to someplace better, not—as most tunnel-visionaries do—the other way around. Fleshing out one's vision of utopia from first principles is no substitute for a plan that gets us from here to there; it is merely to put the cart before the horse.

5.1. A Tale of Two Technophilosophies: Cyberplatonism versus Cybermaterialism

Let me start with some scholarly name-calling that resonates with the central issues raised in the previous chapter. To do justice to Harnad's historical roots, I shall call his position: *Cyberplatonism*. The Platonist's Holy Grail is the frictionless medium of thought that can transcend time and space to get at The Truth. The Cyberplatonist believes he or she has found the Grail in the Internet. There are two issues that need to be teased out before we go any further. First, does the Internet, indeed, approximate the frictionless medium of thought sought by Platonists? Here I use "frictionless" as shorthand for the qualities possessed by the desired medium: i.e., relatively direct and reliable transmission at low cost. Second, do we have an adequate model of how such a medium would enable inquirers to get at The Truth? Harnad simply assumes this to be the case, which leads him to run the two questions together. The model he has in mind is the peer-review system, whereby only qualified members in a field of inquiry evaluate the work proposed for inclusion in the field's body of knowledge and public dissemination.

As we shall see, peer review presupposes material conditions that render it no more than a *Virtual Cyberplatonism*. Nevertheless, according to Harnad, only the presence of paper-consuming intermediaries—the publishing houses—prevents this system from being fully institutionalized and thereby unleashing an era of untrammeled inquiry. This second question may turn out to be more important than the first, especially if academics and other professional knowledge producers remain personally insulated from the costs of maintaining and extending electronic communications. The Achilles' heel of all forms of Platonism is an obliviousness to the material conditions of thought, and Cyberplatonism is no different. The Internet is hardly the frictionless medium of thought Cyberplatonists make it out to be, and more importantly, even if it were, it does not follow that the interests of inquiry would be best served by colonizing it for the peer-review system.

Generally speaking, Cyberplatonists can be found lurking behind any claim that a cognitive or communicative medium enables an "overall saving" in effort or expense. By contrast, my own position on these issues is that of the *Cybermaterialist*, one who does not believe that the search for a frictionless medium of thought is intelligible. Instead, what happens is that one form of friction is exchanged for another, as we pass from one medium to another. In more concrete terms, the costs are merely shifted around, sometimes from one aspect of our lives to another, sometimes from one part of society to another. Of course, a big problem with assessing the exact costs and benefits is that by the time the medium has become institutionalized, people's lives and values will have adapted to it, so that even those who have limited access to the new medium will have a hard time imagining what life could be like without it. Of all aspects of human history, the history of technology is the one that cannot seem to shake off the Orwellian tendency of rewriting the present to make it look like straight-ahead progress from the past. To counteract this tendency, we have the Cybermaterialist's heuristic: *Whenever presented with the prospect of a technological system that provides an "overall saving" in effort or expense, look for what lies outside the system, because that is probably where the costs are being borne.*

The most straightforward way to interpret the Cybermaterialist imperative is in terms of the economist's concept of *externality*. Consider the relatively simple case of two media—print and electronic—whose general virtues trade off against each other. A convenient example is Harnad's own interspersal of his response to my critique of his position in Kling (1995), a familiar feature of electronic exchanges. But *contra* Harnad, such "hypertexting" is not an innovation, but a mere efficiency, of electronic communications. Interlinear (and marginal) commentary to an authoritative text is a practice that reaches back at least to the 12th century. Back then, manuscripts were written with wide margins and interlinear spaces to permit the insertion of the scholastic reader's notes, objections, and (*per* the original meaning of "inquisition") examination answers (Hoskin and Macve 1986). And like electronic hypertext today, as manuscripts were copied and passed on to other scholastics, the comments would often be incorporated into the main body of the text, eventually making it difficult to disentangle exactly who said what. Credit, when assignable, would typically go to the person who assembled the most interesting array of texts, leaving aside issues of original authorship. This medieval practice declined with the introduction of the printing press (McLuhan 1962, Ong 1962). Printing enabled the production of texts that remained invariant as they acquired portability. The invariance resulted not only from the reliability of the printing process, but more importantly from the asymmetry that printing created between authors and readers: Authors appeared in print, while readers were forced to scribble in ever diminishing marginal and interlinear spaces. As a result, it became much easier to assign authorship to a text, and for that assignment to be associated with a proprietary right over a determinate object.

Although I personally welcome the reinvention of medieval hypertextual practices in the electronic medium, they would wreak havoc on the credit allocation schemes that currently operate in the academic world—the very schemes that receive Harnad's enthusiastic support—as virtually all of these depend crucially on the key Gutenberg practice of assigning authorship to text. As we shall see, the legal struggles over defining the Internet suggest that Gutenberg notions of authorship do not sit well with post- (or pre-) Gutenberg notions of hypertextuality. The emerging legal persona of the "infopreneur" seems to owe more to the 12th-century compiler–encyclopedist than to the 19th-century genius–author. It may be that the more we insist on the transformative powers of the electronic medium, the more we unwittingly enable the dissolution of institutions such as authorship around which the peer-review process and other mechanisms of credit allocation in academia revolve. Not being a technological determinist myself, I would not argue that this is a *necessary* consequence, but its probability is sufficiently high to raise concerns that as we wax "Post-Gutenberg," we do not, at the same time, remain "Pre-McLuhan" in our understanding of technology's potential to shape thought. However, a charitable way of interpreting Harnad's desire for some peer-reviewed channels on the Internet may be that he wishes to simulate in the electronic medium some of the virtues that emerged from the print medium, especially a stable text to which authorship can be readily assigned. In that case, it will be interesting to see just how much more regulation ultimately needs to be introduced into peer-reviewed cyberspace so that the integrity of this highly artificial form of communication is maintained (Kahin 1996).

At a more general level, the transition from print to electronic media incurs externalities that accompany the constitution of any social order: How can fallible agents be arranged so that their collective capacity is more, not less, than the sum of their individual capacities? This problem is harder to solve than it may first seem because people are especially good at manufacturing scarcity, both at an object level and a meta-level. In other words, even when people can get what they want, that usually means that what they get is worth less than they thought. In more formal terms, there are two general ways in which the collective capacity of society can be undermined:

(a) If, by either ignorance or design, everybody interferes with each other, so that only some, if any, of them are able to get what they want.

(b) If, by virtue of everyone getting what they want, they unwittingly diminish the value of what they have gotten.

(a) and (b) represent the two kinds of scarcity: (a) an object-level scarcity; (b) a meta-scarcity.

A new technology introduces new opportunities for scarcity, and the Internet is no exception—a point duly noted by Hal Varian, the economist who has probably thought the most about alternative pricing schemes for the Internet (Shapiro and Varian 1998). I will consider only the case of (a) here, though (b) becomes increasingly important once information becomes seemingly "superabundant." Because the Internet involves a "packet-switching" technology, bits of messages from many different sources are transmitted through the same channel at a given time. This enables the channel to become congested, leading to the delay or deletion of transmissions. Moreover, it has proved difficult to regulate congestion because of the potential disparity in the size of transmitted messages (especially when advanced video or audio messages are involved) and the heterogeneity of their sources, as well as the ease with which periods of peak usage shift. Voluntary measures do not seem to work, yet governments appear inclined to privatize, or at least decentralize, whatever control they currently have over the Internet. Nevertheless, historically the only reliable way to prevent the introduction of a new technology from redrawing and sharpening already existing class divisions in society has been government regulation. Clearly, then, we are heading for a crisis in cost accounting for the Internet.

The failure by governments to anticipate the problems of scarcity associated with the Internet partly reflects its secretive roots in Cold War concerns about America's ability to respond to a nuclear first strike. To beef up its communication networks, the U.S. Department of Defense drew upon some work then being done at MIT on resource sharing between computers. From this came the idea of collaboration among different computer user communities. The prototype of the Internet, ARPANET, was thus launched in 1969 to connect Defense Department researchers working all across America. No one at the time had expected that the network would colonize conventional forms of communication. Given this historical background, it would be a mistake to think that the future of the Internet will be resolved by "discovering" what the Internet "really is" and then applying some appropriate legal regime for its cost accounting. Rather, parties with an interest in the future of the medium are now at various bargaining tables proposing that the medium be thought of as, say, a toll highway, a cable television system, a telephone, a radio network, etc.—all in the service of advancing certain pricing schemes that will benefit their respective constituencies.

Those with a sincere interest in making the Internet "the great equalizer" would spend their time wisely by participating in the discussions already underway with the representatives of the information and communication conglomerates, corporate lawyers, government regulators, and high-level university administrators, in whose hands the future disposition of the Internet ultimately lies. These are the people who need to be convinced that it would be in their interest to allow both affiliated and unaffiliated scholars to surf the net with impunity. Simply appealing to its "low cost" is not a particularly strong argument when the pricing mechanism is still up for grabs and the target audience may not be convinced that so much scholarly communication is really necessary in the first place (or who might want to manipulate the pricing mechanism so as to get scholars to communicate in other ways and about other matters).

5.2. The Publishing Industry as the Cyberscapegoat

Harnad is fixated on a piece of folklore of academic life. It pits scholars in the role of Faust against Mephistopheles, played by the publishing industry. In this "Faustian bargain," academics agree to do whatever it takes to get their ideas across, while publishers take advantage of this sincere desire by charging the maximum the market can bear for books and journals. This is probably the closest that academics ever get to the experience of exploitation, and so it provides a ready vehicle for commiserating with the "working classes." But equally, it provides a convenient excuse for why most of us never quite get our message across to all who could potentially benefit from it. Unfortunately, like all such self-serving stories, its grain of truth is buried under a mountain of mystification. The actual history reveals a complex, normatively vexed story of the relationship between academics and the publishers, one in which Mephistopheles often seems more the guardian angel. A plausible plot for the history would be that those with a genuine interest in promoting pure inquiry have stood opposed to *both* authors and publishers. The late 18th century was the watershed period for this complicated issue (Chartier 1994, 32–36).

According to such Enlightenment thinkers as Condorcet, the universal applicability of scientific principles rendered obsolete the very idea of authorship, an echo of a godlike, authoritative origin to knowledge claims. Instead, claims to knowledge—regardless of their brilliance or profundity—should be seen as the result of combining ideas that are, in principle, available to everyone, by virtue of the ideas corresponding to the structure of reality. Thus, from a legal–economic standpoint, it made most sense to reward inquirers for being the first to solve some well-defined problem, as that would capture the element of chance involved in one person rather than some other equally capable person arriving at the correct solution. However, this sporting image of scientific inquiry, though suitable for a period when most science was still conducted by non-academics, was eventually eclipsed by the sober 19th-century image of *Wissenschaft* as a "vocation" that was justified in terms of inquiry being a noble pursuit, regardless of its consequences (Weber 1958). However, a vestige of the old spirit of gamesmanship survives in the priority disputes that continue to punctuate the scientific enterprise.

Designed as it was to maximize the spread of ideas, the Enlightenment ideal of authorless inquiry took seriously the Platonist quest for a frictionless medium of thought. However, almost as soon as it was proposed, the ideal was met with two lines of resistance, one from publishers and the other from authors. Here it is worth recalling that before the end of the 18th century, the "author" of a book most often referred to the impresario who organized and compiled other people's work—little more than the first moment in the book production process.

On the one hand, publishers supported strong copyright laws, as they were beset by chronic book piracy, which often forced them to cut authors' commissions and even replace them with cheaper scribes. (The replacement of authors was quite common, given that publishers commissioned most books, though authors—who would otherwise eke out a living as part-time lecturers or private tutors—were quite prepared to perform such contract labor.) One might say that in this case the ideas were spreading *too freely*.

On the other hand, authors whose ideas were not spreading freely enough also demanded stronger copyright laws, partly to retaliate against publishers, but also to protect themselves from an increasingly fragmented market. Authors argued that the quality of their ideas could not be measured by their sales, or even by their reception more generally, but rather by the originality of their expression. This was a quality that could be recognized immediately (as stylistic distinctiveness) but whose significance could be fully fathomed only through years of reflection. In short, the print may belong to the publisher, but the words are the author's own. A cynic might say that modern copyright laws were thus designed to insure against low demand by upgrading the quality of what the author supplies. In any case, from this came the Romantic image of the "misunderstood genius" whose works appeal only to an esoteric clique. Though it first applied to poets, philosophers and scientists soon refashioned this image for their own purposes.

The connection between the unmarketable Romantic author and the self-policing of academic life known as "peer review" may seem remote, but one way to understand the latter's ascendancy is as simulating a market environment—one where peer citations replace sales figures—for work that would fail to survive in the conventional marketplace of ideas. Peer review was designed, not to allow academics to hide from their sponsors in esoteric splendor, but to dictate the terms on which academics accounted for how they used their sponsors' resources. Instead of letting novel scientific ideas be directly evaluated by those who paid to have them generated (and hence risk immediate rejection for being too difficult or counterintuitive), the peer-review process would forward only those ideas that had already received the stamp of approval of the scientific society: i.e., a version of the "we shall hang together so as not to hang separately" strategy.

Besides promoting a positive public face, there was also the need to erase any latent divisiveness within the peer group. Thus, when the first scientific journals were founded in 17th-century Britain and France, editors were cast in the role of trusted correspondents with the leading scientific minds, whose letters they would edit for gratuitous metaphysical jargon and personal nastiness. In this way scientific writing was first standardized (Bazerman 1988). Eventually the single correspondent was replaced by the editorial board and more specialized referees we have today. Although standardization is often said to be a prerequisite for genuine knowledge growth, a more pressing historical reason for disciplining scientific communication was to ensure that the scientists' aristocratic patrons were not unnecessarily confused or offended. The aristocrats supported scientific societies in order to be amused, edified and, in some cases, technically empowered. Peer review instituted the decorum needed to persuade patrons that their money was well spent. This brief history should serve to remind us that if there is, indeed, a "Faustian bargain" in the life of the mind, it is the one that academics strike with their sponsors that buys them the leisure to collectively pursue their studies.

Throughout the ascendancy of the peer-review process, publishers have often functioned as correctives to the protected markets that constitute academic specialties. They have traditionally encouraged academics to write books that are suitable for either students or general audiences. Of course, publishers have also expedited the specialization of academic journals. But that would not have become such an attractive financial proposition, had academics not been allowed to set their own paths of inquiry in the first place, and hence settle into ever narrower domains whose state-of-the-art is defined by one or two journals. Once academic specialists agree that a certain journal is "essential reading" for their field, they deliver a captive audience to publishers that is too good to resist. The resulting higher subscription prices should perhaps be treated exactly as they are felt, namely, as penalties for scholars veering toward esoterism. However, the ease with which such "penalties" can be imposed has benefited publishing only as a business, but not as an art. Indeed, it has placed at risk the future of the most creative aspect of publishing: *marketing* (Horowitz 1986). Academics tend to ignore marketing altogether, seeing publishing instead as a matter of editing manuscripts, on the one hand, and printing books and journals, on the other. Such dualistic thinking breeds the kind of "Us versus Them" rhetoric which infects tunnel-visionary thinking about publishers.

Nevertheless, the main reason most academics cannot muster the attention of their colleagues to read their works has more to do with the fact that they write too much that interests too few. When publishers increase the price of specialist journal subscriptions, they are merely holding up a mirror to this academically generated practice. In that sense, the rhetoric of "universal access" into which Cyberplatonists tap is little more than false consciousness. Moreover, in their search for new markets, publishers have enabled nonspecialists to locate relevant works that have often served to alter their home fields, thereby contributing to cross-disciplinary fertilization and innovation. Thus, one should think twice before asserting that specialists have any better sense of the ultimate constituency for their work than authors oriented to a broader, less differentiated market. In addition, publishers have helped give voice to groups whose interests cut against those of the established academic fiefdoms. Prominent recent examples include women's studies and cultural studies, two fields that received considerable attention from publishers before receiving formal academic recognition. For all its shortcomings, the publishing industry has operated with standards sufficiently orthogonal to academia's to provide the only consistent check of the "business as usual" attitude fostered by the peer-review system. The offer—some would say "temptation"—of fame, glory, and royalties has periodically succeeded in drawing out scholars, especially in the natural sciences, on what they perceive to be the larger significance of their research, which has then enabled the public to sympathize with work it barely understands. The names of Richard Dawkins, Steven Hawking, Lewis Wolpert, and Steven Weinberg leap to mind in this context.

5.3. Adding Some Resistance to the Frictionless Medium of Thought

The Cyberplatonist Harnad draws an oversharp distinction between "trade" and "esoteric" authorship that is symptomatic of his general failure to see scholarly work in systemic terms. In esoteric publishing, authors supposedly belong to a small community of specialists dedicated to following each other's writings, and hence in principle capable of doing without the production and marketing costs of a publishing house. Harnad provides two criteria for counting a piece of writing as "esoteric": (1) the author does not intend/expect to sell her words; (2) the author's readership is not large enough to constitute a market.

In contrast, the Cybermaterialist deals with the trade/esoteric distinction by looking for a context in which something resembling it makes an empirical difference in understanding the publishing industry, since esoteric publishing does not literally exist. To be sure, Harnad's strategy for demarcating esoteric from trade publishing recalls the hoary sociological distinction between *Gemeinschaft* and *Gesellschaft* (i.e., informal versus formal social relations). Nevertheless, Harnad's criteria for esoteric publishing are sociologically unacceptable for the following corresponding reasons, which will be examined more closely in the rest of this section:

1. No social practice can be sensibly defined simply by referring to the intentions of the particular people who engage in the practice (assuming that Harnad has understood those ade-

quately, which I doubt); one also needs to look at the overall function that the practice serves in a larger social system, however specified. Therefore, even if "esoteric" authors write only because they want to be read by their fellow esoteric authors, it does not follow that the practice of esoteric writing is maintained merely because that is what the relevant authors want to do. Other material conditions need to be in place that highlight the commercial character of esoteric publishing.

2. Any social practice can be construed as a "market" if producers are forced to compete to provide a good that is desired by some group (even if it largely consists of themselves) because "scarcity," in some sense, is present. I take it that new research in an "esoteric" field would count as such a good, that the limited search capacities of consumers would constitute a relevant sense of "scarcity," and that the citation counts that the original producer receives would constitute the price paid by its consumers. In addition, this "peer market" feeds into more traditional labor markets, as publication in a prestigious journal increases the likelihood that the article will be frequently cited, which in turn increases the likelihood that its author will be given a raise, a promotion, or a job at a better university.

In the case of point 1, sociologists who study the publishing industry have found something that vaguely resembles the trade–esoteric distinction, but it is drawn in terms of publishers' investment strategies (Coser et al. 1982, 36–69). Large publishing houses are geared toward short-term profitability. They initially invest a lot of money for securing the author and furnishing and marketing an attractive product, but then expect most of the profits to be registered within the first six months of publication; otherwise, the book is effectively abandoned. In contrast, small publishing houses invest little at the outset but then live off the slow, steady sales of their backlist, which consists of authors whose reputations grow with each passing year. In this context, the French sociologist Pierre Bourdieu coined the expression "symbolic capital" to describe what it is that smaller houses "accumulate" when they invest in a book that they know will sell poorly.

Bourdieu's point (and he has in mind semi-commercial French academic publishers, not subsidized American university presses) is that, in the long term, both the large and small houses may register roughly the same rate of profit, but whereas the former will be punctuated by remarkable gains and losses in a broad market for whom reading books is merely one among several consumer options, the latter will be marked by incremental growth from authors whose market consists mainly of authors of potentially similar caliber who may be drawn into the publisher's stable. This sociological analysis of publishing differs from Harnad's in that writing for publication is always taken to be more than simply corresponding with colleagues. The prospect of wider fame, glory, and royalties is ever present, though manifested differently, depending on the segment of the market to which one's writings appeal. On this analysis, the smaller publishing houses include not only academics but also poets and literary authors who appeal to elite audiences.

Generally speaking, to compare the interests of a publishing house with those of the solitary scholar is to mismatch units of analysis. The relevant point of comparison is between a publisher and the scholar's employer, the university. Both have similar sensibilities about the value-added and profit-making character of scholarly products. Moreover, the production costs of scholarship go beyond the effort it takes to generate text (though phenomenologically a scholar may regard the physical generation of text as the only "cost" he or she bears). In addition, scholarly production requires the computers, laboratories, and libraries—not to mention colleagues and students—that constitute a proper research environment, as routinely provided by universities. A university's investment in these facilities may vary according to the discipline and the anticipated rate of return, but the patterns will not be unlike what we see in publishing. For example, an enormous infrastructure may be set in place for a young chemist with Nobel Prize potential, but within a relatively short period, informal judgments will be made within the chemistry community as to whether the work coming from his lab is living up to expectations. If not, the chemist may well fail to get his grants renewed, rendering his place in the university insecure. However, in the humanities and social sciences, subjects in which a university tends to make relatively small investments to support scholarly production, short-term expectations are correspondingly low, just so long as scholars maintain a rate of publishing and quality of teaching that continue to attract like-minded people to that institution.

In the case of point 2, consider the protected nature of academic markets. When researchers give their words away, they expect something in return. As we saw in the previous chapter, even when researchers directly give credit to others (by citing their work) or enable others to derive credit (by sharing data with them), these are not selfless acts of generosity, but something closer to a Mafia-style "insurance" policy. If one *fails* to give credit at the appropriate moments, sanctions are imposed that will make it difficult for one's work to be published, one's grants to be renewed, and one's students to be hired. This is one of the structural disadvantages of social systems that are relatively impervious to pressures not of their own creation. In academia we dignify them with the name "autonomous." Moreover, there are hardly any studies of the significance of the peer-reviewed knowledge produced in academic markets for anything outside itself or the careers of its producers (a point repeatedly stressed by Daniel 1993).

What we do know, however, is that the general public is prone to distrust, say, medical professionals for obscuring and withholding potentially useful information so as to increase the public's reliance on them. Many people, especially those with serious illnesses, seem perfectly willing to risk their own lives on treatments that have not passed all the proper scientific tests and government regulations. Moreover, there may be nothing especially irrational or desperate about this practice, since the efficacy of medical treatments depends on much more than strict laboratory conditions and other trappings of the scientific method.

Collins (1979) argues that were medicine not protected by a strong, government-backed professional association, the public would take a more active interest in pursuing medical knowledge themselves, up to the point of personally experimenting with new treatments. Typically, the public would like to see the track record of a treatment's consequences—something on the model of *Consumer Reports*—but is much less impressed by the research credentials of the laboratory or the impeccability of the methodology with which the treatment was first developed and tested. This "credential libertarian" stance is extending to public attitudes toward science in general, as a "value-for-money" mentality leads governments to divest support from an increasing number of peer-reviewed programs that fail to meet consequentialist criteria. However, it is not clear that the divested projects can survive in an unprotected private sector, especially when they may be competing (in the case of psychology and maybe even physics) with "New Age" knowledges that boast

ATTITUDES TO MARKETING	"TRADE" PUBLISHING	"ESOTERIC" PUBLISHING
CYBERPLATONIST (Harnad)	*Gesellschaft* (marketing needed because demand created)	*Gemeinschaft* (marketing not needed because demand natural)
CYBERMATERIALIST (Fuller)	Profit in *short* term (*a lot* up front for marketing: results judged in sales in first six months)	Profit in *long* term (*little* up front for marketing: results judged in subsequent author recruitment)

Figure 3.4.
Opposing scholarly attitudes to marketing

many satisfied, even if scientifically ill-informed, customers (Hess 1993).

In Figure 3.4, I focus the strands of the argument between the Cyberplatonist and Cybermaterialist over the last three sections into a debate about the need to market professional knowledge products, namely, academic books and journals. In terms of this figure we may identify two "diagonal" tendencies. The combination of a Cyberplatonist view on trade publishing and a Cybermaterialist one on esoteric publishing implies that marketing serves a proactive function on the research frontier, whereas the combination of a Cybermaterialist view on trade publishing and a Cyberplatonist view on esoteric publishing implies that marketing is reduced to a more reactive publicity function. The differences between the proactive and reactive views of publishers are summarized below.

Publishers as Proactive

1. Correct academics' often parochial and self-serving evaluations with "unobtrusive indicators" of emerging tendencies, through course enrollments, library adoptions, etc.: marketing as meta-scientific research.
2. Cut against established peer-review regimes by funding journals in emerging areas, which helps create "symbolic capital" for innovative scholars: e.g., success of women's studies and cultural studies.

3. Encourage authors toward the textbook market, which forces them to write accessibly and incorporate innovations into the curriculum.
4. Restrict authors' ability to recycle material (e.g., by holding the copyright to the work), thereby forcing them either to target their message to particular audiences or to develop novel implications of their research.

Publishers as Reactive
1. The research function of marketing is reduced to targeting:
   - Two courses with 500 students each is better than 1000 globally dispersed scholars
   - Big advances to "big names" who function as "market attractors"
2. If a new journal manages to find a market niche, it is encouraged indefinitely, as long as it provides return on investment. There is no publisher-based incentive for cognitive euthanasia of a "cash cow."
3. As book prices rise and copyright becomes more restrictive, courses increasingly rely on just one all-purpose textbook, which effectively curbs the incentive of publishers to support innovation—thereby reversing the main intellectual benefit of the Gutenberg Revolution, which was to create a presumption that prior research would be within easy reach of readers (Eisenstein 1979).
4. Copyright and other publisher restrictions encourage academics to think of their work as consisting of discrete products rather than as an ongoing process, in which the same points may be raised in different conversations.

5.4. Why Paperlessness Is No Panacea

The mark of the tunnel-visionary is the capacity to raise phenomenology to the level of ontology: to treat the immediate as profound. For Harnad, "paperlessness" is the means by which the Internet will bring publishers to their knees, ushering in the fabled frictionless medium of thought. No one can deny that rising paper costs make life increasingly difficult for publishers—and especially their customers, who ultimately absorb these costs. But to refuse the services of publishers in favor of posting one's works on the World Wide Web would hardly reduce the amount of paper consumed. All it would do is diffuse the source of paper consumption, as each person prints out materials downloaded from the Web onto his or her own personal computer. Pool (1983, 189–225) has argued that the flight from hard copy to virtual copy will actually increase the amount of paper consumed, the costs of which will be borne either by the individual user or by the institution that maintains the user's computer. Of course, it may be that these costs will turn out to be less than the ones currently passed on to consumers by publishers. In that case, we would see the continuation of the "Xerox effect," whereby increased paper consumption (i.e., number of photocopies) is accompanied by lower overall costs to the consumer.

However, even this prognosis is probably hasty, since people use computers at least as much to *produce* text as to retrieve it. When scholars still worked on typewriters, it was common to write successive rounds of corrections on the margins of a single paper draft, saving the generation of a second paper draft for the final, "clean" version. The advent of computers has altered scholarly sensibilities about paper use, so that now it is common to generate a new paper draft for each round of corrections, and to store the final, "clean" copy in cyberspace. Admittedly, this development is very much in keeping with the Cyberplatonist view that the ideal form belongs in a place that transcends corruptible matter—but to get there, it seems that the Cyberplatonist needs to wade through more, not less, of the corrupt papyrus than the scholarly typist used to.

Can this attachment to paper be severed simply with an extended lesson in the latest computer applications? The answer is no—and the reasons do not require imagining the average computer user to be an idiot. Paper persists, not out of nostalgia or unexamined habit, but out of genuine convenience and, more importantly, risk management. It remains rational to keep generating hardcopy as long as computer systems crash as often as they do and remain as vulnerable to playful and not-so-playful viral intruders. Only once those problems are tackled will it make sense to embark on a campaign to wean computer users away from their attachment to paper. More generally, the liberatory rhetoric associated with scholars posting their works on the World Wide Web "free to all" will become a literal reality only once all scholars have (and retain, through changes in the political economy) unimpeded access to the Internet. Until that time, the postal service remains the most "equalizing" medium for communicating with fellow scholars, however much we may wish it to be otherwise.

The illusion of a frictionless medium of thought is also kept alive at the phenomenological level by the hidden institutional costs of maintaining the average scholar's computer system. Simply put, if you don't personally pay the costs, you treat them as if they weren't there. Consider this bit of Cyberplatonist "analysis": "When things get cheap enough, they get absorbed into the overheads. Does your department charge you for every pencil you take from the office? Back two decades ago, when I was graduating, it was common for universities to have strict accounting of long-distance calls.... Nowadays, with telephone call costs lower, charges up to some limit are typically absorbed into the general overheads" (Odlyzko 1995). This testimony, unsurprisingly, comes from someone who works at an Ivy League university, not a community college. The situation is even worse for such financially vulnerable institutions as primary and secondary schools because an unusually large percentage of their transmissions contain multimedia imagery, which travel in large packets that can easily congest the Internet, regardless of the speed at which they are transmitted (Fuchs 1996). Encouraged by both public and private sector investment in the 1980s and early 1990s, schools built substantial information infrastructures that ultimately aimed to meet all of their instructional needs. At that time, school administrators were led to believe that government would either continue subsidizing the information infrastructure or regulate the markets in which it is transacted. However, the advent of Internet privatization has thrown this tacit commitment into doubt, leaving schools literally adrift in the aethernet.

Ultimately, the ideal of a frictionless medium of thought is based on one of the many philosophical distinctions—in this case, between medium and message—that fails to make a material difference. Harnad's very insistence that the Internet is necessary for future academic productivity unwittingly betrays the fact that scholars *already* depend on this particular medium for transmitting their thoughts, so that it would be difficult for the scholarly community to revert to another medium, should Internet accessing fees rise significantly for universities (as in the case of Carnegie Mellon University, whose fees jumped from $30,000 to $300,000 per year with the privatization of the Internet). Universities would either have to make scholars bear the costs themselves on the model of rents (as in the Scandinavian practice of deducting rent on university office space from the monthly salary) or ration Internet access by some formula that will probably be to the advantage of scholars whose productivity has already been enhanced by electronic communication.

Either scenario would bear witness to what in the previous chapter I called the *commodification of knowledge*, or the hidden political economy of public goods. In the case of the Internet, there are at least two other ways of capturing the dependency of thought on medium.

(a) Successive technologies tend to be more expensive than the ones they replace, even though their own costs tend to go down over time. Thus, while computers drop in price, they are still more expensive than typewriters, which are, in turn, still more expensive than pens. In economists' terms, the "entry costs" for each new technology are higher, thereby potentially disenfranchising a larger segment of the population each time around. Of course, computers are much more versatile than typewriters or pens, but the additional power provided by computers had not been constitutive of normative scholarly practice when typewriters or pens were the dominant medium of knowledge production. Rather, scholarly norms adapted to the capacities of the new technologies, and so we see Harnad extolling the virtues of a quick turnaround time in editorial judgment, as if that had been a scholarly desideratum down through the ages, when in fact its desirability is intimately linked with the "Publish or Perish" imperative of contemporary academic survival.

(b) Information industries tend to converge on all sectors of the information market (Pool 1983, 23–54). Whereas in 1880, one could still identify distinct firms that fell along the orthogonal axes of "products versus services" and "content versus conduit," today, largely as a result of the revolution in electronic communications, an historically service-oriented firm such as American Telephone and Telegraph (AT&T) competes in every sector with an historically product-oriented firm such as International Business Machines (IBM) (Cronin 1988). Given this history of categorical fluidity, publishers should have little trouble adjusting their *raison d'etre* in cyberspace from that of manufacturing a product to that of providing a service—especially if publishing houses continue to be sold to newspaper chains with multinational interests in providing financial services and cable communications (Aitkenhead 1995). Moreover, the integrity of books and journals—let alone the distinction between them—may yield to the customized pay-per-view world of hypertext and Web links, which, if anything, will diminish the likelihood that anyone will possess a complete text of any single work. Rather, once publishers colonize cyberspace, it will be more common to have personal access to the equivalent of several photocopied pages of many different works that have been consulted for specific research needs.

5.5. Does Cyberspace "Deserve" Peer Review?

An important historical aim of peer review has been to preempt efforts to make scientific research more directly responsive to the public interest by assuring non-specialists that a guiding hand is already in place, however invisible it may appear. The appeal to peer review was made with an eye more toward whom to exclude (patrons, politicians, and people who might alert them) than toward whom to include. Peer review has been successful, at least rhetorically, in that the expression has exchanged its original connotation of "clubbiness" for "autonomy." Nevertheless, peer review remains empirically elusive, with the parameters of peerage for a given academic specialty often amounting to little more than the choices that journal editors make to have certain people review certain articles (Chubin and Hackett 1990, 83–124; Daniel 1993). Since these people have typically worked in the specific area, peer review seems well designed to reproduce existing disciplinary boundaries, if nothing else. Yet, editorial agreement on appropriate reviewers for a given article, and even agreement among reviewers on the criteria by which the article should be judged, by no means ensures that a common verdict will be reached. But what to make of such dissensus, the value of multiplying reviewers (which usually means multiplying judgments), and, most importantly, the very pursuit of reviewer consensus? The last may be a spurious goal, since there is little correlation between articles that reviewers rate highly and articles that subsequently receive high citation counts (Daniel 1993, 5).

Given these uncertainties, which features of the peer-review system would be worth transferring from the print to the electronic medium? Here Chubin and Hackett (1990, 85–91) provide considerable guidance in noting that most of the praiseworthy features of academic journals have little or nothing to do with the peer-review process as such. The communication of results, the allocation of credit, and the creation of an archive all reflect the *publicity* function of journals. What peer review supposedly adds is a means for authenticating the results and evaluating their significance, which in turn licenses the scientific society to take collective responsibility for the individual scientist's (or team's) work. In other words, peer review issues to authors intellectual insurance policies in case their results are attacked. If the results are shown lacking, the deficiency will be attributed to honest error and not incompetence or fraud.

However, in practice (at least as judged by reviewers' reports), relatively little authentication takes place during peer review, mainly because it would demand too much effort from the reviewer, who typically believes he or she can judge authenticity simply from the text of the article. Instead, reviewers spend their time negotiating with authors the size of the knowledge claim that their articles entitle them to make. Not surprisingly, authors wish to claim more than the reviewers will allow them. Of course, in principle, this haggling could transpire in public. However, most editors and reviewers seem to believe that if peer review itself were absorbed into the publicity function of journals, the variability of its workings from case to case would undermine the legitimacy of the entire process.

The upshot, then, is that it is not clear what peer review adds to the knowledge system, aside from a certain kind of professionally sanctioned regularity at the subsystem level of academic disciplines and specialties. However, it remains unclear how such regularity bears on other quality measures. In that case, peer review should be foisted upon the Internet only if the present "functional differentiation" of the knowledge system is deemed appropriate. Even then, there is sufficient sociological variation in the constitution of these fields that it is unlikely that a mechanism as purely formal as that of peer review could account for the research advances these fields have made. Thus, there is little reason to think that the success of journals in fields as different as high-energy physics and Harnad's domain of cognitive science can be explained in terms of their common characteristics. Whereas high-energy physics is probably the most intellectually focused and socially stratified specialty in science today, cognitive science is a very active, but relatively amorphous, interdisciplinary field. The elites in high-energy physics coordinate their activities to dictate to the rest of the field, and sometimes to the entire physics community (Redner 1986, 122–165). By contrast, the success of *Behavior and Brain Sciences* may be better explained in terms of the bandwagon effect caused by several elite cognitive scientists from different parts of the field publishing early in the journal's history.

5.6. Conclusion: Purifying Cyberplatonism's Motives

It should be clear that Harnad's call for the peer-review system to migrate to the Internet constitutes a corrupt version of the Cyberplatonist utopia, one that would simply transfer existing academic hierarchies to the new medium; hence its status as a "Virtual Cyberplatonism." Were we to take Cyberplatonism at its word, then not only should paper publishing go by the wayside, but also the whole idea of seeking personal credit for as many articles as possible in peer-reviewed journals. Peer review is not essential to pure inquiry but the result of academics having to account for their activities in a competitive environment involving the allocation of scarce resources.

Even Harnad's superficially populist call for everyone to post their articles on the World Wide Web plays to this point, as such a move would only strengthen the knowledge system's elitist tendencies. Faced with a plethora of titles on a common topic, an author's name recognition will count more than ever. The sheer availability of a work does not guarantee that it will get into the hands of the people who could most benefit from it. (Here marketing can make all the difference, thus providing a fresh challenge for the 21st-century publisher.) Nowadays, a relatively democratic cross-section of the academic community can be found on the "listservs" and "usenets" that structure the Internet. Teachers, administrators, and students do not merely consume the knowledge that cutting-edge researchers generously deposit on the World Wide Web. They are themselves knowledge producers, and often incisive critics of what passes for quality in the print and electronic media. The result is a multiple-registered, rough-and-tumble atmosphere that has put off some elite inquirers but has empowered many more. Admittedly, women and minorities remain underrepresented, but that is being quickly remedied. Virtual Cyberplatonists such as Harnad tend to downplay the heterogeneity of the Internet, perhaps hoping that it will all eventually come under the decorous thumb of peer review, or if not, at least enough of it will to entice major researchers across the disciplinary spectrum to submit their works to cyber-scrutiny.

Intellectual property lawyers have been struggling to draft appropriate "zoning ordinances" for regulating the Internet's virtual real estate, even though the status of "owners," "renters," "producers," and "consumers" is continually shifting. For example, Jaszi (1994) has proposed that the freedom to cut, splice, and forward material across listservs and usenets may cause the concept of "authorship" to revert to its 18th-century meaning of a packager of other people's material—an "infopreneur," in the current term-of-art—that could make copyright almost unenforceable. Whether this prospect encourages or discourages people taking their best ideas to cyberspace remains to be seen. However, were we to take Plato's Socratic dialogues as a model for "free inquiry," such legalized anarchy would not seem so bad: Anyone would be allowed to participate in any line of thought wherever it may lead. There would be no expectation of a discrete publication, but if one did happen to result, it would be only after considerable discussion, by which time it would be difficult to identify who deserves credit for which idea. Crackpots and ignoramuses—assuming we know who they are—would be given their say, but then one would do the obvious: refute, ignore, or delete. The filtered world of anonymous refereeing would thus dissolve into open peer commentary, thereby erasing a distinction that may not be particularly clear even in the minds of peer review's defenders. After all, one way to explain the negative correlation between reviewer ratings and citation counts for journal articles is to say that articles are highly cited because they attract criticism, which, in the private context of peer review, could have led to the paper not being published in the first place.

In short, elements of the pure Cyberplatonist vision *are* worth pursuing. For example, tardy referees are not the worst problem facing journal editors today. More troubling is that authors read referees' reports pretty much as editors do, namely, as a red or green signal for publication. Harnad's enthusiasm for quick turnaround times from acceptance to publication only nurtures this mentality. However, the reports may wind up playing little or no role in shaping an author's thought, at least as long as there are other journals to which the author can submit a rejected piece with minimum alterations. No wonder referees find theirs to be a thankless lot! The source of the problem is simply that authors are encouraged to submit their work in a finished form. By that time, they have normally become so attached to it that they are psychologically incapable of grappling with substantial criticism. However, because there is so little to which one can become attached on the Internet, authors are more prone to submit drafts with holes that others may be better positioned to fill. Thus, a genuinely collaborative inquiry may be fostered. However, this purer version of Cyberplatonism will be confined to Plato's Heaven, unless academics pay greater attention to the political economy of electronic communications and the historical sociology of peer review.

6. Postscript: Capitalized Education as the Ultimate Information Technology

In recent years, social scientists have converged on an historical scheme for understanding the impact of technology on the production and consumption of goods and services in capitalist economies (cf. Harvey 1989): The scheme consists of four stages: (1) *holistic craft*; (2) *divided labor*; (3) *mass production*; (4) *customized consumption*. It can also be used to illustrate what happens to the production and consumption sides of *education*—or, respectively, teaching and learning—once they become "technologically mediated." In what follows, we shall see that education's economic environment gradually prepares the way for the acceptance of new information technologies that alter the relationship between knowledge producers and consumers.

In stage 1, the *holistic craft*, the producer sees her product from inception to completion and typically faces the consumer whose (dis)satisfaction with the product is directly registered to the producer. The producer largely sets her own standards of performance, given the relative scarcity of competitors. For their part, consumers are likely to regard the producer in possession of a special "talent" because of the many different things that she must do before her product is sold (as well as the fact that they are pretty much at the producer's mercy). Consequently, something received from this person is regarded as a unique and highly valued possession. The corresponding stage in education is personal study with a guru or all-purpose philosopher, which was common when education was organized around charismatic schools rather than multiply staffed faculties. The "product" was more than just information or even knowledge, but that elusive quality, "wisdom." Even something as mundane as the "content" of a university course originally referred to whatever the lecturer said in the room that "contained" his speech. It did not refer to a specific subject matter that could be delivered in many different ways by many different people (and things, such as books and computers), as it does today.

In stage 2, *divided labor*, the number of producers of a good or service becomes sufficiently large that a competitive environment is created. Producers must therefore distribute their labor to other people and things in order to minimize production costs. It becomes important to design a scheme for dividing labor that makes any given person or thing, in principle, replaceable, so that production can continue apace, even in the wake of personnel changes. In the history of education, this period began when universities established distinct subject matters in which lecturers had to qualify. Thus, staff were hired in terms of their appropriateness to a subject rather than some more general criterion of personal brilliance. Later, standardized textbooks were introduced that enabled students to access the relevant subject matters without having to suffer through poor lecturers (or good ones who timed their lectures at an unfortunate hour). Although, in strict historical terms, this stage occurred more than a century ago, we can already see the path being paved for the introduction of computers in educational settings. In the face of a competitive environment, the teachers' first line of defense was to change their own work orientation rather than to change the learners' orientation. One no longer hired the whole person, but rather an embodiment of a needed expertise that was seen as relatively self-contained and easy to assess—the human equivalent of an expert system. Qualifications for academic employability thus became better defined, including the need to pass certain examinations and explicit licensing procedures. Once hired, academics developed teaching and research profiles within a relatively narrow range of topics.

In stage 3, *mass production*, the value of a product is determined more by the quantity of its sales than by the quality of what is sold. This is largely the result of increased competition among producers. However, once the conditions of production have been standardized, producers can induce a fundamental shift in the attitudes of consumers, a shift historically associated with advertising and other sophisticated marketing techniques. Consumers come to believe they must have a product because everyone else has, and in that way the product is rendered a necessary part of a normal existence. This new attitude encourages consumers to adapt their behavior to the standardized product. The corresponding changes from an educational standpoint are exemplified by the passage of legislation designed to regulate students. For example, classroom attendance is made compulsory and the possession of academic degrees becomes an employment requirement. Eventually, students come to accept the artificiality and difficulty of academic work as a necessary evil that "pays off in the end." Once students think this way, they are ready to adjust to the highly constrained settings in which human–computer interactions still typically take place. These settings, which involve the user staring in one direction for extended periods, turn out to be not so very different from the depersonalized lecture-based system in which students encounter human instructors in today's scaled-up public universities.

In stage 4, *consumer customization*, consumers regain a measure of control over the products they are sold by being more discriminating in their response to standardization. For example, small firms start thriving on the margins of big corporations by producing goods that target consumer groups with special needs. Even the big corporations increasingly permit potential consumers a say in the design of products. Indeed, once customization reaches full swing, consumers may be able to rework the products they possess to their complete satisfaction. In that sense, the distinction between producer and consumer can become blurred. However, one consequence of production becoming so fixated on consumer satisfaction is that products that permit consumers to satisfy their needs with relatively little effort drive out products that force consumers to expand their basic skills and perspectives.

This situation has very important consequences for the emerging role of computers in education. As instructional software packages become more "expert" and hence take over more of the jobs previously performed by classroom instructors, and more users become capable of reprogramming the software, it may soon become difficult to determine whether students have genuinely mastered a course of study or, rather, have simulated this mastery by programming the computer to provide the desired results. For example, once students were allowed to use calculators in examinations, it was observed that some "clever" students programmed their calculators to compute complex equations at the press of a button, though the students were supposedly being tested on their personal mastery of such equations. More generally, educators promote the World Wide Web as a vast resource of information for theses at all levels of academic accreditation, yet the Web also renders plagiarism virtually effortless, as students need only download the relevant texts into their own text and make appropriate stylistic changes to avoid detection.

Figure 3.5 summarizes the stages through which technology transforms a sphere of economic activity, first by being entirely outside of it but eventually becoming the medium in which all such activity occurs. It should be clear that this sequence of stages constitutes "progress" in a rather ironic sense of the term. Specifically, the subordination of education to the economic imperatives displayed in this sequence threatens an important feature of traditional academic culture whose preservation is necessary for any genuine sense of social progress: namely, the relative autonomy of knowledge production from the interests of knowledge consumers (Bourdieu 1997). This is not an argument against the largely salutary trend to render academics more "accountable" to students and other "users and beneficiaries" (to invoke the jargon of the state research funding councils). Rather, it is an argument against only, or even mainly, potential consumers determining the standards of accountability, which marks the transition from stages 3 to 4 in the scheme.

Nowadays it is unfashionable to claim that the character of a particular technology constrains the possibilities for social and political action. Of course, it is difficult to predict very specifically what people will do with a given technology in a given setting. Nevertheless, general trends can be discerned. For example, it is not too bold to claim that a new technology—whatever else it may do—generally makes it easier for those in its possession to get what they want, while those not in its possession find it harder to get what they want. Economists do not balk at this tendency because they rarely have the

	SHAPER	SHAPED
PRODUCER	1. Holistic craft (pre-Taylorist)	2. Divided labor (Taylorist)
CONSUMER	4. Customized consumption (post-Fordist)	3. Mass production (Fordist)

Figure 3.5.
Technology's transformation of economic activity (and the corresponding phases in the history of capitalism)

historical vision to consider the changes that a new technology might cause in the power relationships in society, or even how members of that society might come to redefine their interests and what it would mean to have them satisfied. Rather, economists tend to operate with a static sense of global efficiency that is vindicated by observing that the introduction of a particular technology makes it easier for an entire society to manufacture a larger amount of a widely desired product.

Finally, let us consider these matters in the context of the computerization of education. We often hear that computers can help academia catch up in "a rapidly changing world" by adapting instructional resources to match employment needs. This rhetoric betrays a lack of concern (or awareness) that academics may have their own reasons for wanting to keep a strategic distance from these goals. Perhaps the most important reason why education has tended to make students more critical and reflective is that they are taught to achieve their goals in ways that force them to alter their natural modes of thought and behavior. In that sense, criticism and reflection short-circuit drives toward efficiency, at least in the short term. To be sure, instead of learning for themselves how to solve a math problem or how to construct an intelligent argument, many students could "more efficiently" pay someone else to do it for them. Indeed, humanity's oldest written records typically arose from the patronage of wealthy illiterates. The age of customized computerization seems to be returning many of us to that original state, only now the acquisition of knowledge is "outsourced" to a portable machine rather than a humble scribe. Of course, nothing in the nature of computers prevents them from being used for critical and reflective purposes, rather than eliminating opportunities for the expression of those purposes. But that would mean disembedding the educational system from the technological trajectory outlined in this chapter and the often subtle transformation of values that has accompanied it.

4

A CIVIC REPUBLICAN THEORY OF KNOWLEDGE MANAGEMENT

1. The Historical and Philosophical Bases of Civic
   Republicanism   197
2. A Distinguished False Lead: Michael Polanyi's "Republic
   of Science"   203
3. In Search of Republican Vehicles for Knowledge
   Management   211
   3.1. Knowledge Worker Unions   212
   3.2. Consensus Conferences   213
   3.3. Universities: The Ultimate Republican Institution   216

4. Historic Threats to the Republican Constitution of the
   University   220
5. The Challenge of Contract Academic Workers to the
   University's Republican Constitution   225
6. Conclusion: A Civic Republican Agenda for the Academic
   CEO of Tomorrow   229

1. THE HISTORICAL AND PHILOSOPHICAL BASES OF CIVIC REPUBLICANISM

In much of my work on knowledge production, I have preferred the term *governance* to *management* (e.g., Fuller 2000a; contrast Fuller 1993b, Chapters 7, 8). I shall revert to that practice in this chapter. In an important respect, "governance" relates to "government" as "management" does to "economics": In both cases, the former term is meant to complement the dominant tendency represented by the latter, though they do so from opposing directions. Thus, "governance" suggests the need for greater autonomy and self-organization in a world where "government" would otherwise clearly distinguish between the rulers and the ruled. On the other hand, "management" implies that more order needs to be imposed on the business world than would be suggested by the idealized free market, in which rational economic agents spontaneously engage in exchanges with each other. In the case of knowledge production, I believe—especially in the current economic climate—that it is better to presume the need to carve out a space for autonomy in a world of control, rather than vice versa. So, let us begin: In what respects do the history and philosophy of civic republican politics provide a model for the governance of knowledge production? The answer turns out to have deeper consequences for management more generally than one might think.

The original models for the free-standing organization, the corporation, were the churches, trade guilds, and universities of the medieval European cities (Weber 1954, 169–170). The Latin word attached to these corporate entities, *universitas*, implied that the organization's members pursued ends beyond their individual interests that could be pursued in perpetuity by the subsequent membership of others. The implied contrast here was with a *societas*, the root of the English word "society," such as allies in combat, whose association is meant to terminate once their common goal has been met.

From Max Weber to today's transaction economists, it has been generally agreed that a necessary condition for capitalism's development was the idea that wealth production could be legally protected on a basis beyond the occurrent needs of particular individuals or households. This transition in economic thought from a *societas* to a *universitas* conception of business was a legacy of civic republicanism from Athens and Rome. But its future is currently under threat as the project network replaces the firm as the unit of management, a reversion to *societas* that, as we saw in Chapter 1, the KM literature largely encourages. My appeal to republicanism in this chapter is meant to counter this trend, indeed, by suggesting that the university, rather than an aberration, may be the ideal case of a corporation.

Republicanism is ultimately a theory of *liberty* (Pettit 1997). The theory states that liberty is freedom from domination by another's will, where "domination" goes beyond actual interference to include the perceived threat of interference that inhibits people from doing and saying what they would like. The republican sense of liberty is enforced by a constitutional agreement to submit to what the 17th-century English philosopher James Harrington originally called an "empire of laws, not men." Republicans regard the actions taken by either a solitary tyrant or a democratic majority as equally the product of an "arbitrary will" that knows no law other than its own desire. In this sense, there is nothing "natural" about republican liberty: it must always be socially constructed—hence the significance attached to a written constitution and the need for regular elections in democracies to decide the fate of existing policies, *even when no one is complaining*. In this respect, republicanism incorporates the reflectiveness that warrants the label, associated with the U.S. Constitution, "philosophically designed order."

Because republican liberty is the explicit product of a legal system, citizens are *obliged* to uphold and test (for purposes of improving) the system. This implies significant civic participation. Most fundamentally, people agree to couch their political disagreements in terms amenable to resolution by legally recognized procedures; hence, republicans have set great store by an education in rhetoric. Republicans are loath to refer to their personal interest in the outcome of a debate, since the long-term value of appearing honorable in the polity outweighs any short-term personal advantage. The way George W. Bush and Al Gore handled themselves in the aftermath of the disputed 2000 U.S. presidential election—ever translating personal feelings into legal arguments—epitomized republicanism in action. Thus, when republican theorists speak of the value of "civility," they are not referring to some outmoded ideal of courtliness, but rather to what the political theorist Jon Elster (1999, 396–398) has called the "civilizing force of hypocrisy." In the long term, people come to believe the reasons they are forced to use to justify their actions. This means that, for republicans, political rationality is tantamount to mass hypocrisy. In more florid terms, republicanism's much vaunted "civil religion" is a belief in the transubstantiation of private vices into public virtue via the administrative alchemy of the law.

But the republican sense of obligation goes beyond the norms governing free public expression. While republican regimes have been opposed to the existence of standing armies (or police), they have endorsed universal military training and rotating service in the armed forces. Also, republicans reject the idea of career politicians—especially that a life in politics can be a vehicle of upward social mobility. There lies the corruption of the individual and the captivity of the polity. (This republican legacy explains the relatively low salaries of legislators and ministers in democracies.) Sometimes republicans have supported the random selection of civil officeholders, akin to the selection of jurors in trials, combined with compulsory voting in elections. The presupposition here is that regardless of their other differences, citizens are peers in matters of public affairs (what the Romans meant by *res publica*) and, more to the point, *are obliged to act that way*. In that sense, the obligation to exercise one's freedom is a democratized version of *noblesse oblige*.

Behind this compulsory conception of freedom is the idea that the competences involved in managing one's own and society's affairs are micro and macro versions of the same skills. Thus, proven competence in the management of one's estate establishes the sense of social responsibility necessary for holding political office, and compulsory military training enables one to stand up for oneself in the public forum, especially in the face of majoritarian intimidation. It is often forgotten that before the introduction of state-mandated mass education in the late 19th century, the only clear grounds for compulsory training was defense of the commonwealth. Not surprisingly, the strongest republican voice in the last two centuries, John Stuart Mill, upset the "pure democrats" of his day by arguing that extending the right to vote was useless unless people were capable of performing the duties entailed by the right. Mill was thus quite happy to couple the right to vote with an obligation to be educated.

Given such qualifications for citizenship, it is unsurprising that republicanism has held an ambivalent place in democratic political theory (Everdell 2000). If liberty is a social achievement, and not a natural entitlement, then it must be earned. Thus, classical republican regimes fiercely ensured the maintenance of equality among those already free, but they did precious little to extend the circle of liberty. Stories of the founding of republics typically begin by recounting the revolutionary overthrow of a tyrant by an indignant middle class. But republics often end up either becoming empires that support a complacent middle class on the backs of a far-flung and stratified social order (e.g., Rome and arguably the United States) or allowing their volatility and divisiveness to expose them to an external stabilizing force (e.g., the fate of classical Athens and Weimar Germany).

To be sure, many republican practices anticipated socialist ones, most notably the redistribution of inherited wealth and agricultural surpluses. This aspect of republicanism is often lost on the burgeoning "social capital" literature that otherwise derives inspiration from the movement (e.g., Putnam 1993). The redistributionist imperative reflects the concrete situation of traditional republican regimes, namely, that liberty adhered to land owners in a specific region who were ipso facto equal stakeholders in the region's future, which was the domain of public affairs. Thus, redistributionist policies were necessary to ensure that economic power could not turn into political power over time. This often meant that the first-born male inherited his father's livelihood but relatively little of the wealth he accumulated in its practice. Moreover, the rotating nature of civil and military service anticipated the Maoist strategy for acquainting freed people with the full range of societal tasks so as to prevent the subversion of egalitarianism by certain jobs acquiring either too much expertise or too little status.

Nevertheless, as citizenship was extended beyond a small middle class, liberty tended to get either "thinned" or "thickened." In Isaiah Berlin's (1958) terms, the thinned version of republicanism is *negative liberty*, the thickened version *positive liberty*—or, respectively, *liberalism* and *communitarianism*, as they are ideologically defined in Fuller (2000a, Chapter 1). Interestingly, Berlin saw these two kinds of liberties as pure types, rather than alternative degradations of republican liberty, as I would urge. This helps us to understand the alien character of republicanism in our time. Republicans would regard as an historical Fall from Grace what modern political theorists would see as the progressive clarification of polar ideals.

Negative liberty has supported unlimited freedom of contract in democratic societies, including the "freedom" to contract oneself into wage slavery and other forms of servitude, in which self-worth is effectively exchanged for money. Thus, in liberal regimes, non-domination is reduced to non-interference, a point originally urged by Thomas Hobbes in his demystified definition of the law as the state's monopoly of force in society. When Jeremy Bentham declared that the republican appeal to "rights" amounted to "nonsense on stilts," he was reinventing Hobbes in a world where mass enfranchisement meant that the state would have to meddle objectionably in people's lives in order to regain the kind of self-determination vaunted in republican regimes.

Indeed, this Hobbesian reluctance to have the state interfere more than is absolutely necessary has been even carried over into the welfare state. The benchmark is John Rawls' (1972) "difference principle," whereby inequalities in "wealth" (understood broadly to include both money and talent) are justified if the rich are in a better position to benefit the poor than the poor themselves are. Such a policy licenses the "spontaneous" emergence over time of a paternalist social order that would be anathema to republican sensibilities. Moreover, it sets the groundwork for a form of positive liberty that would "free" people from entertaining false expectations about their own life chances. Thus, the state would ascribe roles that enable people to participate "appropriately" in reproducing the social order. An updated version of this strategy is the use of aptitude tests or genetic screening to delimit people's career horizons. According to this communitarian mentality, the worst situation to befall both the individual and the collective is what Emile Durkheim originally called "anomie," the lack of social rootedness that results when people have lost their ties to such traditional institutions as the family or religion, without having established an identity within the more modern institutions defined by the market, the professions, or party politics.

Republicans oppose what negative and positive liberty jointly uphold, namely, the allowance of non-coercive forms of domination justified in terms of either the explicit choice or the "best interests" of the people concerned—that is, the republican diagnosis of negative and positive liberty, respectively. Republicans use the legal system to foreclose these undesirable possibilities. On the one hand, labor–management legislation and a guaranteed citizens' income counteract the desperation and abuses associated with unlimited freedom of contract; on the other, affirmative action and antitrust legislation counteract the advantage accumulated by wealthy groups and corporations over time. This distinctive legislative posture epitomizes republicanism's adherence to three propositions:

1. There need not be a tradeoff between individual and collective well-being. Indeed, promotion of the individual may be the best way to promote the collective.
2. Individual and collective well-being should not be identified, respectively, with short- and long-term benefit. Rather, individuals become better people by thinking in terms of what is best for society in the long term.
3. Collectively minded individuals need not aim for an absolute consensus of opinion, only for the reversible resolutions of differences, the proliferation of which is to be encouraged.

Those who relish paradoxes may sum up the republican position as favoring the "artifice" of state intervention over the "natural" emergence of domination in the absence of state intervention. Historically, this amounts to a view of politics that combines "liberty before liberalism," in Quentin Skinner's (1998) apt phrase, and what I call "social responsibility after socialism"—at least in the sense that the disagreements fostered in a republican environment are meant ultimately to serve the larger good in a way communitarians could not envisage. In most extreme terms, republicans uphold a maxim invoked by various thinkers from Goethe to Popper—that our ideas should always die in our stead, so that to risk an idea is never to risk one's life (Fuller 2000d).

Both liberals and communitarians implicitly deny this maxim. The negative conception of liberty championed by liberals gravitates toward a recklessly risk-seeking "survival of the fittest" mentality, whereas the positive conception championed by communitarians is an extended exercise in risk avoidance. To a republican, either extreme is tantamount to reducing the status of humans to that of ordinary animals. Admittedly, this is a popular strategy in these Neo-

TYPES OF LIBERTY	REPUBLICAN LIBERTY	POSITIVE LIBERTY (COMMUNI-TARIANISM)	NEGATIVE LIBERTY (LIBERALISM)
SLOGAN	The right to be wrong	Freedom is the recognition of necessity	Anything not prohibited is permitted
LIBERTY'S ANTITHESIS	No legal protection from implicit threats	Anomie bred by false self-understanding	Actual interference from other people
FUNCTION OF LAW	Guarantee rights	Define identity	Prevent harm
DEFORMATION	Liberalism or communitarianism	Duty to perform a role	Right to be a slave

Figure 4.1.
Republican liberty and its devolutions

Darwinian times, but it forgets the spirit of gamesmanship that has animated so much of collective human endeavor, which led the medievalist Johan Huizinga (1949) to speak of *Homo ludens* (cf. Fuller 2000c). The republican is the consummate player, someone who always expects a second chance. A more prosaic account of the differences in conceptions of liberty is presented in Figure 4.1.

2. A Distinguished False Lead: Michael Polanyi's "Republic of Science"

The chemist Michael Polanyi was probably the most important philosophical theorist of science policy to emerge from the Cold War era. Polanyi (1962) is relevant to our discussion because he first floated the idea of a "republic of science" that is the basis of the peer-review system of scientific governance, more about which in the appendix to this chapter. However, Polanyi meant "republic" in a very specific sense—not the sense which makes the United States and other non-monarchies "republics." Rather, his "republic of science" harks back to the class of philosopher-kings in the utopia defined in Plato's *Republic*. According to Plato, the community of inquirers (or Polanyi's "society of explorers") functions as the highest court of appeal on matters concerning efficacy, rationality, and, most fundamentally, reality itself. This image of science as the ultimate ideological authority goes very much against the spirit of civic republicanism.

The Platonist sharply distinguishes between the unified front of scientific authority that is presented for public consumption and whatever differences of opinion may exist behind the scenes—indeed, often within the soul of a given philosopher-king (cf. Elster 1986). We can cast the republican alternative to the Platonic way of thinking in sharpest relief by drawing from the conceptual resources of constitution-making. A true republican would allow the legislature to absorb judicial functions, whereas Polanyi's pseudo-republican would try, wherever possible, to reduce legislative functions to judicial ones. The former tends to expand the sphere of contestation by enabling the expression of countervailing forces; the latter tends to contain the sphere by resolving differences before going public. It is not by accident that, during the Cold War, when scientists tried to constitute themselves as a political body, a court—as opposed to a legislature—struck them as the most natural model.

Moreover, the distinction between civic republicanism and Polanyi's pseudo-republicanism is regularly played out in the peer-review practices of the social and natural sciences, respectively. This helps explain why, generally speaking, social science journals reject such a high proportion of their submissions compared to natural science journals. In the more republican social sciences, "errors" are committed openly in the peer-review process, whereas in the more Polanyiesque natural sciences, authors will have been trained to present their knowledge claims so as to avoid "errors" before submission (Fuller 1997, 19–23). Incidentally, this also explains the paradox that the perceived "hardness" of a science varies directly with the acceptance rate of articles for journal publication: the harder the science, the *easier* to get into print. The differences between the natural and social sciences are summarized in Figure 4.2.

However, matters become a bit more complicated, once we factor Cicchetti's (1991) observation that while rejection rates in the social sciences (and, interestingly, in interdisciplinary forms of natural science) are very high, it is also true that eventually most articles find a place in some journal or other. Whether this is a good result depends on what I have called the *social ecology of science* (Fuller

	NATURAL SCIENCE	SOCIAL SCIENCE
Article Rejection Rate	Low	High
Criteria of Peerage	Clear	Unclear
Research Writing	Topic-neutral	Topic-sensitive
Cause of Rejection	Incompetence	Politics
Verdict	Professionalism?	Amateurism?

Figure 4.2.
Peer review in natural and social science

1994a, cf. Hawley 1950). A truism of classical political theory is that two material conditions preclude the existence of society: extreme abundance renders society unnecessary, whereas extreme scarcity renders it impossible. Now imagine "society" to be the community of inquirers. In that case, it might be said that, in terms of the relationships that inquirers are encouraged to cultivate with each other, social science exists in the anti-social extremes, whereas natural science exists in the middle "sociable" realm. Thus, social scientists exist in a state of either splendid isolation (a breakaway journal) or mortal combat (mainstream peer review), while natural scientists are primed to peacefully carve out a niche in explicit relation to what others have done, so that one's own work complements theirs. It is the sort of "market" mentality that a classical free trader such as David Ricardo would have recognized, in which an efficient division of labor is spontaneously generated on the basis of knowledge producers individually determining what would provide a "comparative advantage" for them (cf. White 1981). However, this policy of "mutual adaptation," which Polanyi (1957) himself modeled on the medieval monastery, can lead to the reinforcement of already existing beliefs rather than attempts to transcend them in ways that may cause internal dissent.

In science, the material resources needed to insulate one's ideas from one's survival—to let one's ideas die in one's stead—have markedly changed with the rise of "Big Science." In this context, the republican spirit can move in either of two opposing directions (cf. Fuller 1993b, 281–300):

1. On the one hand, republicans may make the preservation of diversity of opinion a *sine qua non* of science policy. In this vein, the late Paul Feyerabend (1979) advocated the devolution of state funding for science to local authorities. Yet, Feyerabend's self-styled anarchist rhetoric belied its aristocratic precedents. In effect, he called for a return to the spirit in which science had been pursued in the "Little Science" era of table-top experiments and personal observations of nature. But back then, the pursuit of knowledge was treated as a leisured activity, which reflected the pursuer's own economic security, which in turn implied that research costs were to be measured more by time than by money. Reinstating this ethos in our own time would require a further devolution of the state into Rousseauian communities large enough to pursue what satisfies the majority but small enough to enable dissenters to form their own like-minded communities (Fuller 2000a, 38–42).

2. On the other hand, republicans may operate in the spirit of the American founding fathers and take "bigness"—in both government and science—as not merely given but even desirable, in that it provides a "natural" basis for expressing countervailing forces (Dahl 1989). They would then construct means to ensure that majorities cannot irreversibly disempower minorities. My own republican theory of science pursues this perspective. In this context, there are two key republican mechanisms.

One republican mechanism is coalition formation, whereby different groups can pursue their interests simultaneously. For example, if a Big Science project is likely to absorb most of the research budget, then a necessary condition for its approval should be that several research interests are satisfied by it, as would be the case if anthropologists and sociologists were earmarked to roam around the site of a particle accelerator. I call this the principle of "fungibility" of research (Fuller 2000a, 143–145). The second mechanism is the provision of a regular and explicit procedure, perhaps modeled on elections, for registering one's debts, allegiances, and opponents. In short, opportunities to reverse historically contingent advantage would be built into the politics of science, so as to prevent such advantage from accumulating and thereby exerting authority by default (Fuller 2000a, 25–26).

Once again, we see that republicanism is not compatible with all species of democracy. To show that science currently exists as an anti-republican form of democracy, consider the uses made of the *Science Citation Index* (SCI), which systematically lists all the references cited in every major scientific (including humanistic and social scientific) article. The SCI's main republican failure is precisely what has made citation counts so attractive to both scientometricians and policy-makers, namely, their seemingly spontaneous self-organizing charac-ter. Here citation counts are seen as votes cast in an ongoing election over whose work matters. If the research frontier shifts over time, it is presumed that will be because individual researchers have decided for themselves that it should change, and their numbers have become sufficiently large to have the desired effect.

However, neglected in this interpretation are the various local reasons for citing others' work, which have more to do with shoring up one's own current position than prescribing for the future. Con-sequently, citation counts can turn out to be very backward-looking measures, as they award credit to those whose past work puts them in a good position to judge the citer's future work. In short, the citers do not operate in an environment where their own fates are suffi-ciently insulated from the decisions they make (Fuller 2000a, 85–89; cf. Fuller 1997, 69–74). While Polanyi would have deplored the policy uses made of the crassly quantitative SCI, nevertheless I believe he would have agreed with the underlying theory that informs its use. Specifically, Polanyi's vision of "tradition" as the principal determining tendency of science can be understood as akin to the spontaneously self-organizing process that the SCI attempts to capture.

Citation counts are determined by the citers, the vast majority of whom are not themselves cited. Each citer can make as many cita-tions as s/he wishes, which means that the biggest debtors exert the most influence over the citation counts. Thus, dependency is taken as an indicator of recognition: i.e., the more of you who depend on me for legitimacy, the more recognized I am. Sometimes this is finessed by saying that citation is evidence not for affiliation but *dif-ferentiation*: i.e., I cite others to distinguish myself from them. Unfor-tunately, the same problem arises if everyone tries to differentiate themselves from the same people: In the long term, they will be seen merely as having contributed to the significance of the person from whom they distanced themselves. As we saw in Chapter 2, these perverse consequences occur because citation often serves as insurance against risk or a Mafia-like "protection" function whereby one pays tribute to others who could influence his or her fate in non-publication settings (e.g., grants or jobs). A possible solution is to restrict citers to one citation apiece that can be distributed across several authors as the citer specifies—i.e., a system of fractional voting that accords each person one vote.

Republicans recognize the value of personal wealth as an insulator from corrupting influence, yet they are equally adamant that wealth needs to be earned by each generation and not simply treated as an automatic inheritance. In that respect, Polanyi's sense of "tradition" grants the past too much control over the future. Thus, republican societies have engaged in practices that we would now see as akin to "affirmative action." For example, a deceased person's wealth might be redistributed to others in the society whose merit had yet to be rewarded, which may or may not include that person's relatives. Moreover, republics have discouraged the establishment of fixed social classes by, say, requiring universal military training while prohibiting any standing armies. In the case of science, this could have interesting consequences, as it would decouple an interest in general science education from one in professional specialist training. For example, the various "wars" waged against disease over the past century may be taken a bit more literally in a republican regime, as involving the conscription of rather diversely trained people to tackle a specific problem rather than, as we tend to do today, supposing that there is already a class of specialists appropriate for the task.

But probably the most telling sign of Polanyi's unrepublican sensibility is that representation in his scientific polity is defined in terms of partially overlapping domains of inquiry, each of which is treated as a fiefdom of expertise. Admittedly, science's peer-review processes typically conform to this model. Dispute occurs, if at all, at the margins between two fiefdoms. Thus, the chief policy question routinely facing Polanyi's "republic of science" is deciding the jurisdiction for evaluating a piece of interdisciplinary research. In contrast, republican regimes operate with an interest-based conception of representation, one which presupposes that each representative is competent to promote his or her own group's interests but in matters where the other representatives are equally competent to promote theirs. Public debates over a nation's foreign policy or annual budget can be easily understood this way.

These radically contrasting sensibilities can be explained in terms of what Polanyi and the true republican each take as uniting and differentiating their respective scientific polities. Polanyi's polity is united by a vision of fundamental ontology as abstract real estate in which fields of inquiry are modeled on plots of land. Entitlement to such a field is communicated through that form of inheritance known as apprenticeship. Emergent differences of opinion are treated as relatively superficial and solvable through a mutual adjustment of the parties concerned, since the representative of each party is presumed to be a legitimate heir. In striking contrast, republican polities are united by exigencies—be they foreign aggressors or tight budgets—that force otherwise diverse groups to mobilize around a common strategy. Thus, while disagreement is likely to be much more intense in a genuinely republican regime than in Polanyi's realm, republicans would also have a more explicit sense of the criteria needed for approving policy proposals. One would not simply rely, as Polanyi might, on someone's training or even reputation as a basis for trust in what they happen to say. Rather, regardless of whose proposals are approved, these would be subject to a period of experimentation, followed by a vote to ratify—or not—the consequences. The difference between the types of republicanism discussed in this section are summarized in Figure 4.3.

Science policy thinking remains stuck in Polanyi's pseudo-republican mentality. A theoretical and a practical example come to mind. First, argumentation and negotiation—rhetoric, in a word—are still not regarded as intellectually respectable activities in the philosophy of science and epistemology (Fuller 2000b, 313–317). In the heyday of positivism, this was because these activities failed to conform to known canons of deductive or inductive reasoning. In our more sociologically informed times, such matters of rhetoric remain sidelined, but now in favor of observing scientists' interactions with things. Even relatively sophisticated social epistemologies of science tend to divide scientific authority into two jointly exhaustive categories: one's own expertise and one's knowledge of the relevant experts in other fields (e.g., Kitcher 1993; cf. Fuller 1996, for a critique).

For practical evidence of the influence of Polanyi's sensibility, consider the ease with which scientists continue to be caught unawares by gross error, fraud, and other forms of research misconduct, coupled with a belief that all such misconduct is eventually spotted and corrected. Because it is difficult to publish disconfirmations of

	POLANYI	FULLER
HISTORIC MODEL	Plato's *Republic*	Civic republicanism
FLOW OF GOVERNANCE	Legislature → judiciary	Judiciary → legislature
FLOW OF POLITICS	Reduce sphere of contestation in training	Expand sphere of contestation without training
DEFINING PROBLEM	Who are the experts? Dispute occurs on the margins	How to resolve competing interests? Everyone is competent to judge
UNIFYING PRINCIPLE	Ontology = real estate	Exigency = common fate
DISCIPLINARY EXEMPLAR	Natural science	Social science

Figure 4.3.
The two "republics of science"

earlier research, there is little professional incentive for scientists to check each other's work, in any literal sense, on a regular basis. In the main, research validation occurs at one step removed from actual testing—in the realm of "virtual witnessing," as Steven Shapin aptly puts it. This essentially literary exercise constitutes the core of peer-review judgement. And it is here that Polanyi's image of science as a fiduciary institution comes out most clearly, since referees seek textual signs of an author's trustworthiness, which may include treating an author's name as if it were a more or less reliable commercial brand.

Of course, what promises to usher us out of Polanyi's trusting world is research on which a lot of money or lives have been staked. Thus, Walter Stewart and Ned Feder's publicly proactive efforts at "fraud-busting" at the U.S. National Institute of Health in the late 1980s and early 1990s must count as among the most un-Polanyiesque activities imaginable. For, while Polanyi was cognizant of the scaled-up stakes in scientific research in the 20th century, he nevertheless seemed more concerned with protecting the conduct of research from external social factors than protecting society from the impacts—intended or unintended—that such research might have. (For the other side of the coin, Polanyi's concern to protect society from science, see the discussion of science as a "moral community" in Fuller 2000b, 139–149.) Perhaps in the middle of the 20th century, Lysenkoism more directly threatened the integrity of science than, say, genetically modified foods threatened society as whole, but certainly this is not how things seem today.

3. IN SEARCH OF REPUBLICAN VEHICLES FOR KNOWLEDGE MANAGEMENT

Republicanism highlights the ever-present need to constitute the object of governance. There is nothing "natural" about the polity that dictates how it should be governed. Rather, the "who" and "how" of political participation must be formally defined, continuously enacted, and subject to periodic review. This explicitly artificial (or "constructivist") approach to politics is focused more on the quality of the political process than on the quantity of its products— less on the actual number of voters and more on the character of their participation in the electoral process. Transferred to the scientific realm, republicanism offers a welcomed counterbalance to current discussions of the "governance of science," which presume that "science" exists simply as a body of systematic knowledge that may be institutionalized by any number of means, ranging from individual minds through state-funded universities to privately funded "research parks." Thus, a large body of knowledge management research has been devoted to developing knowledge-bearing indicators or "outputs," such as the number of scientific papers, patents, or university graduates. Serious study has yet to be given to the relationship among these indicators and the institutions generating them, wherein lie hidden hierarchies and suppressed perspectives.

Nevertheless, whenever attempts have been made to study science from the standpoint of its participants rather than its products, the results have revealed that the aggregate measures do not reflect the interests of most of those who are presumed to have contributed to them. A simple case in point is the survey that the American Physical Society conducted of its membership in 1991 on their degree of support for the Superconducting Supercollider, which was strongly pushed on Congress by various Nobel Prize–winning physicists. It turns out that the Supercollider was ranked only third, with many expressing reservations that Congressional funding of the world's largest particle accelerator would undermine the support received for less glamorous, but more populous, branches of the discipline, as well as skew the teaching of physics so as to inflate the larger social significance attached to particle physics.

Even more to the point was a survey conducted in 1990 by the U.S. Carnegie Foundation for the Advancement of Teaching in response to perceived pressure on faculty at all tertiary educational institutions to emulate the high-publication model of research universities (Boyer 1990). Published under the title of "Scholarship Reconsidered," the survey revealed that despite the perception that all faculty are pressured to publish a lot, only institutions strong in graduate training required it for tenure and promotion. Nevertheless, except for the most elite universities, most faculty (70% overall) saw their "scholarship" better expressed through teaching than through academic publications. Moreover, strong graduate-oriented institutions tended to perceive a tradeoff in quality between teaching and publication that was not perceived in the rest of higher education. And while there remained considerable disagreement over scholarly standards across tertiary sector institutions, nevertheless there was virtual unanimity that "exciting developments" were taking place in one's own field. In the end, more than two-thirds held that means other than publication needed to be developed to evaluate scholarly performance. A civic republican approach to knowledge management would aim to preserve these different interests *in order to* advance more collective aims of knowledge production. But how is this particular circle to be squared?

Ultimately, the practical success of civic republicanism depends on the ability to settle on an institution as the unit of governance, in terms of which criteria for participation and standards of accountability can be developed. There are three possibilities: the *knowledge worker union*, the *consensus conference*, and the *university*. None of these institutional sites should be seen as excluding the others, but their historical viability as vehicles of republicanism varies significantly, as indicated below.

3.1. Knowledge Worker Unions

The first possible unit of governance is Marxist-inspired. It involves taking discipline-based professional associations as the basis for unionizing the sciences. In that case, science policy would become a form of labor–management relations. Aside from the Marxist baggage, the main obstacle to realizing this possibility nowadays is that the work conditions of scientists trained in a particular discipline have become so diversified as to undermine a plausible case for the kind of "class consciousness" that unions are supposed to foster. This negative unintended consequence of our inhabiting a post-industrial "knowledge society" has been brought out in the Carnegie Foundation Report. Yet, there is a silver lining in this cloud. Insofar as the diverse work conditions of scientists reflect those of society at large, then a democratically governed professional association can function as the launch pad for a social movement within which standing conflicts in the society can be expressed, elaborated, and to some extent, resolved. For example, the full range of public attitudes can be found within the community of professional biologists, whose internal debates mirror larger societal struggles.

3.2. Consensus Conferences

A second possibility is that academics should be seeding republican projects at large as an extension of the idea of the "open society" that is essential to the spirit of critical inquiry, a.k.a. "deliberative democracy" (Fishkin 1991, Bohman 1996). Too often when we speak of the need for society to become "scientifically literate" or "knowledgeable," we think purely in terms of increasing the amount of formal training people receive. Here, however, the emphasis would be placed on expanding the opportunities people have to participate in defining the scientific agenda. Too often in knowledge-intensive public issues, the blockage of political expression is read as a stable cognitive attitude. For example, the popularity of Creationist approaches to the origins of life is glibly dismissed as the product of ignorance—rather than, say, knowledgeable rejection—of Neo-Darwinism. More mandatory education in biology is presumed to be the remedy, as opposed to forums for negotiating legitimate and informed differences of opinion. Similarly, the public's apparent tolerance of scientific and technological developments may be equally symptomatic of apathy as of endorsement (cf. Noelle-Neumann 1982). Just as advertising agencies in the 1920s began to create previously unknown demands for goods, and political pollsters in the 1930s invented the entity known as "public opinion," so now the idea would be to institutionalize the public's thought processes.

This may be seen as a continuation of the "extension agency" model of academic public service pioneered by the land-grant colleges in the United States in the 19th century (Collier 1998). However, in this case, outreach would focus on ideological, rather than technological, innovation. The ideal vehicle is the consensus conference, sometimes called the "citizens jury," whereby a cross-section of the public takes testimony from various experts and interested parties in order to draft policy guidelines for legislation governing a science- or technology-based issue of widespread social concern. (Typically, these have been related to health or the environment. Loka 2001 provides a list of consensus conferences worldwide.) The citizen-jurors do not themselves make policy—that remains in the hands of popularly elected representatives—but in effect they draft the constitutional framework within which the representatives should make policy. In this respect, the name "consensus conference" is somewhat of a misnomer, since the goal is not a first-order meeting of minds, but rather a second-order agreement on the terms on which such a meeting should occur. (WIHSC 1998 provides a recipe for organizing a consensus conference.)

From the standpoint of lay interest in democratizing science, consensus conferences have continued the contribution of academics to political movements in the larger society. Yet, consensus conferences have also generally produced results that leave the experts "pleasantly surprised," especially in terms of the public's diligence and fairness in drafting a workable policy framework. (This has been especially true in Japan, which does not have a strong tradition of participatory democracy: Ayano 1999.) Indeed, politicians are virtually alone in objecting to the insertion of consensus conferences as an institutional "wild card" into the policy process. Specifically, they pose three objections, which I list and answer below:

1. Consensus conferences would seem to usurp the authority of the legislature, indeed, by interpolating academics (who are the typical organizers of these conferences) to act as convenors of a mini-constitutional convention. I respond that the appropriate way of viewing these conferences is as a counterbalance to the "de-republicanizing" tendencies of representative democracy, whereby people come to believe (often with the help of

their elected officials!) that their duty is done once they have voted for their representatives. The long-term effect of such de-republicanization has been that parties come to stereotype what is politically possible, and voting comes to be seen as little more than a symbolic ratification of one's vague faith in the political system as a whole. (It is worth recalling that such complacency on the part of the electorate has been defended, under the name of "plebiscitarianism," as the appropriate response in a complex world best left to expert politicians.) In this respect, consensus conferences ensure that the democratic polity is republican, not just in the legislative chamber, but "all the way down."

2. Consensus conferences cannot get around the problem of what counts as an adequate "cross-section of the public," the perennial problem of representative democracies in general. I respond that this objection misses the point of the exercise. There is nothing intrinsically valuable about having citizens juries constituted in certain proportions of the population. A "cross-section of the public" is valuable only insofar as it results in a framework that adequately distinguishes between the personal interests of the jurors and the diverse interests of the larger society, with the understanding that the full range of those interests can never be represented by a single jury. There is evidence from Japan that this is the case, namely, that while jurors do not start by distinguishing their own interests from the collective good, they do so by the end of the consensus conference. In fact, often they became clearer about their own reasons for, say, refusing gene therapy for themselves yet allowing others to receive such treatment if they wish (Ayano 1999).

3. By what authority do academics—as opposed to anyone else—claim to conduct consensus conferences? What makes them the unique keepers of republican democracy? I respond that first one needs to look at the competition. In Tony Blair's Britain, it is common to conduct "focus groups" before legislation is proposed. Marketing consultants and think-tank dwellers (often armed with sociology degrees) are employed for this purpose. Their basic strategy is to start with the government's general policy aim and then adjust its expression according to the focus group's response, so as to ensure maximum agreement. In other words, the public is not offered the chance to

make an independent assessment or to resolve internal disagreements in non-consensualist terms. In contrast, the relatively detached situation of academics (i.e., their jobs do not depend on the outcomes of the conference) enables them to avoid this pattern. Moreover, the perennial pedagogical concern of academics with the next generation of societal leaders means that their sense of "policy" is bound to be broader than that of any particular government, or consultancy working on its behalf. The breadth of the academics' temporal horizon is significant, since any major legislative initiative is likely to have consequences beyond the voters in the next election.

This last point raises the third possibility, namely, the university as the principal site of republican governance of science, which will be the focus of the remainder of this chapter.

3.3. Universities: the Ultimate Republican Institution

Universities were originally chartered in medieval Europe as politically autonomous, self-funding, limited liability corporations, with many of the same characteristics as the ancient republics. Unlike the often much larger academies of Islam, India, and China, the medieval universities were not directly beholden to state or private benefactors and hence could survive changing conditions in the larger society. Indeed, universities were often encouraged to fill vacuums in political and economic leadership, as long as they did not attempt to subvert the keepers of the legal system that enabled their existence. Thus, universities came to perform at least three functions: They completed the family's role in educating the next generation of elites; they offered professional training for civil and ecclesiastical posts; and they continued the ongoing project of synthesizing disparate forms of knowledge into a common cultural inheritance. As we shall see in Section 4, in the modern period, these three functions have come to be differentiated and set against each other, representing what, after Bjorn Wittrock (1985), I call the *British, French*, and *German* models of the university, respectively.

Both universities and classical republics are predicated on the presence of an external enemy that threatens all their members equally. Regardless of their other differences, academics and citizens, respectively, can always focus their political energies on how to deal with this foe. In the history of republics, the foe has tended to be a larger empire or political entity that threatens to obliterate the republic's autonomy and hence the liberties enjoyed by its citizens. The common foe that has confronted the university has been alternatively called "error," "falsehood," "prejudice," or "ignorance." The university has traditionally tackled this common foe through *curriculum design*, which functions much as "foreign affairs" does in republics. In both cases, it provides the backbone of governance, underwriting both the autonomy and dynamism of republics and universities. Deft curriculum design has prepared the conditions for the wider reception of the innovative and often controversial research done by the faculty. Even during the Scientific and Industrial Revolutions, when the universities were rarely the source of new discoveries or inventions, they nevertheless helped to normalize those developments as part of the public knowledge of the day—if only by immunizing the next generation of elites against a knee-jerk negative reaction to innovation and controversy.

Thus, rather than being a burden on the free spirit of research, teaching has conferred legitimacy and relevance on ideas and techniques that would otherwise fall victim to either benign neglect or charges of blasphemy. Toward this end, curriculum design has compelled the maintenance of a lingua franca for a single academic subject and sometimes even the entire university (cf. MacIntyre 1990, which claims that the discourse of Christian doctrine was the university's lingua franca before the Enlightenment). This has enabled the expression of intellectual disagreement in ways that have had larger societal import. Indeed, one should not underestimate the long-term role that the scholastic artifice of reducing complex differences of opinion to binary oppositions has played in fueling the political imagination. The intellectual basis of virtually every modern social movement is an "us-versus-them" dichotomy such as "nature versus nurture," "rulers versus ruled," or simply "traditional versus modern."

Moreover, just as republicans would have it, universities have been traditionally run according to a system of checks and balances in which faculty and students exercised mutually countervailing powers. Faculty determined the curriculum, but students could voice their objections by refusing to pay for lectures, which would ultimately—albeit indirectly—affect course content. In the medieval period, the university's corporate character was modeled on the trade guilds, where students were positioned as apprentices in their field of study. However, the British settlers in 17th- and 18th-century America innovated the idea of the university as an *independent church* that, lacking either a state monopoly or a natural clientele, had to actively solicit its student base as a constituency that would support the institution even after graduation. This "evangelical" attitude has anchored higher education policy in the United States more generally, even in the public sector, most notably through the philanthropic mission of university alumni associations. While the best American private universities officially charge the world's highest tuition fees, few students actually pay them because their education is subsidized by generous alumni who want others to have the same formative experiences they had.

This point raises the important issue of the political economy under which universities have been able to retain their autonomy as republican institutions—especially in the face of a changing environment. We have already seen that the republican sense of liberty is typically lost under these circumstances; hence the rise of positive and negative liberty as alternative ideals. In the history of the university, there have been two basic autonomy strategies, which have involved academics in, respectively, a *priestly* and a *monastic* mission.

In the priestly mode, universities *expand* to become sovereign states in their own right, or at least to acquire many of the powers typically held by states. During the politically disorganized Middle Ages, this was a common path for universities to take, given that they were in the business of training the next generation of civil and religious officials. In the 19th century, this strategy was updated for a modern secular society in the land-grant mission of American universities (Collier 1998, Chapter 2). In the monastic mode, universities *contract* so as to be free of benefactors who might try to pervert the path of inquiry with their donations. Fuller (2000a, Chapter 6) proposes an updated version of this ascetic orientation, namely, that universities would refuse big corporate grants in favor of functioning as critics, quality control checks, and "reverse engineers"—all in the aid of removing barriers to the free flow of knowledge. In this respect, the innovative function of universities would be limited to opening up channels for the distribution of already existing knowledge. In Chapter 1, I referred to this in terms of universities as producers of "metapublic goods."

The two autonomy strategies are traceable to the period immediately preceding the founding of the first universities. Two 12th-century French clerics, Bernard of Clairvaux and Peter Abelard, are the "patron saints" of the priestly and monastic strategies, respectively. Bernard's academics would stamp out heresy and consolidate religious orthodoxy as part of the proselytizing mission of the Church, whereas Abelard's would relentlessly pursue dialectics to bring out the strengths and weaknesses of both sides of any issue, so as to drive home the fallibility of any humanly designed orthodoxy. To be sure, both the priestly and monastic modes are susceptible to pitfalls analogous to those that befell the religious orders on which they are modeled. In theological terms, the priestly mode is susceptible to *simony*, the monastic mode to *acedia*. On the one hand, an expanding university is open to corruption as potential benefactors try to buy their way into the research and teaching agenda; on the other, a contracting university may withdraw into itself in a cynical spirit that doubts the ultimate efficacy of the university's mission, which many today associate with the "postmodern condition." The existence of these pitfalls points to the sorts of environments in which the priestly and monastic modes tend to operate. The former requires a permeable boundary between the public and private spheres, whereas the latter requires a much harder boundary. I believe that much of the ideological content of the "culture wars" in U.S. universities over the past quarter century can be captured in these starkly polarized terms, if we think of St. Bernard as the patron saint of the "Right" and Peter Abelard as that of the "Left."

However, matters elsewhere have not been so clear-cut, and so more complex models might be welcomed. For example, Fuller (2000b, Chapter 2) considers the Faustian bargain struck in the early 20th century by Max Planck and other defenders of the German universities, in the face of growing public demands, coupled with a growing dependency of universities on public resources to support their own activities. Basically, the bargain—one replayed in all the other major national university systems—consisted of academics agreeing to set examinations and curricula that provided the new ("democratic") basis for societal reproduction and stratification, in return for a largely free research culture. In other words, the dynamic function of the university was contained to an increasingly esoteric arena (the research culture) that was removed from the stabilizing function that the curriculum now had to make its public face. This bargain remained intact throughout most of the 20th century, and indeed inspired the sociological side of paradigms presented in Kuhn (1970). However, with the end of the Cold War and the divestment of what Alvin Gouldner originally called "the welfare–warfare state," the Faustian bargain is unraveling. It is to this that we now turn.

4. HISTORIC THREATS TO THE REPUBLICAN CONSTITUTION OF THE UNIVERSITY

However, the status of the university as a regulative ideal of institutionalized inquiry is in danger of being lost today, as academic culture comes to be divided between what European science policy gurus, after Michael Gibbons et al. (1994, cf. Nowotny et al. 2000), have dubbed "Mode 1" and "Mode 2" knowledge production. These two modes effectively reenact, respectively, the communitarian and liberal devolutions of republican liberty previously outlined in Figure 4.1. The full array of differences among the three modes of science governance is captured in Figure 4.4.

In the history of the university, the difference between communitarianism and liberalism is most clearly reflected in the difference between *too much* and *too little* concern about the disruptive consequences of innovation for society. Kuhn's conception of "paradigm" as resistant to innovation until a research tradition has run its course is perhaps the clearest example of the conservatism of Mode 1, to which Mode 2 is supposed to provide welcomed relief by opening up knowledge production to a wider range of influences. Indeed, most interdisciplinary fields in the natural sciences (and even some in the social sciences, including cybernetics and some area studies) owe their existence to academics frustrated with the disciplinary boundaries of their universities and hence susceptible to the lure of strategic research initiatives from both the public and private sectors. However, although the innovations may have been made outside the academy, their institutionalization ultimately depended on the establishment of degree-granting programs at universities.

Thus, Mode 2 is at most a *temporary* antidote to Mode 1. This is a point that we are in serious danger of losing, as universities are increasingly forced to compete on a "leveled playing field" with other institutions that attempt to fulfill only one of the university's many traditional functions, such as science parks (for research) and online

SCIENTIFIC POLITY	REPUBLICAN	COMMUNITARIAN	LIBERAL
MODE OF KNOWLEDGE PRODUCTION	Mode 0 or 3?	Mode 1	Mode 2
MOTTO	"Right to be wrong"	"Safety in numbers"	"Survival of the fittest"
INSTANTIATION	Dynamic university	Fixed paradigm	Temporary network
DEFINING VIRTUE OF SCIENCE	Inclusive reliable access	Certified reliable knowledge	Increasingly effective action
INTRINSIC VALUE OF KNOWLEDGE	"Public good" (indivisible and non-positional good)	Consensus (divisible good)	Utility (positional good)
EXTRINSIC VALUE OF KNOWLEDGE	Critique (inquiry serves by changing social practices)	Ideology (inquiry constrains other social practices)	Technology (inquiry subserved to other social practices)
METASCIENCE	Institution-centered social epistemology	Domain-centered epistemology	Individual-centered research ethics
ATTITUDE TO RISK	Collectively encouraged	Collectively avoided	Individually absorbed
CUMULATIVE ADVANTAGE	Regularly redistributed	Academic lineage	Track record
SOURCE OF DISADVANTAGE	None	Ideological (political correctness)	Financial (unfunded grants)

Figure 4.4.
Three modes of science governance

degree courses (for teaching). The 19th century is the source for the three modern models of the university, each associated with the historical experience of a European nation: Britain, France, and Germany. Each tradition evokes a totemic figure: Cardinal John Henry Newman, Napoleon Bonaparte, and Wilhelm von Humboldt. I shall review each type and then comment on more recent developments that have altered (perverted?) the ideal it represents. The three types are summarized in Figure 4.5.

These three ideal types basically accentuate aspects that had been integrated together in the training of elites in the ancient Greek academies and original medieval universities. However, Europe's political reorganization around a system of competitive nation-states undermined this pre-modern unity of mission. Interestingly, within its own borders, the United States has permitted each type to flourish, respectively, as liberal arts colleges, land-grant colleges, and research universities. But then again, as a federally constituted republic, the

IDEAL TYPE	BRITAIN	FRANCE	GERMANY
TOTEMIC FIGURE	Cardinal Newman	Napoleon Bonaparte	Wilhelm von Humboldt
WHAT IS PROMOTED?	Development of the whole person	The interests of clients	The advancement of the discipline
STUDENT COMMITMENT	Lifelong	Temporary	Either or both
FACULTY COMMITMENT	Collegial	Contractual	Departmental
QUALITY CONTROL	Entrance exams	Licensing board	Peer review
ECONOMIC MODEL	Fiduciary institution	Monopoly	Multi-product firm
INCOME SOURCE	Rent (of reputation)	Profit (from contracts)	Wage (for work)
RECENT IDEOLOGY	Principal-agent theory	Credential society	Economies of scope and scale
RECENT THEORIST	Arthur Stinchcombe	Peter Drucker	William Baumol
ACHILLES HEEL	Academic bullionism	Poor accountability	Competing standards

Figure 4.5.
Modern deformations of the university's republican spirit

United States has never pretended to have a coordinated national system of education and research.

According to the British ideal, the university (think Oxbridge) is located on a campus and is governed "collegially," which is to say, on the basis of academics inhabiting a common space without necessarily having common intellectual interests. These colleagues relate to students as an extended family (*"in loco parentis"*) through a personalized tutorial system. Students are evaluated as much for their "good character" as for their academic performance. The pursuit of knowledge is clearly a means for creating the well-rounded person. In less flattering terms, the university is a glorified "finishing school." Thus, students typically come from wealthy backgrounds and are expected to assume leadership positions upon graduation.

According to the French ideal, higher education is led by glorified polytechnic institutes that are explicitly entrusted with advancing the fortunes of the nation that subsidizes their existence. Thus, faculties of these *grandes ecoles* may be organized around, say, "agriculture" and "mining," as opposed to such conceptually defined object domains as "physics" and "chemistry." Value-for-money at the level of teaching and research translates to a system of clients and contracts. Here we see the greatest concern with demonstrating an overall increase in "human capital" ("credentials," for short) as determined by state licensing boards.

According to the German ideal, the university is dedicated primarily to the pursuit of knowledge for its own sake. This explains why its institutional structure appears arcane to non-academics, organized as it is around disciplines and not social functions. Yet, at least at the level of rhetoric, this model seems to have had the most lasting impact. Here the university is officially detached from the concerns of state and regulated primarily by "peer-review" mechanisms. This autonomy is justified on the grounds that policy would benefit most from knowledge that has undergone specialist scrutiny, resulting in its collective authorization by a specialist journal. Not surprisingly, Ph.D. training turns out to be the cornerstone of this model.

Each model implies a distinctive political economy, which by the end of the 20th century has exhibited its own distinctive "deformation."

The British model envisages the university as a fiduciary institution, in which students pay academics to make choices on their behalf that they themselves do not feel competent to make—with incompetence potentially carrying a heavy toll (cf. Stinchcombe 1990, Chapter 9). The choices concern the sort of knowledge that students need to succeed in life. As the students' entrusted agent, the university then engages in informed speculative investments, namely, the hiring of the most distinguished faculty. However, this process can be deformed, if there is no clear relationship between the accumulation of "big names" and the quality of education that students receive. A good example, discussed in the first chapter, is the sharp distinction in performance standards used in teaching and research, with the latter carrying greater symbolic and financial value. The result is what Adam Smith would have recognized as "academic bullionism," that is, the possession of big names who look good on university brochures but do little to increase the competence of those who pay their salaries.

On the French model, higher education is a state-sanctioned monopoly that licenses the practice of the liberal professions: law, medicine, engineering, and more recently something called "business." The attractiveness of this model lay in the provision of quality control in areas where academic knowledge interfaces with public and private interests. Yet, interestingly, the person most closely associated with the idea that ours is a "knowledge society," Peter Drucker (1993, 104), has long denounced the deformation attending this model: namely, the university becomes a place where excessive fear of charlatanry and the jealous guarding of guild privileges stifle the spirit of experimentation and innovation.

Finally, the German model of the university is that of a multiproduct firm—in this case, one devoted to both teaching and research. This multiplicity of functions constitutes the "scope" of the university. In theory, the university should become better in performing both functions as it gets larger, since that would allow for "synergies" between teaching and research. The exposure of more students to the latest research should produce at least a more supportive public environment for new research and perhaps even new recruits to the ranks of researchers. Thus, an increase in the scale and scope of the university should be positively correlated (Baumol 1977). But, once again, this rosy picture is deformed by the divisive performance standards for teaching and research, in which the former pulls toward ever more credentially enhanced students and the latter toward ever more multiply cited publications. Consequently, academics and students face each other more as obstacles than as enablers of their respective ends.

5. THE CHALLENGE OF CONTRACT ACADEMIC WORKERS TO THE UNIVERSITY'S REPUBLICAN CONSTITUTION

The suboptimal academic worlds generated by the British, French, and German schemes may be summarized as follows. The British university retains its autonomy by mystifying its relationship to society, while the French university loses its autonomy by becoming an extension of society. The German university arrives at a hybrid ("Faustian") conception of autonomy, whereby it agrees to provide the basis of societal reproduction in a democratized polity, while it abdicates all responsibility for the circulation of its knowledge products. Thus, research autonomy comes to be equated with the freedom to ignore the consequences of one's research. This mentality probably reached its apotheosis in U.S. Cold War academia. However, with the end of the Cold War and the gradual devolution of traditional academic functions to the private sector, we see the rise of "contract academic workers" who are temporarily funded by some combination of academic and non-academic interests. To Mode 2 devotees, these workers are the wave of the future—but the future of what?

Here are three relevant facts:

1. As an increasing percentage of new researchers (or Ph.D. recipients) are unable to get regular academic posts immediately, they must rely on some sort of external funding for their livelihoods. How can the interest of such contract-based researchers be sustained in the peer-review processes by which academics have traditionally decided which potential contributions to knowledge are worth funding and publicizing? These itinerant workers are typically equipped with the most up-to-date knowledge and skills in their fields, yet the conditions under which they work are not conducive to the support of peer review and allied academic practices.

2. Most government-based research councils require that a grant's "principal investigator" hold a regular academic post, which rules out anyone employed on a temporary basis. Most articles

submitted for publication to academic journals are refereed by established academics on whom the editor has previously relied. These people are not only distinguished in their fields but also employed in environments that recognize the significance of their participation in such reviews. Contract-based researchers do not enjoy this indulgence: Any time spent refereeing a colleague's article is time taken away from completing one's own time-dependent project or writing a proposal to ensure one's continued employment.

3. Most universities will not accord the same welfare and legal coverage to temporary staff as they do to regular staff. This is an open invitation to worker exploitation, not only in terms of the number of hours that may be demanded of contract researchers but more importantly the appropriation of such researchers' intellectual property by the universities that temporarily house them. Peer review is thus not unreasonably regarded as a euphemism for the proverbial "old-boys network," where the old get richer, the young poorer.

Given these three conditions, universities may soon become the site of class conflict of a magnitude previously experienced only by the industrial sector of the economy. However, this conflict is unlikely to be manifested in work stoppages, property damage, and strikes. Instead, it will be marked by a gradual withdrawal of services from the universities by many of the most academically talented people of the current generation. Their contract-based status will encourage them to see teaching in opposition to research, and hence the university as little more than a necessary evil for the proper conduct of their work. Indeed, these people may be among the first to call for greater public accountability for universities in ways that may eventually serve to undermine the autonomy of academic institutions altogether.

Unfortunately, academia continues to harbor considerable snobbery toward contract-based research, including a widely held folk psychology of contract researchers (a.k.a. "Thatcher's Children" and "Reagan's Children") as more interested in the pursuit of profit than knowledge. We often presume the inherent attractiveness of contemporary academic life to such an extent that we can only ascribe base motives to those who might resist its charms. Yet, these charms are largely byproducts of the very thing that contract-based researchers lack, namely, secure employment with clear career prospects. Absent those conditions, one is simply presented with an indeterminate labor market where one must live by his or her wits by taking advantage of opportunities as they arise. By those standards, it is not surprising that the dynamic environment of corporate culture increasingly lures people whose ties to academia have become tenuous.

Moreover, when academics try to defend themselves from the onslaught of corporate culture, they rarely seek to protect the university as such; rather, they aim more parochially to shore up the integrity of discipline-based inquiry, as against the interdisciplinary and (allegedly) methodologically sloppy work produced by client-driven, contract-based research. In short, Mode 2 is met with Mode 1—not a more republican Mode 0 or 3. Here we see the most pernicious feature of the Myth of the Modes: The two modes are seen as not merely mutually exclusive, but also jointly exhaustive—that is, not admitting of other possibilities. In particular, missing is the idea of the university as an autonomous site for knowledge production that constitutes a whole that is greater than the sum of its disciplinary parts. This idea, the foundation of liberal education, kept disciplinary proliferation in check by regularly forcing academics to consider how their disparate research agendas contributed to a common curriculum that would be imparted to the incoming cohort of students. This curriculum, in turn, provided a basis for the university to present a unified image of itself as a critical force in society's self-reproductive processes.

To be sure, the historical realization of this ideal has been always less than perfect, but at least one could rely on the presence of some academics to defend the ideal and provide institutional buffers to its complete corruption. Such was the case when academic administrators were recruited from the ranks of the teaching and research staff. However, increasingly academic administration is itself seen as requiring skills akin to those needed to manage business firms with a similar range of personnel and organizational structure. Perhaps not surprisingly, these administrators actually encourage academics to conceptualize their work in terms of the discipline-based criteria associated with Mode 1 knowledge production, partly because that is the easiest way to get academics to mimic the productivity orientation that governs Mode 2 knowledge production.

But as universities shed the ideological and institutional trappings that traditionally distinguished them from business, can they be reasonably expected to compete with business in attracting and keeping the best research talent? Academia continues to send mixed messages about the need to publish in peer-reviewed journals while, at the same time, encouraging the pursuit of intellectual property that typically takes research out of the public domain and may even mask the contributions of the original researchers. In business, the situation is more brutally straightforward: Research is primarily aimed at intellectual property, and researchers are paid sufficiently well that the reversion of patent rights to the company is not regarded as an injustice.

This problem here is traceable to the terms on which the experimental natural sciences were incorporated into the universities in the late 19th century, originally in Germany. The natural sciences were not part of the original framework for the constitution of liberal education that justified the university as an autonomous institution of higher learning. Not surprisingly, Thomas Kuhn found physics and chemistry to be most conducive to his conception of scientific inquiry as paradigm-driven, which approximates the insular ideal of Mode 1 knowledge production. Yet, within a generation of their admission as proper subjects for academic training, the natural sciences were involved in large-scale projects collaboratively sponsored by government and industry. In Germany, this was epitomized by the Kaiser Wilhelm Institutes, the precursors of today's Max Planck Institutes. They marked the institutional dawn of Mode 2 knowledge production.

In short, Mode 1 and Mode 2 were born largely as opposite sides of the same coin, which was the recognition of experimental natural science as proper academic subjects. The humanities, which up to that point had dominated the universities, were never as narrowly insular as Mode 1 implies, but neither were they as readily adaptive to external pressures as Mode 2 implies. Self-declared "postmodernists" in the humanities too often forget that common to the multiple coinages of the expression "the postmodern condition" in the 1970s by Daniel Bell, Stephen Toulmin, and Jean-Francois Lyotard was a belief that 20th-century developments in the natural sciences (broadly construed to include mathematics and computer science) had irreversibly destroyed the unity of knowledge ideal, which Lyotard quite explicitly associated with the constitution of the university.

6. CONCLUSION: A CIVIC REPUBLICAN AGENDA FOR THE ACADEMIC CEO OF TOMORROW

The days of appointing a university's chief executive officer ("president" in the United States, "vice-chancellor" in the United Kingdom, "rector" in continental Europe) from the ranks of senior academics is quickly drawing to a close. There is no reason to think that the average successful department chair, or even faculty dean, has the competence needed to defend the university's autonomy in the face of competing institutions and pressure from both the public and private sectors. However, this need not mean turning over the reins of the university to a "professional manager" (in the Robert McNamara mold) who thinks that organizations of comparable scale and scope can be run in largely the same way, whether they are in the business of making cars, bombs, or knowledge. Rather, it means that academic administration requires its own course of study and accreditation, which would in turn be the new breeding ground for the republican spirit.

The victory of both liberalism and communitarianism over republicanism in higher education today can be measured by the KM caricature of universities as "dumb organizations." This dumbness is most clearly manifested in the enforcement of mutually exclusive, even competing, standards for the evaluation of teaching and research, thereby ensuring that the university will appear to be a sub-optimally performing—if not downright incoherent—institution. Academic administrators seem to be little more than glorified custodians who make sure that the university's space is efficiently managed and that staff are sufficiently happy to remain in their allotted places.

To be sure, the past 20 years of public sector liberalization have forced universities to set goals that transcend the interests of their constituent disciplines. Unfortunately, instead of setting their own organizational aims, university administrators have allowed those aims to be dictated by others who would see academic institutions as means to their own ends. Moreover, the result still fails to impress, only now knowledge managers openly wonder whether each competing demand might not be more efficiently served by such "post-academic" institutions as electronically administered degree programs or privately funded research parks. Even economists, who are officially wedded to rather idealized visions of knowledge as a public good, increasingly focus their debates over the university's optimality in terms of whether it actually enhances (i.e., "adds value to") versus merely selects (i.e., "signals") productive people for prospective employers (Rothschild 1973, Johnes 1993).

The republican antidote to this pervasive anti-university mentality is a reassertion of the university's corporate identity, above not only non-academic interests (Mode 2 liberalism) but also narrowly disciplinary ones (Mode 1 communitarianism); hence the following three-point agenda:

1. Universities must treat expansion or contraction as genuinely alternative modes of survival. Bigger is better only if there is no state support, and hence universities must turn to the private sector. This state-of-affairs would probably indicate a contraction of state control more generally, and hence universities should enter into an expansionist mode as a statelike corporation, providing services to the larger society that are not likely to be provided by a purely market-driven corporate entity. However, if there is strong state support, then universities best retain their autonomy by remaining small and critical of the dominant market-driven forms of knowledge. Both possibilities have the advantage of avoiding the Faustian bargain that universities have struck in the 20th century, which I discussed briefly at the end of Section 3.

2. Assuming, in our post-welfare-state world, that university expansion is the more realistic alternative, there are two radically different models for conceptualizing the "private sector" corporation. One is the fast-food franchise based on satisfying specific but transient consumer demand; the other is the independent church based on servicing vaguer but deeper dispositions in people's lives. Despite the dominance of the former model, I would strongly urge the latter. This means *inter alia* shifting the burden of funding from market-driven student tuition fees to lifelong alumni support (which is then used to finance scholarships). To motivate this shift, consider that a church that devoted all its resources to baptism in the faith and schooling in its catechism but ignored the interests of adult members would be always struggling to make ends meet and probably deemed dysfunctional. Here the United States enjoys a definite historical advantage. Even strong state-subsidized universities in the United States have long flourished as *de facto*

churches (where football games function as Mass). However, recent calls across the world to privatize state-run universities typically aim to reduce the utility curves for teaching and research to the short-sighted ones associated with fast food. The "religiosity" of churches seems to blind people to their organizational virtues.

3. Finally, to regain their republican potential, universities must take a principled stance against the inheritance of academic advantage. To be sure, affirmative action and positive discrimination in the selection of students and staff contribute to this end. However, the principle must be applied thoroughly, so as to prevent the emergence of academic dynasties whose overthrow is justified only when the dynastic heirs have failed in their own terms. (This is basically the conservative theory of revolution as caused by the need to restore natural order, the scientific version of which is Kuhn's theory of paradigm change.) Fuller (2000a, Chapter 8) makes a number of proposals designed to subvert inherited advantage. These are summed up in the word *fungibility*, namely, that no form of inquiry should command so many resources as to crowd out most competitors. There are many ways to satisfy the fungibility condition, not the least of which involve regularly scheduled elections to determine the distribution of research and teaching resources—and, as illustrated in the German academic tradition, this may extend to the selection of the university's own chief executive officers.

Appendix:
What's Living
and Dead in
Peer-Review
Processes?

1. Introduction: The Scope of Peer Review   232
2. Defining Peers   235
3. Recruiting Peers   238
4. Systematically Recording Peer Judgments   241
5. Ethically Monitoring Peer Judgments   242
6. "Extended Peer Review": The Universal Solvent?   245
7. Does Peer Review Have a Future? Implications for
   Research and Policy   248
   7.1. Methodological Note   251

1. Introduction: The Scope of Peer Review

"Peer review" is the general name given to the principle that research should be evaluated by people bound by mutual trust and respect who are socially recognized as expert in a given field of knowledge. Peer review has been used to accomplish several distinct goals associated with knowledge production. Its full complexity is brought out in the multiple and often cross-cutting functions typically performed in a single editorial judgement over a piece of work:

- Standardize the conduct of research
- Exercise quality control over research
- Enforce ideological conformity among researchers
- Restrict entry into the ranks of researchers
- Extend the learning experience of researchers
- Reward completed research
- Influence the future direction of research
- Assume collective responsibility for research results
- Maximize the impact of research results: speak in one voice

This list can be streamlined into a three-stage sequence, presented in rough historical order:

1. A mechanism for certifying research activity as knowledge and crediting researchers with having produced knowledge (e.g., editorial policies)
2. A mechanism for protecting the knowledge base from error contamination and the public from the application of unsound research (e.g., state regulatory bodies; ethics review panels)
3. A mechanism for the efficient and equitable allocation of the scarce resources available and needed for conducting research (e.g., state funding agencies)

Since 2 and 3 are of much more recent origin than 1, author track record as a validity marker has tended to cut against author anonymity as a fairness marker. Point 1 is illustrated by the Royal Society and other early scientific associations, which used peer review to solidify an interest group. Here editors such as Henry Oldenburg, Pierre Mersenne, and in our own time, Stevan Harnad function as community-building visionaries. Point 2 emerges as scientific knowledge is formally harnessed to the great nation-building projects of the 19th century, especially Bismarck's Germany, in which the editor operates more as a disciplinary guardian who preempts state interference by enforcing specifically "epistemic" norms. Point 3 comes into its own in the Cold War period, when a scaled-up scientific enterprise comes to depend on the state for funding, the fruits of which are designed to shore up the nation's defense. Here peer reviewers are perhaps most aware of serving multiple masters. Given this history, there has been a tendency to see 2 and 3 through the lens of 1. Not surprisingly, the use of peer review in 2 and especially 3 has been much more controversial than its use in 1.

There are three categories of research that are notoriously difficult to accommodate within peer-review processes. Specifically, what are the criteria for work of (a) international quality, (b) interdisciplinary relevance, and (c) critical incisiveness of existing research? In terms of (a), how does one judge the relative merit of *applying* or translating a foreign trend in one's own national setting vis-à-vis *starting* a line of research that is regarded as seminal overseas but exerts little influence on the domestic scene? Who decides the "international" status of research: domestic or foreign peers? In terms of (b), exactly what decides the matter of relevance: one's own discipline or the other discipline—or some combination of the two? Specifically, how does one judge the relative merit of *importing* ideas and findings from another discipline into one's own vis-à-vis *exporting* ideas and findings from one's own discipline into another? Finally, in terms of (c), who judges—and what value is placed on—work that is explicitly critical in intent, such as the reanalysis of data, the replication of an experiment, or a methodological or theoretical "audit" of a field (a.k.a. "meta-analysis": cf. Shadish and Fuller 1994, Chapter 7)?

Finally, because peer-review processes invariably involve the combination of different people's judgements, there is a tendency for decisions to hold consensus above every other collective value. Consider the fate of two proposals, X and Y. Here is a summary of each of their peer judgements:

X: Uniformly rated as methodologically sound and likely to advance knowledge in a well-established field.

Y: Some rate it as methodologically innovative and intellectually bold; others rate it as flawed in places and too speculative to support a sizeable grant.

Because there is less disagreement over X—no one thinks it's flawed though no one thinks it's a work of genius—X is gets funded, while Y is either denied funding or referred back for resubmission at a later date. This conclusion is generally justified on grounds of what psychologists call "inter-rater reliability" and the systemic need to ensure that the existing knowledge base is not contaminated by unsubstantiated research. But is there any way to get beyond the clearly conservative bias of this line of reasoning?

2. DEFINING PEERS

There are two general ways of defining what it means to be a "peer." On the one hand, peers may be seen as people who treat each other's views with the respect they accord their own views: i.e., *not* the relation of teachers marking students' assignments. On the other, peers may be seen as people who can reciprocally function as marker and marked for each other. The former model seems to imply that peer review is just an input to a final decision, but not the mechanism by which the decision (to fund or publish) is made. In contrast, the latter implies that peer review can be used to make the final decision. The first model may suit journal publication, but the latter fits funding decisions, where funders do not themselves have a working knowledge of the field or even know if the field is worth funding. The former casts the peer as an expert witness, the latter as more of a juror.

Unfortunately, reviewer instructions typically send mixed signals that fail to specify which of the two roles should be stressed. If reviewers are being asked to deliver a verdict on a proposal's fundability, then they should have some sense of the number of competitors, their composition, the funds available for disbursement and whatever other constraints may influence the funding agency's decisions. On the other hand, if reviewers are simply offering expert judgement, then the agency should make clear the types of judgement in this vein that it considers helpful and unhelpful.

At a finer-grained level, we can distinguish two types of peers in the peer-review process: *absolute* and *relative* peers. The absolute peers of someone who submits a grant proposal or article for publication are people working in the same field as that person. In contrast, relative peers do not work in the same field but know a significant amount about it and are potential beneficiaries and/or critics of such work. Both types of peers are essential to the functioning of the peer-review process, and each type poses its own special problems.

The concept of "peer" implies an equality of status but, as Orwell would say, some peers are "more equal" than others. People working in a given field who are well-known, institutionally better placed, and (not a trivial feature) actually willing to take the time to review their peers exert a disproportionate amount of influence on the entire system. Much of this is the product of institutional inertia: Editors and funders rely on those who can be relied on, and typically these are people who have done the job in the past. These people are also relied upon to provide the names of potential recruits to the ranks of peer reviewers.

Empirical studies of peer-review processes tend to show that of all the forms of discrimination that beset the system, the hardest to reverse are those based on *nepotism* (Wenneras and Wold 1997), that is, personal networks, be they of "old boys" or "new girls"— or old boys supporting new girls! From a sociological standpoint, nepotism is a form of generalized provincialism: In other words, if I work in the same field as X and I have not yet had contact with X or anyone who has had contact with X, then X must not be worth having contact with. Therefore, in practice, absolute peerage turns out to be hierarchically biased toward older and better-connected peer reviewers. Most members of any given field are rarely, if ever, involved as reviewers, and few of those involved really know how peer-review judgements contribute to publication and funding decisions. Nevertheless, because knowledge production has become so professionalized and research so resource-intensive, virtually every academic must now subject herself to this frankly elitist and gerontocratic process. However, if *everyone* working in a given field—"absolute peers" in the literal sense—contributed to selecting the pool of peer reviewers, both the people selected and the judgements reached would be substantially different from what we now see.

A researcher's "relative peerage" may be subject to considerable prejudice. For example, anecdotal evidence suggests that feminist researchers rarely peer-review men, regardless of overlap in substantive interests, whereas men may be periodically asked to evaluate feminist research because of such overlap—and are generally asked to review proposals farther afield than women are. Yet, to involve more women in peer review—only so that they can review other women—is little more than to ghettoize women's knowledge practices. In this respect, relative peerage is the final frontier of anti-discriminatory knowledge policy. A perhaps even more fundamental problem of relative peerage is that it presupposes a "map of the field" that enables specialties to be divided into separate domains, like nation-states, each with its own territorial sovereignty. Of course, this cartographic metaphor allows for there to be "regions" and "empires" that enable the practitioners of certain specialties to have intellectual purchase over more than simply their own official domain of knowledge.

The use of peer review to evaluate grant proposals is one of the few occasions when knowledge-producing communities come close to formal self-governance. By analogy with legislative bodies, we can distinguish between a *one-chamber* and *two-chamber* representation of peers. In the one-chamber approach, the same set of peers decide on the absolute and relative merit of proposals. A typical procedure is that the peers (who know each other's identities) are sent all the grant proposals competing in a given funding round. They first privately score the proposals and then meet together to compare scores and decide the proposals' fates. Of course, this allows the possibility of peers changing—or reinterpreting the significance of—their scores, once they have gathered together. According to Wenneras and Wold (1999), who managed to get their reforms accepted by the Swedish Medical Research Council, gender bias was dramatically reduced, once reviewers had to electronically transmit their scores on all proposals before convening to decide on which should be funded. In the past, women would receive middle-to-high scores, yet be damned with faint praise in the accompanying narrative. (However, nepotism has proven harder to tackle, even if interested reviewers are prohibited from participating in funding decisions.)

In the two-chamber approach, each grant proposal is first sent to several peer reviewers, each of whom knows neither the competing grants nor the identities of the grant's other reviewers. These peers are supposed to establish the absolute merit of the proposal. Once they have done their work, the relative merit of the proposals is established in a procedure akin to the one-chamber approach, except that the peers here (a different set of people) will not be simply scoring the proposals but assigning relative weights to the scores expressed by peers in the first chamber. What principles should determine the composition of the panel? To what extent would issues of gender, age, rank, ethnicity, specialty, geographical region, institutional affiliation matter?

3. RECRUITING PEERS

Because peer review has traditionally worked best in the context of making judgements about past performance (i.e., completed work that one wishes to publish), special measures are needed to ensure that judgements that are fundamentally about the future—the direction of the research agenda and its larger public import—are not held entirely captive to the past, a.k.a. the "old boys network." Most cases of discrimination, fraud, and other errors in collective scientific judgement are ultimately traceable to peer-review judgements relying too heavily on what researchers have achieved in the past as a guide to present and future performance. In that sense, peer review's tendency to inhibit the publication of researchers without a distinguished track record is the flip side of its tendency to enable researchers with distinguished records to promulgate fraudulent or insufficiently validated findings, in the superstitious guise of "repeating past success." Indeed, perhaps the most important conceptual and practical problem surrounding peer review is how to overcome this retrospective bias.

Even at the level of state research councils, there is still too much reliance on such "self-organizing" means of soliciting peer opinion as word-of-mouth, grant-holding history, and past participation in peer-review processes. Such self-organization is too often a euphemism for self-perpetuation. Proactive peer recruitment is imperative because an increasing percentage of academically trained researchers are on short-term contracts which often prevent them from obtaining their own grants and hence entering the usual peer-review networks. Yet, perhaps because of the precariousness of their employment, they are among the most talented, creative, and enterprising knowledge workers around. People working on fixed contracts now form the vast majority of new researchers in most countries, and they constitute most members in some disciplines. Moreover, since many contract workers do not anticipate entering regular academic careers, they are not intrinsically motivated to participate in peer-review processes, which are characteristically seen as only benefiting tenured university staff. However, since the contract sector of the academic community is skewed toward its most recent entrants, peer-review processes run the risk of losing precisely the expertise that will be instrumental in defining the future shape of research—both in and out of academia.

Many contract workers see the peer-review system as responsible for fostering the "old boys network" that contributes to their own status as an academic underclass, the so-called "unfaculty." This suspicion of the "old boys" side of peer review is often tied to a lack of trust in "track records," which often boil down to a trail of exploitation: How many other people have you been able to organize to do work for which you then take much or most of the credit? At the same time, even more traditional academics question a long trail of publications and grants as masking "salami slicing" (i.e., the same research published in slightly different ways in many forums) and misdirected money-grubbing (i.e., inflated budgets for results that could have been reached at a much lower cost).

To be sure, track records are sometimes regarded like the principle of natural selection in evolutionary theory, namely, a mark of survival that is intrinsically worthy of respect. But if Professor Fart has been doing largely the same research—albeit reliably—over the past two decades, perhaps he should have to do something different before securing his next grant. In that case, track record constitutes, at least in part, a liability that should be penalized, or "taxed," so that a senior researcher's accumulated advantage is effectively redistributed. Otherwise, the grant system would appear to reproduce the worst features of an unregulated market (cf. Horrobin 1990). Thus, there might be an upper limit on the amount of grant money that an individual can hold at any given time. Research requiring large resource allocations would therefore necessitate the collaboration of other individuals and institutions who would jointly hold the grant. To make this proposal work, researchers may need to declare their entire grant and consultancy income more formally than they currently do. Another possibility is that tenured and non-tenured researchers would not be allowed to draw from the same pool of research funds, given the disparity in their conditions of employment. Tenured researchers would automatically receive a small fund that is increased or decreased based on research performance. Non-tenured researchers would be allowed to vie for funds under their own names in open competitions.

One way of adjusting the significance accorded to track record is by considering more than simply the number of publications amassed. You could also examine what bibliometricians call the "impact factor" of the journals where researchers publish. In other words, each journal publication would be weighted according to the frequency with which research in that journal is generally cited. In the case of grants, you could go beyond fixating on their monetary value and look instead at the "publication per dollar" ratio, or "bang for the buck." Sometimes it seems that researchers spend more time writing up grant proposals and managing the people contracted under the grants than actually producing research. Such a metric would provide a way of detecting this problem.

Finally, peer recruitment may be able to exploit the partial division of labor between people who publish a lot in a field and those who publish much less but read much more widely in the field. These are people who have withdrawn from, if they ever spent time at, the front lines of research. Mainly teachers or administrators, they constitute the "silent majority" of users and beneficiaries of research, even within the academy. Because these people are not personally invested in the future of particular lines of research, they may be better able to offer dispassionate peer evaluations. Moreover, as Boyer (1990) demonstrated, they may even provide novel criteria for peer evaluation, such as "teachability" and "applicability," which often elude the evaluative capacities of ordinary research-oriented peers.

One way around this problem is to allow contract researchers to qualify as principal investigators on grant proposals, in exchange for their inclusion in a national registry of researchers who are periodically called upon to participate as peer reviewers, just as registered voters are sometimes requested to participate in jury-based trials. Such a strategy has been successfully used by Brazil's national research councils. The "Plataforma Lattes," named for a distinguished physicist, Cesare Lattes, is a scheme of unprecedented comprehensiveness that ranges from providing centralized databases for Brazilian researchers in all the disciplines to standardizing information and communication technologies across all regions of the country (Lattes 2001). The system works in large part because the Brazilian state has traditionally enjoyed a virtual monopoly on research funding, and hence it has been in nearly everyone's interest to share information about their knowledge-producing activities.

An obvious question for any new attempt to compile a national peer-review registry is how would registrants demonstrate their expertise. Publications perhaps constitute the most obvious proof, but other means must be allowed to capture all the contexts where academics work, most of which do *not* privilege publication in academic periodicals. For example, white papers and other reports resulting from funded research should count, as well as an extensive teaching portfolio that includes recent course outlines which establish the registrant's familiarity with the cutting edge of the field where she claims expertise. Perhaps one could also take an examination in the area where one claims expertise. There may be a special incentive for people in traditionally subordinate academic roles—such as contract researchers—to obtain such a license, as it would then count as a credential to improve their employment prospects. It may be that the examination could be designed so as not to be prejudicial against those who teach or read widely in a field but who have not amassed a track record of original research.

4. Systematically Recording Peer Judgments

But beyond proactive recruitment, peer-review processes require adequate accounting mechanisms for monitoring the long-term consequences of peer judgements on the research frontier. A good benchmark is the extent to which an untested low-status person can prove herself over time as a grant-holder (even without moving to a high-status institution), while a high-status person can lose his initial advantage by repeatedly failing to deliver the goods (even without downshifting to a low-status institution). Empirical studies of the peer-review process tend to show that "status" is the ultimate barrier to fair peer assessment of grant proposals (cf. Peters and Ceci 1982, which showed that given a change in the reviewed's affiliation, reviewers would reject articles they previously accepted).

Among the preconditions necessary for tracking the implications of peer review are serious record-keeping and accessing facilities (e.g., previous funding history, ideally via databases coordinated across funding agencies in both the public and private sectors). Since the peers who review a proposal generally have only an impressionistic sense of track record, there should be an independent means of judging track record. This may include sophisticated accounting schemes that produce in-house ratings for grant applicants based on their grant history. In that case, the funding of less tested applicants with promising proposals could be justified by subjecting the grantees to a probationary term when they must deliver some goods before receiving the entire grant.

As for grant applicants, they should be informed about the total number in the applicant pool, some of the pool's more salient characteristics, and the likelihood that a given member in that pool will be funded. Sometimes this information is provided, but rarely systematically. Also, feedback needs to be given to applicants, *even if they are successful.* There is much folklore and even superstition attached to peer-review processes, mainly because success is never officially explained. Even funded applicants need to know why they succeed, since in most cases an application will stand out from the rest of the pool in some but not all respects.

We can also distinguish between the *absolute* and *relative* merit of grant proposals in the following way. Absolute merit has to do with the proposal's ability to meet certain scientifically desirable criteria, regardless of the proposals it is competing against and the overall pool of resources available. Relative merit has to do with the status of the proposal compared to its competitors with respect to a specific finite pool of resources. The distinction is meant to keep open the possibility that a proposal scoring high on absolute merit may not fare so well in relative merit, perhaps because the juxtaposition of competing proposals alters what the peer reviewers regard is at stake.

Finally, both those reviewing and those reviewed should be told the extent to which aspects of the application process are negotiable with the funding agency, say, by offering to fund a pilot study smaller than requested, appointing an advisory board to oversee controversial research, or proposing research partners to economize on effort. Most academic journals permit a judgement of "revise and resubmit" to a manuscript, which effectively enables the author to negotiate the terms under which publication would occur. Why not extend this practice to the evaluation of grant applications? Indeed, in what state should a research proposal be presented before the agency sets terms for providing a grant? A related issue is whether a funding agency should negotiate with researchers the size of grants, e.g., saying that it will fund research if certain proposed expenses are increased or cut from what has been officially offered.

5. ETHICALLY MONITORING PEER JUDGMENTS

Given the principle that peer review should judge more the work than the worker, peer review in academic journals has increasingly moved toward rendering a manuscript's author anonymous. One may therefore ask whether reviewers of grant proposals need to know the exact identities of the proposers, or whether it is possible—and desirable—to render the proposals at least somewhat anonymous. Of course, the same question can be asked in reverse, and perhaps would receive a different answer: How much should researchers who submit their proposals and work for review know of those who are reviewing it? For example, in Sweden, researchers whose proposals have been reviewed by state funding agencies have access to the full text of reviewer judgements, via a "Freedom of the Press Law." In both cases, the issue addressed is inappropriate discrimination. You may not want the reviewer to know the identity of the reviewed in order to prevent discrimination, whereas you may want the reviewed to know the reviewer's identity in order to enable the reviewed to redress discrimination.

Because extramural funding is now necessary for most forms of sustained research, the competition for grants has become more intense than ever. Funding agencies have typically responded to this situation by demanding more details about proposed projects, so that they can be peer-reviewed in more depth. Indeed, it is not uncommon for a well-crafted grant proposal to provide the conceptual framework for the entire project that will resurface in publications subsequently associated with the grant. This suggests that the writing up of grant proposals is itself a substantial research endeavor. Universities have begun to acknowledge this fact by allowing staff to list grant applications—both successful and failed—in their curriculum vitae. However, at most, this provides a basis for rewarding effort but not priority and originality.

Intellectual property law may help model the moral dimensions of peer review. Recalling our discussion in Chapter 2, there are two general ways of conferring value on intellectual property. On the one hand, value may come from being the first to come up with an idea or finding that is of value to a disciplinary community or the larger public. Usually, it is assumed that several people have been seeking what the researcher has found. Such concerns over priority provide the philosophical basis for *patent* law. On the other hand, value may come from claims to originality, regardless of the ultimate utility of the idea or finding for a larger community. This is the basis for *copyright* law. Ethical problems with peer reviewing normally arise in relation to matters of priority. In one sense, the ideal peer reviewer is someone working in the same field as the researcher whose work is under review. However, such a reviewer is also in an ideal position to undermine the researcher's project by stalling funding or publication, and then appropriating ideas or techniques for the reviewer's own purposes. Even something as simple as a researcher's bibliography can be "mined" to enable the clever reviewer to quickly reach a level of competence comparable to the researcher under review. Given that the reviewed is typically not told the reviewer's identity, it would be difficult to establish charges of intellectual property theft.

How, then, to prevent intellectual property theft during peer review? Here are four proposals:

(A) Peer reviewers should be forced to reveal how close the article or proposal under review is to their own current research interests. (This information would be made available to the researcher under review.) If they admit significant closeness, then (in the case of grant proposals) they would be asked whether they would agree to work with the researcher under review on a joint project. If they say no, they would have to explain why. Presumably, the response to this question would reveal differences in orientation that may prove useful when it comes to interpreting the significance of the reviewer's remarks.

(B) The number of peer reviewers should be multiplied, reflecting a broad range of absolute and relative peers. Although this increases the bureaucratic dimension of the peer-review process, in return one would be sure that judgements were obtained from people who do not directly stand to benefit from a researcher's work. Such judgements would be especially useful as checks on attempts to delay publication or funding for reasons that may not be as disinterested as they first seem.

(C) This applies primarily to grant proposals, but there may be a version applicable to a journal's editorial decisions. The idea would be for a grant proposal to be regarded as a partial claim to knowledge that can be registered or published, alongside suitably edited and attributed comments by the peer reviewers. In this way, none of the parties involved in the peer-review process—neither reviewers nor reviewed—would feel they have wasted their time by participating in the process.

(D) The editor or funder may tell the peers reviewing a particular application who the other peers are, without revealing that information to the applicant. The threat of potential witnesses to intellectual property theft may well be enough to dissuade unscrupulous peers from going down that road. At the same time, the "anonymity" or "blindness" of peer review from the applicant's end would be preserved.

6. "EXTENDED PEER REVIEW":
THE UNIVERSAL SOLVENT?

As academia is increasingly asked to be more responsive to non-academic concerns ("users and beneficiaries," as we say in the United Kingdom), the idea of extending peer review to non-academics has become more attractive. Part of the intellectual justification for this extension is a move away from a "production line," or "linear," model of knowledge growth, whereby academics would produce knowledge among themselves and then apply it in various settings to grateful and compliant consumers. In many quarters ranging from local communities to multinational corporations, it is now fashionable to say knowledge is "co-produced," "co-constructed" and that the line between production and consumption is not very clear (Funtowicz and Ravetz 1992). All of this favors the extension of peer review.

However, in practice, extended peer review raises many serious policy issues about the changing status of academia. In the first place, the idea of extending peer review to non-academics normally presupposes that all academics are already involved in peer review. But in fact, peer-review processes typically involve only a small, typically elite, subset of the entire academic community. One can easily imagine a phenomenon akin to "uneven development" in Third World countries occurring, once the doors are open to considerable non-academic involvement. Individuals and institutions that already fare well in peer-review processes will have the social capital to work well with comparably elite peers outside academia, resulting in mutually enhancing partnership. But those academics who never fared well in peer-review processes may fall behind once non-academics enter the picture. In short, until safeguards are taken to diversify the academic interests that are represented in normal peer-review processes—say, by establishing the national registry mentioned earlier—it is not clear that extending the process to non-academics will result in knowledge that is truly socially responsive. According to Boyer (1990), it is wise to assume that the full range of institutions that comprise the higher education sector together constitute a microcosm of society's interests. From that standpoint, most peer-review processes are unequivocally elitist, but they could be easily made more democratic simply by including more of academia's own members.

Another problem with extending peer review is that its academic and non-academic participants are often not reciprocally accountable. Usually, it is assumed that academics need to be more open to problem-oriented "real world" research, and that the injection of community or commercial standards of research evaluation will propel that shift in mindset. Much less is said of what non-academics are supposed to get from academics, aside from help in solving their problems. The fact that academics are allowed time and space to publish in their specialist journals is usually taken as enough to show that a fruitful academic–non-academic partnership has been forged. However, little is made of the possibility of non-academics acquiring certain virtues—say, a respect for rigorous reasoning, thorough research, and thinking beyond the short term—through their encounters with academics. If contacts with business can leave their mark on how academics conceptualize research quality, why cannot this happen vice versa, with business rethinking commercial quality in light of its contacts with academics? As academic work is increasingly tied to non-academic interests, that staple of peer evaluation—publication quality—will need to be supplemented and, in some cases, superseded by other objects and criteria of evaluation that (one hopes) will not automatically revert to those of the non-academic partner. In Chapter 1, I discussed this prospect in terms of the academic infiltration of corporate values in the design of the Executive Ph.D. program.

A more general problem is how one evaluates the impact of academic work outside the formal academic publication channels. In government settings, this problem typically arises in the context of so-called *evidence-based policy making*, which purports to use peer-sanctioned knowledge claims to give direction and stability to state policies. The time-honored strategy in this vein goes back to the Charter of the Royal Society, which first made explicit the division of labor between science and politics, and culminated in the "value neutrality" that German academics took to be a guild right by the late 19th and early 20th centuries (Proctor 1991). The idea was for the spheres of knowledge production and knowledge application to play to their own strengths: the former would present feasible alternatives, and the latter would select one for action. Meanwhile, peer-review processes would launder out particular inquirers' controversial ideological commitments, since an entire disciplinary community effectively staked its reputation on the knowledge claims contained in its peer-reviewed publications.

However, this strategy has been gradually undermined through increased specialization in both spheres, so that nowadays scientists and politicians often face each other in mutual incomprehension. Thus, recent calls for evidence-based policymaking have emphasized that knowledge claims need to be stripped of their distinctive theoretical and methodological formulations (a.k.a. jargon) before being presented to policymakers. Yet, this is tantamount to removing all traces of the peer-review processes that enabled them to acquire the status of "policy relevance" in the first place. Moreover, stripped of these epistemic markers, the "hard evidence" often appears so equivocal in its policy implications that politicians can easily revert—albeit through a rather circuitous route—to their default mode of simply being responsive to immediate political concerns.

Despite my reservations, extended peer review may nevertheless serve to advance the civic republican knowledge policy presented in Chapter 4. It may especially bolster the use of consensus conferences, whereby a lay jury deliberates on a public policy issue with significant scientific and technical content. However, the widespread adoption of this form of extended peer review may result in judgements that differ significantly from the expectations of its boosters. Because consensus conferences are still relatively rare, and sometimes are conducted in response to a public outcry, the lay panel often concludes with cautious policy guidelines designed to constrain the ambitions of the state, business, or the scientific community.

But this caution may be nothing more than a contextual artifact. The long-term prospect of regularized consensus conferences may be to immunize the populace against resistance to new scientific and technological developments. It would thus serve to increase the sphere of responsibility for public action. Put vividly, the public would accept larger risks in the natural environment if the public felt

	PROMISE	PITFALL
EXAMPLE	Consensus conference	Focus group
CONSTITUTION OF PEERAGE	Add Non-academic Interests	Presume academic interests already represented
INTERNAL DYNAMICS	Public open to more adventurous policies	Public co-opted to dominant view
EXTERNAL RELATIONS	Consumption elevated to co-production	Power asymmetries reproduced

Figure A.1.
The promises and pitfalls of extended peer review

their deliberations were integral to the relevant decisions. What may appear *prima facie* to be either scientific ignorance or a nascent ecological ethic may really be an expression of alienation from the political process that may be remedied by involvement in consensus conferences. However, as indicated in Figure A.1, the style of "homeopathic" politics implied here may easily shade into the dreaded "rule by focus groups" that characterizes many social democracies today. Here the lay panel is not allowed sufficient discretion in either the interpretation of expert testimony or the design of policy guidelines. In effect, the panel's charge is simply to fine-tune a preordained piece of legislation.

7. DOES PEER REVIEW HAVE A FUTURE? IMPLICATIONS FOR RESEARCH AND POLICY

The future of peer review can be envisaged under three political economies. The first, related to Stevan Harnad's Cyberplatonism discussed in Chapter 3, would continually transfer current peer-review processes—including their default elitism—from more to less expensive information technologies. According to this aristocratic future, commercial publishers are bourgeois upstarts who threaten time-honored traditions of epistemic authority. In response, I argued that even if publishers are bourgeois, in relation to the academic aristocracy that may not be such a bad thing—at least if one thinks in

Marxist terms about the issue. The second political economy, exemplified above by the Brazilian "Lattes" approach, would have the nation–state consolidate peer-review processes, resulting in a unified knowledge production front. Despite the obvious attractions to this approach, as we saw in the case of evidence-based policy, it does not guarantee that knowledge producers will exert either a stronger or a steadier hand in policy decisions. Moreover, the scheme may work best in a country such as Brazil, whose relatively tight fiscal regime for research makes peer-governed consolidation a welcomed research policy solution. Finally, there is the strategy of the Executive Ph.D. program raised in Chapter 1, whereby academic values would be transferred—and perhaps even reinvented—in business settings as a counterbalance to ever-dynamic markets. Along with the consensus conference as a form of extended peer review, this may be the best bet for retaining a civic republican sensibility in knowledge production in the contemporary capitalist world.

The challenges to the current peer-review system vary somewhat between natural and social sciences, and whether peer-review functions to initiate research (as in a funding council) or reward research (as in a journal publication). Nevertheless, they can be summarized as follows:

1. The problem of motivating the increasing percentage of contract researchers in the sciences—often the most up-to-date people in these fields—to participate in unrewarded peer-review work.
2. The continued discrimination in peer-review processes against traditionally disadvantaged groups, especially in terms of the extent of their peerage (e.g., women are less likely to review materials that range beyond gender-based areas than men).
3. The difficulties in peer reviewing interdisciplinary and critical work without simply requiring the work to pass muster by ordinary disciplinary criteria: i.e., how can peer review be used to encourage, rather than discourage, interdisciplinary transformations of existing academic structures?
4. The potential for "extended peer-review" processes to align powerful academic players with powerful non-academic players (in government, business, etc.), thereby intensifying the existing "class divisions" both inside and outside academia.

5. The general lack of accountability in peer-review processes to the academic communities the peers purportedly represent (e.g., peers are always appointed, never elected).

In terms of further avenues for research into peer-review processes, it is worth noting that most empirical research to date on this matter has been confined to the biomedical sciences, which is not surprising, given their unique mix of high cost and high impact. Yet, even in the United States, the last substantial study of peer review (Chubin and Hackett 1990) draws on research conducted 15 years ago. So, there is plenty of scope for research projects here. Three stand out:

■ A survey of how research quality is defined by people working across all institutional settings in the tertiary educational sector (the precedent is Boyer 1990, which found considerable variation across settings, with "teachability" standing out as a research quality outside the top research universities). This will provide a precise sense of just how representative—or not—the "old boys network" is of academics at large.

■ A sustained study of a peer-review context that potentially provides evidence of "collective learning" in a knowledge-producing community, such that its members display more overall sophisticated peer judgements over time, despite the lack of clear procedural guidelines and the idiosyncrasies of particular reviewers. For example, one might examine the emergence of peer-review standards within a single agency or journal (the latter may be an easier source of material, especially if the journal is the house organ of an academic department or professional society).

■ A comparative study of consensus conferences as exercises in extended peer review. A comprehensive listing of them is already available (Loka 2001). Under what conditions do they get beyond the ventriloquist mode of focus groups, such that extending the peer group results in judgements that genuinely challenge the "conventional wisdom" of both expert and lay groups?

An interesting related development is that in 1999, the U.S. General Accounting Office undertook an audit of peer-review processes in the federal government (GAO 1999). It found that most federal agencies use peer review in evaluating grant proposals and results. However, grants directly funded by the U.S. Congress, often among the largest, do not regularly use peer review. From an academic standpoint, a revealing finding was that the use of peer review was related to the absence of formal criteria for evaluating research proposals and results, especially when projects did not have an applied focus. Often this was because the research in question involved mixed or unclear methods. The peers tended to tie the ultimate value of such research to the resolution of these methodological ambiguities.

7.1. Methodological Note

The United Kingdom's public social science funding agency, the Economic and Social Research Council, commissioned me to organize a cyberconference on "peer review in the social sciences," which was held from 28 May to 14 June 1999. It was the second one I had done for them. (The first, on the "public understanding of science," took place over two weeks in February and March 1998: cf. Fuller 1998.) The cyberconference was framed around 30 interconnected statements to which people were invited to reply, revealing as much or little of their identities as they wished. The general tenor of the conference—both by intent and in consequence—was supportive of peer-review processes. The conference was hosted by the electronic server at the Science Policy Support Group, London, which (as of this writing) continues to post the results (SPSG 1999). I wrote the 30 opening statements, which generated 70 substantial responses. In the 18-day period of the conference, 417 people from 30 countries, representing every continent, visited the site 1272 times. There was a high ratio of lurkers to participants among the visitors, including users with U.S. military and NATO electronic addresses.

CONCLUSION: THE MIXED ROOT METAPHOR OF KNOWLEDGE MANAGEMENT

The emergence of knowledge management as a field of inquiry has brought into view two conflicting intuitions that have informed Western conceptions of knowledge since the time of the Greeks. I have encapsulated this conflict as the *military–industrial metaphor* (Fuller 1997, 49–50). The military side of the metaphor is that the pursuit of knowledge has clear goals that inquirers approximate to varying degrees. The industrial side is that knowledge is perpetually generated and accumulated, so that, like money, one can never have enough of it. The military metaphor attracts more sporting virtues, such as doing the most with the least, whereas the industrial metaphor attracts craft virtues such as hard work and attention to detail in product design. The former is aristocratic in origin, the latter

252

plebeian, and, with the advent of scientific professionalization, it has now become bourgeois. Knowledge is "achieved" according to the military metaphor, "produced" according to the industrial one.

The military–industrial metaphor appears in a rather confused form in contemporary philosophy and economics. On the one hand, lip service is still paid to the idea that knowledge aims at the truth, which would seem to imply a commitment to the military side of the metaphor. On the other hand, this truth is often portrayed as unknowable in principle or approachable only "asymptotically," such that more and more needs to be done to achieve less and less. Here we find an appeal to the industrial side's commitment to endless effort. Even an idea as seemingly clear as the "functional differentiation" of knowledge can be interpreted from either the military or the industrial side of the metaphor. Is the specialization of academic disciplines a sign that inquiry is acquiring more focused goals, or that it is proliferating in indefinitely many directions? Military or industrial?

In terms of larger cultural debates, the differences between "modernists" and "postmodernists" have largely turned on which side of the military–industrial metaphor carries the more intuitive weight in making sense of the nature of knowledge. Generally speaking, modernists take the military side, postmodernists the industrial side. Thus, when one speaks of the "demystification" of knowledge wrought by recent sociological studies of science and technology, one usually draws attention to the labor involved in producing knowledge, which goes beyond simply making statements that happen to correspond to the way things are. However, knowledge management is not reducible to this postmodern turn. Indeed, knowledge managers attempt to reinvent the military side of the military–industrial metaphor. But now the material stakes are higher than they have ever been, and what it means "to do the most with the least" has accordingly become more complicated. There are opportunities here for both an intelligent democratization of inquiry and a mindless "natural selection" of knowledge producers and products. The reader of this book will participate in determining which possibility becomes a reality.

REFERENCES

Abbott, A. (1988). *The System of Professions*. University of Chicago Press.

Abelson, R. (1986). "Beliefs are like possessions," *Journal for the Theory of Social Behaviour* 16: 224–250.

Ackermann, R. (1985). *Data, Instrument, Theory*. Princeton University Press.

Adorno, T., and Horkheimer, M. (1972). *The Dialectic of Enlightenment*. Continuum.

Aitkenhead, D. (1995). "Farewell the gentleman publisher: Now read on," (London) *Independent on Sunday*, 16 April, p. 5.

Andrews, E. (1989). "Equations patented; some see danger," *New York Times*, February 15, pp. 29–30.

Argote, L., and Epple, D. (1990). "Learning curves in manufacturing," *Science* 247: 920–924.

Argyris, C. (1957). *Personality and Organization*. Harper and Row.

Argyris, C. (1991). "Teaching smart people how to learn," *Harvard Business Review*, May–June.

Argyris, C., and Schon, D. (1978). *Organizational Learning: A Theory of Action Perspective*. Addison-Wesley.

Arkes, H., and Hammond, K., eds. (1986). *Judgment and Decision Making*. Cambridge University Press.

Asch, S. (1987). *Social Psychology*. Cambridge University Press. (Orig. 1952.)

Averch, H. (1985). *A Strategic Analysis of Science and Technology Policy*. Johns Hopkins University Press.

Ayano, H. (1999). "The Consensus Conference on Gene Therapy in Japan and Understanding Advanced Technologies," paper presented at the annual meeting of the Society for Social Studies of Science, San Diego, California.

254

Bartley, W.W. (1990). *Unfathomed Knowledge, Unmeasured Wealth.* Open Court Press.

Bates, B. (1988). "Information as an economic good: The sources of individual and social value," in Mosco and Wasko (1988), pp. 76–94.

Bauman, Z. (1993). *Postmodern Ethics.* Blackwell.

Baumol, W. (1977). "On the proper cost tests for a natural monopoly in a multi-product industry," *American Economic Review* 67: 809–822.

Bazerman, C. (1988). *Shaping the Written Word.* University of Wisconsin Press.

Beck, U., Giddens, A., and Lash, S. (1994). *Reflexive Modernization.* Polity Press.

Belk, R. (1991). "The ineluctable mysteries of possessions," *Journal of Social Behavior and Personality* 6(6): 17–56.

Bell, D. (1960). *The End of Ideology.* Free Press.

Bell, D. (1966). *The Reforming of General Education.* Doubleday.

Bell, D. (1973). *The Coming of Post-Industrial Society.* Harper and Row.

Bem, D. (1967). "Self-perception," *Psychological Review* 74: 183–200.

Beniger, J. (1986). *The Control Revolution.* Harvard University Press.

Berlin, I. (1958). *Two Concepts of Liberty.* Oxford University Press.

Block, F. (1990). *Postindustrial Possibilities.* University of California Press.

Bloor, D. (1976). *Knowledge and Social Imagery.* Routledge and Kegan Paul.

Boehme, G. and Stehr, N., eds. (1986). *The Knowledge Society.* Kluwer.

Bohman, J. (1996). *Public Deliberation.* MIT Press.

Botwinick, A. (1990). *Skepticism and Political Participation.* Temple University Press.

Bourdieu, P. (1984). *Distinction.* Harvard University Press.

Bourdieu, P. (1997). *Practical Reason.* Polity Press.

Bourdieu, P., and Passeron, J.C. (1977). *Reproduction in Education, Society, and Culture.* Sage.

Boyer, E. (1990). *Scholarship Reconsidered.* Carnegie Foundation for the Advancement of Teaching.

Brannigan, A. (1981). *The Social Basis of Scientific Discoveries.* Cambridge University Press.

Brenner, R. (1987). *Rivalry: In Business, Science, among Nations.* Cambridge University Press.

Brown, J.S. (1991). "Research that reinvents the corporation," *Harvard Business Review,* January–February.

Callon, M. (1994). "Is science a public good?" *Science, Technology, and Human Values* 19: 345–424.

Campbell, D. (1988). *Methodology and Epistemology for Social Science.* University of Chicago Press.

Carley, K., and Kaufer, D. (1993). *Communication at a Distance.* Lawrence Erlbaum Associates.

Cartwright, N., Cat, J., Fleck, L., and Uebel, T. (1996). *Otto Neurath: Philosophy between Science and Politics.* Cambridge University Press.

Cassirer, E. (1923). *Substance and Function.* Open Court.

Castells, M. (1996). *The Network Society.* Blackwell.

Chancellor, E. (1999). *Devil Take the Hindmost: A History of Financial Speculation.* Macmillan.

Chartier, R. (1994). *The Order of Books.* Polity Press.

Chisholm, R. (1966). *Theory of Knowledge.* Prentice Hall.

Chubin, D., and Hackett, E. (1990). *Peerless Science.* SUNY Press.

Cicchetti, D. (1991). "The reliability of peer review for manuscript and grant submissions," *Behavioral and Brain Sciences* 14: 119–150.

Cicourel, A. (1968). *Cognitive Sociology.* Penguin.

Clark, C. (1957/1940). *The Conditions of Economic Progress,* 3rd ed. Macmillan.

Coleman, J. (1990). *The Foundations of Social Theory.* Harvard University Press.

Collier, J. (1998). *The Structure of Meta-Scientific Claims: Toward a Philosophy of Science and Technology Studies.* Ph.D. Virginia Tech (Dept of Science and Technology Studies).

Collins, H. (1990). *Artificial Experts.* MIT Press.

Collins, H., and Pinch, T. (1982). *Frames of Meaning.* Routledge and Kegan Paul.

Collins, R. (1979). *The Credential Society.* Academic Press.

Collins, R. (1998). *The Sociology of Philosophies.* Harvard University Press.

Collins, R., and Ben-David, J. (1966). "Social factors in the origins of a new science: The case of psychology," *American Sociological Review* 34: 451–65.

Coser, L., Kadushin, C., and Powell, W. (1982). *Books: The Culture and Commerce of Publishing.* University of Chicago Press.

Cozzens, S. (1985). "Comparing the sciences," *Social Studies of Sciences* 15: 127–153.

Cronin, B. (1988). "The Information Industry in AD 2000," in J. Whitehead (ed.), *Information Management and Competitive Success* (Aslib), pp. 222–250.

Cronin, B. and Davenport, E. (1988). *Post-professionalism: Transforming the Information Heartland.* Taylor Graham.

Croskery, P. (1989). "The intellectual property literature," in Weil and Snapper (1989), pp. 268–281.

Crouch, C. (1983). "Market failure," in A. Ellis and K. Kumar (eds.), *Dilemmas of Liberal Democracies.* Tavistock.

Dahl, R. (1989). *Democracy and Its Critics.* Yale University Press.

Daniel, H.-D. (1993). *Guardians of Science: Fairness and Reliability of Peer Review.* VCH.

Dasgupta, P., and David, P. (1994). "Toward a new economics of science," *Research Policy* 23: 487–521.

Davidson, D. (1986). "A nice derangement of epitaphs," in E. L. Pore (ed.), *Truth and Interpretation.* Blackwell.

Davidson, D. (1989). "Reverse engineering software under copyright law," in Weil and Snapper (1989), pp. 147–168.

De Mey, M. (1982). *The Cognitive Paradigm.* Kluwer.

De Romilly, J. (1992). *The Great Sophists in Periclean Athens.* Clarendon.

De Soto, H. (2000). *The Mystery of Capital.* Bantam.

Dennett, D. (1987). *The Intentional Stance.* MIT Press.

Dennett, D. (1996). *Kinds of Minds.* Phoenix.

Diamond, A. (1996). "The economics of science," *Knowledge and Policy* 9 (2/3): 1–48.

Dogan, M., and Pahre, R. (1990). *Creative Marginality: Innovation at the Intersections of Social Sciences.* Westview Press.

Douglas, M. (1987). *How Institutions Think.* Syracuse University Press.

Downes, S. (1987). "A philosophical ethnography of human–computer interaction research," *Social Epistemology* 1: 27–36.

Drahos, P. (1995). "Information feudalism in the information society," *The Information Society* 11: 209–222.

Dreyfus, H. (1992). *What Computers Still Can't Do*, 2nd ed. (Orig. 1972.) MIT Press.

Dreyfus, H., and Dreyfus, S. (1986). *Mind over Machine*. Free Press.

Drucker, P. (1954). *The Practice of Management*. Harper Brothers.

Drucker, P. (1988). "The coming of the New Organization," *Harvard Business Review*, January–February.

Drucker, P. (1993). *Post-Capitalist Society*. Harper Collins.

Eisenstein, E. (1979). *The Printing Press as an Agent of Change*. Cambridge University Press.

Ellul, J. (1965). *The Technological Society*. (Orig. 1954.) Doubleday.

Elster, J. (1979). *Logic and Society*. John Wiley and Sons.

Elster, J. (1980). *Ulysses and the Sirens*. Cambridge University Press.

Elster, J. (1983a). *Explaining Technical Change*. Cambridge University Press.

Elster, J. (1983b). *Sour Grapes*. Cambridge University Press.

Elster, J. (1999). *Alchemies of the Mind: Rationality and the Emotions*. Cambridge University Press.

Elster, J. ed. (1986). *The Multiple Self*. Cambridge University Press.

Engestrom, Y., Brown, K., Engestrom, R., and Koistinen, K. (1990). "Organizational forgetting: an activity-theoretical perspective," in Middleton and Edwards (1990).

Everdell, W. (2000). *The End of Kings: A History of Republics and Republicans*, 2nd ed. (Orig. 1983.) University of Chicago Press.

Ezrahi, Y. (1990). *The Descent of Icarus*. Harvard University Press.

Faust, D. (1985). *The Limits of Scientific Reasoning*. University of Minnesota Press.

Febvre, L., and Martin, H.-J. (1976). *The Coming of the Book*. London: New Left Books.

Festinger, L. (1957). *A Theory of Cognitive Dissonance*. Stanford University Press.

Feyerabend, P. (1975). *Against Method*. Verso.

Feyerabend, P. (1979). *Science in a Free Society*. Verso.

Fields, C. (1987). "The computer as tool," *Social Epistemology* 1: 5–26.

Fishkin, J. (1991). *Democracy and Deliberation*. Yale University Press.

Ford, K., and Agnew, N. (1992). "Expertise: socially situated, personally constructed, and 'reality' relevant," paper presented at the AAAI Spring Symposium on the Cognitive Aspects of Knowledge Acquisition.

Foucault, M. (1970). *The Archaeology of Knowledge*. Harper and Row.

Frank, R. (1984). "Are workers paid their marginal products?" *American Economic Review* 74: 541–579.

Fuchs, I. (1996). "Networked information is not free," in Peek and Newby (1996), pp. 165–180.

Fuller, S. (1985). *Bounded Rationality in Law and Science*. Ph.D. dissertation, University of Pittsburgh: Department of History and Philosophy of Science.

Fuller, S. (1986). "User-friendliness: friend or foe?" *Logos* 7: 93–98.

Fuller, S. (1988). *Social Epistemology*. Indiana University Press.

Fuller, S. (1992a). "Social epistemology and the research agenda of science studies," in Pickering (1992), pp. 390–428.

Fuller, S. (1992b). "Epistemology radically naturalized: Recovering the normative, the experimental, and the social," in Giere (1992), pp. 427–459.

Fuller, S. (1993a). *Philosophy of Science and Its Discontents*, 2nd ed. (Orig. 1989.) Guilford Press.

Fuller, S. (1993b). *Philosophy, Rhetoric, and the End of Knowledge: The Coming of Science and Technology Studies*. University of Wisconsin Press.

Fuller, S. (1994a). "Social psychology of scientific knowledge: Another strong programme," in W. Shadish and S. Fuller (eds.), *Social Psychology of Science*. Guilford Press, pp. 162–178.

Fuller, S. (1994b). "Making agency count: A brief foray into the foundations of social theory," *American Behavioral Scientist* 37: 741–753.

Fuller, S. (1996). "Recent work in social epistemology," *American Philosophical Quarterly* 33: 149–166.

Fuller, S. (1997). *Science*. Open University Press and University of Minnesota Press.

Fuller, S. (1998). "The first global cyberconference on public understanding of science," *Public Understanding of Science* 7: 329–341.

Fuller, S. (2000a). *The Governance of Science: Ideology and the Future of the Open Society*. Open University Press.

Fuller, S. (2000b). *Thomas Kuhn: A Philosophical History for Our Times*. University of Chicago Press.

Fuller, S. (2000c). "Increasing science's governability: Response to Hans Radder," *Science, Technology and Human Values* 25: 527–534.

Fuller, S. (2000d). "Governing science before it governs us," *Interdisciplinary Science Reviews* 25: 95–100.

Fuller, S., and Gorman, D. (1987). "Burning libraries: cultural creation and historical consciousness," *Annals of Scholarship* 4 (3): 105–122.

Fuller, S. ed. (1995). Special issue on "simulating science," *Social Epistemology* 9: 1–88.

Funtowicz, S., and Ravetz, J. (1992). "Three types of risk assessment and the emergence of post-normal science." In S. Krimsky and D. Golding (eds.), *Social Theories of Risk*. Praeger, pp. 251–274.

Galbraith, J.K. (1967). *The New Industrial State*. Houghton Mifflin.

Gallarotti, G. (1995). *The Anatomy of an International Monetary Regime: The Classical Gold Standard, 1880–1914*. Oxford University Press.

Gambetta, D. (1994). "Inscrutable markets," *Rationality and Society* 6: 353–368.

Gambetta, D., ed. (1988). *Trust*. Blackwell.

GAO (1999). *Federal Research: Peer Review Practices at Federal Science Agencies Vary*. U.S. General Accounting Office. Letter Report, 17 March 1999, GAO/RCED-99-99. http://www.gao.gov.

Geertz, C. (1983). *Local Knowledge*. Basic Books.

Gibbons, M., Limoges, C., Nowtony, H., Schwartzmann, S., Scott, P., Trow, M. (1994). *The New Production of Knowledge*. Sage.

Giddens, A. (1990). *The Consequences of Modernity*. Polity Press.

Giere, R., ed. (1992). *Cognitive Models of Science*. University of Minnesota Press.

Gigerenzer, G. and Murray, D. (1987). *Cognition as Intuitive Statistics*. Lawrence Erlbaum Associates.

Gigerenzer, G., Todd, P., and the ABC Research Group (1999). *Simple Heuristics That Make Us Smart*. Oxford University Press.

Gouldner, A. (1970). *The Coming Crisis in Western Sociology*. Basic Books.

Grafton, A. (1990). *Forgers and Critics*. Princeton University Press.

Greenbaum, J., and Kyng, M., eds. (1991). *Design at Work*. Lawrence Erlbaum Associates.

Guston, D. (2000). *Between Politics and Science*. Cambridge University Press.

Habermas, J. (1984). *The Theory of Communicative Action*, Vol. 1. (Orig. 1981.) Beacon Press.

Hacking, I. (1975). *The Emergence of Probability*. Cambridge University Press.

Hacking, I. (1983). *Representing and Intervening*. Cambridge University Press.

Haddock, K., and Houts, A. (1992). "Answers to philosophical and sociological uses of psychologism in science studies," in Giere (1992).

Hagstrom, W. (1965). *The Scientific Community*. Basic Books.

Haraway, D. (1991). *Simians, Cyborgs and Women*. Free Association Books.

Hardin, G. (1959). *Nature and Man's Fate*. New American Library.

Harnad, S. (1998). "The invisible hand of peer review," *Nature On-Line*, http://www.cogsci.soton.ac.uk/~harnad/nature2.html

Harvey, D. (1989). *The Condition of Postmodernity*. Blackwell.

Haug, M. (1977). "Computer technology and the obsolescence of the concept of profession," in M. Haug and J. Dofray (eds.), *Work and Technology*. Sage.

Haugeland, J. (1984). *Artificial Intelligence: The Very Idea*. MIT Press.

Hawley, A. (1950). *Human Ecology*. The Ronald Press Company.

Hayek, F. (1948). *Individualism and Economic Order*. University of Chicago Press.

Hayek, F. (1952). *The Counter-Revolution in Science*. University of Chicago Press.

Head, J.G. (1962). "Public goods and public policy," *Public Finance* 3: 197–219.

Held, D. (1987). *Models of Democracy*. Polity Press.

Hellstrom, T. (2002). "Governing the virtual academic commons." *Research Policy* 31.

Hess, D. (1993). *Science in the New Age*. University of Wisconsin Press.

Hirsch, F. (1977). *Social Limits to Growth*. Routledge and Kegan Paul.

Hirschman, A. (1976). *The Passions and the Interests*. Princeton University Press.

Hoch, P. (1987). "Institutional versus intellectual migrations in the nucleation of new scientific specialities," *Studies in History and Philosophy of Science* 18: 481–500.

Horowitz, I.L. (1986). *Communicating Ideas*. Oxford University Press.

Horrobin, D.F. (1990). "The philosophical basis of peer review and the suppression of innovation," *Journal of the American Medical Association* 263: 1438–1441.

Hoskin, K., and Macve, R. (1986). "Accounting and the examination: A genealogy of disciplinary power," *Accounting, Organizations and Society* 11: 105–136.

Huber, P. (1990). "Pathological science in court," *Daedalus* 119, 4: 97–117.

Huizinga, J. (1949). *Homo Ludens*. (Orig. 1938.) Routledge and Kegan Paul.

Jacob, M., and Hellstrom, T., eds. (2000). *The Future of Knowledge Production in the Academy*. Open University Press.

Jansen, S. (1988). *Censorship: The Knot That Binds Power and Knowledge*. Oxford University Press.

Jaszi, P. (1994). "On the Author Effect: Contemporary copyright and collective creativity," in M. Woodmansee and P. Jaszi (eds.), *The Construction of Authorship: Textual Appropriation in Law and Literature* (Duke University Press), pp. 29–56.

Johnes, G. (1993). *The Economics of Education*. Macmillan.

Kahin, B. (1996). "Scholarly communication in the networked environment: Issues of principle, policy and practice," in Peek and Newby (1996), pp. 277–298.

Kelly, R. (1989). "Private data and public knowledge: intellectual property rights in science," *Legal Studies Forum* 4: 365–380.

Keynes, J.M. (1936). *The General Theory of Employment, Interest, and Money*. Harcourt Brace.

Kitcher, P. (1993). *The Advancement of Science*. Oxford University Press.

Kling, R., ed. (1995). Special issue: "Electronic journals and scholarly publishing," *The Information Society* 11: 237–344.

Kling, R., and Lamb, R. (1996). "Analyzing alternate visions of electronic publishing and digital libraries," in Peek and Newby (1996), pp. 17–54.

Knorr-Cetina, K. (1981). *The Manufacture of Knowledge*. Pergamon.

Kolakowski, L. (1972). *Positivist Philosophy: From Hume to the Vienna Circle*. Penguin.

Kransdorff, A. (1998). *Corporate Amnesia*. Butterworth–Heinemann.

Krause, E. (1996). *Death of the Guilds*. Yale University Press.

Kuhn, T.S. (1970). *The Structure of Scientific Revolutions*, 2nd ed. (Orig. 1962.) University of Chicago Press.

Kuhn, T.S. (1977). *The Essential Tension*. University of Chicago Press.

Lash, S., and Urry, J. (1987). *The End of Organized Capitalism*. Sage.

Latour, B. (1987). *Science in Action*. Open University Press and Harvard University Press.

Latour, B. (1988). "The politics of explanation," in Woolgar (1988b).

Latour, B., and Woolgar, S. (1979). *Laboratory Life: The Social Construction of Scientific Facts*. Sage.

Lattes (2001). The Lattes Platform.
http://www.cnpq.br/plataformalattes/index.htm

Lea, S., Tarpy, R., and Webley, P. (1987). *The Individual in the Economy: A Survey of Economic Psychology*. Cambridge University Press.

Lepage, H. (1987). *Tomorrow, Capitalism*. Open Court.

Levine, J. (1989). "Reaction to opinion deviance in small groups," in Paulus (1989), pp. 187–232.

Loka (2001). *Citizens Panels*. Loka Institute.
http://www.loka.org/pages/panel.htm

Lynch, W (1989). "Arguments for a non-Whiggish hindsight: Counterfactuals and the sociology of knowledge," *Social Epistemology* 3: 361–366.

Lyotard, J.-F. (1983). *The Postmodern Condition*. (Orig. 1979.) University of Minnesota Press.

Machlup, F. (1984). *The Economics of Information and Human Capital* (Vol. III of *Knowledge: Its Creation, Distribution, and Economic Significance*). Princeton University Press.

MacIntyre, A. (1990). *Three Rival Versions of Moral Enquiry*. Duckworth.

Manicas, P. (1986). *A History and Philosophy of the Social Sciences*. Blackwell.

Mannheim, K. (1936). *Ideology and Utopia.* (Orig. 1929.) Routledge and Kegan Paul.

Mannheim, K. (1940). *Man in an Age of Reconstruction.* Routledge and Kegan Paul.

Marcuse, H. (1964). *One-Dimensional Man.* Beacon Press.

Marx, K. (1970). *Capital.* (Orig. 1865.) Lawrence and Wishart.

McLuhan, M. (1962). *The Gutenberg Galaxy.* University of Toronto Press.

Merton, R. (1973). *The Sociology of Science.* University of Chicago Press.

Middleton, D., and Edwards, D., eds. (1990). *Collective Remembering.* Sage.

Miller, A., and Davis, M. (1983). *Intellectual Property: Patents, Trademarks, and Copyright in a Nutshell.* West.

Minsky, M. (1986). *The Society of Mind.* Simon and Schuster.

Mirowski, P. (1989). *More Heat than Light.* Cambridge University Press.

Monk, P. (1989). *Technological Change in the Information Economy.* Pinter.

Mosco, V., and Wasko, J., eds. (1988). *The Political Economy of Information.* University of Wisconsin Press.

Nagel, E. (1961). *The Structure of Science.* Harcourt and Brace.

Noelle-Neumann, E. (1982). *The Spiral of Silence.* University of Chicago Press.

Nonaka, I. (1991). "The knowledge-creating company," *Harvard Business Review*, November–December.

Norman, D. (1993). *Things That Make Us Smart.* Addison-Wesley.

North, D., and Thomas, R. (1973). *The Rise of the Western World: A New Economic History.* Cambridge University Press.

Nowotny, H., Scott, P., and Gibbons, M. (2000). *Re-thinking Science.* Polity Press.

O'Connor, J.R. (1973). *The Fiscal Crisis of the State.* St. Martin's Press.

Odlyzko, A. (1995). "Payment for publication," (London) *Times Higher Education Supplement*, 9 June, p. vii.

Oldroyd, D. (1986). *The Arch of Knowledge.* Methuen.

Olson, M. (1965). *The Logic of Collective Action: Public Goods and the Theory of Groups.* Harvard University Press.

Ong, W. (1982). *Orality and Literacy.* Methuen.

Page, J. (1990). "Tort law and deterrence," *Harvard Journal of Law and Public Policy* 13: 30–35.

Paulus, P., ed. (1989). *Psychology of Group Influence*, 2nd ed. Lawrence Erlbaum Associates.

Peek, R., and Newby, G., eds. (1996). *Scholarly Publishing: The Electronic Frontier*. MIT Press.

Perelman, M. (1991). *Information, Social Relations, and the Economics of High Technology*. St. Martin's Press.

Perrolle, J. (1987). *Computers and Social Change: Information, Property and Power*. Wadsworth.

Peters, D., and Ceci, S. (1982). "Peer review practices of psychological journals: The fate of published articles submitted again," *Behavior and Brain Sciences* 5: 187–255.

Pettit, P. (1997). *Republicanism*. Oxford University Press.

Peukert, D. (1993). *The Weimar Republic*. Penguin.

Pfaffenberger, B. (1990). *Democratizing Information*. G.K. Hall.

Phillips, J., and Firth, A. (1995). *Introduction to Intellectual Property Law*, 3rd ed. Butterworths.

Pickering, A., ed. (1992). *Science as Practice and Culture*. University of Chicago Press.

Polanyi, K. (1944). *The Great Transformation*. Beacon Press.

Polanyi, M. (1957). *Personal Knowledge*. University of Chicago Press.

Polanyi, M. (1962). "The republic of science: Its political and economy theory," *Minerva* 1: 54–73.

Pollock, J. (1986). *Contemporary Theories of Knowledge*. Hutchinson.

Pool, I. de S. (1983). *Technologies of Freedom*. Harvard University Press.

Popper, K. (1957). *The Poverty of Historicism*. Harper and Row.

Popper, K. (1963). *Conjectures and Refutations*. Harper and Row.

Popper, K. (1970). "Normal science and its dangers," in I. Lakatos and A. Musgrave (eds.), *Criticism and the Growth of Knowledge*, pp. 51–58. Cambridge University Press.

Popper, K. (1972). *Objective Knowledge*. Oxford University Press.

Prendergast, C. (1986). "Alfred Schutz and the Austrian School of economics," *American Journal of Sociology* 92: 1–26.

Price, D. de S. (1978). Toward a model of science indicators. In Y. Elkana et al. (eds.), *Toward a Metric of Science*. Wiley-Interscience.

Proctor, R. (1991). *Value-Free Science?* Harvard University Press.

Putnam, R. (1993). "Bowling alone: America's declining social capital," *Journal of Democracy* 6: 65–78.

Quine, W.V.O. (1960). *Word and Object*. MIT Press.

Rawls, J. (1955). "Two concepts of rules," *Philosophical Review*. 64: 3–32.

Rawls, J. (1972). *A Theory of Justice*. Harvard University Press.

Redner, H. (1986). *The Ends of Science*. Westview Press.

Ringer, F. (1979). *Education and Society in Modern Europe*. Indiana University Press.

Rorty, R. (1979). *Philosophy and the Mirror of Nature* Princeton University Press.

Roszak, T., ed. (1967). *The Dissenting Academy*. Random House.

Rothschild, M. (1973). "Models of market organization with imperfect information," *Journal of Political Economy* 81: 1283–1303.

Rudmin, F. (1990). "The economic psychology of Leon Litwinski: a program of cognitive research on possession and property," *Journal of Economic Psychology*. 11: 307–339.

Salmon, W. (1967). *The Foundations of Statistical Inference*. University of Pittsburgh Press.

Samuelson, P. (1969). "Pure theory of public expenditures and taxation," in J. Margolis and H. Guitton (eds.), *Public Economics* (Macmillan), pp. 98–123.

Scarbrough, H., and Swan, J. (1999). "Knowledge management and the management fashion perspective," paper presented at the British Academy of Management Conference, "Managing Diversity," Manchester, 1–3 September.

Schaefer, W., ed. (1984). *Finalization in Science*. Reidel.

Schiller, D. (1988). "How to think about information," in Mosco and Wasko (1988), pp. 27–43.

Schumpeter, J. (1950). *Capitalism, Socialism, and Democracy*, 2nd ed. (Orig. 1942.) Harper and Row.

Schumpeter, J. (1954). *History of Economic Analysis*. Oxford University Press.

Schumpeter, J. (1961). *The Theory of Economic Development.* (Orig. 1912.) Galaxy Books.

Schutz, A. (1964). "The well-informed citizen: An essay in the social distribution of knowledge," in A. Schutz, *Collected Papers*, Vol. II, pp. 120–134. (Orig. 1932.) Martinus Nijhoff.

Senge, P. (1990). *The Fifth Discipline.* Doubleday.

Shadish, W., and Fuller, S., eds. (1994). *The Social Psychology of Science.* Guilford Press.

Shapin, S. (1994). *The Social History of Truth.* University of Chicago Press.

Shapin, S., and Schaffer, S. (1985). *Leviathan and the Air-Pump.* Princeton University Press.

Shapiro, C., and Varian, H. (1998). *Information Rules.* Harvard Business School.

Simmel, G. (1978). *The Philosophy of Money.* (Orig. 1907.) Routledge.

Simon, H. (1981). *The Sciences of the Artificial*, 3rd ed. (Orig. 1972.) MIT Press.

Skinner, Q. (1969). "Meaning and understanding in the history of ideas," *History and Theory* 8: 3–53.

Skinner, Q. (1998). *Liberty before Liberalism.* Cambridge University Press.

Smith, A.D. (2001). "Drug giants forced to swallow bitter pill," *The Independent*, 20 April, p. 17.

Smith, B. (1994). *Austrian Philosophy: The Legacy of Franz Brentano.* Open Court Press.

Smith, C. (1981). *The Mind of the Market.* Rowman and Littlefield.

Soros, G. (1998). *The Crisis of Global Capitalism: Open Society Endangered.* Little, Brown.

Sowell, T. (1972). *Say's Law.* Princeton University Press.

Sowell, T. (1987). *A Conflict of Visions.* Morrow.

Spence, M. (1974). *Market Signaling: Information Transfer in Hiring and Related Screening Processes.* Harvard University Press.

SPSG (1999). "Cyberconference on Peer Review in the Social Sciences." Science Policy Support Group.
http://www.sciencecity.org.uk/cyberconference.html

Stehr, N. (1994). *Knowledge Societies.* Sage.

Steiner, H. (1998). "Silver spoons and golden genes: Talent differentials and distributive justice," in J. Burley (ed.), *The Genetic Revolution and Human Rights*. Oxford University Press, pp. 133–150.

Stewart, T. (1997). *Intellectual Capital: The New Wealth of Organizations*. Nicholas Brealey.

Stigler, G. (1961). "The economics of information," *Journal of Political Economy* 69: 213–235.

Stinchcombe, A. (1990). *Information and Organizations*. University of California Press.

Swedberg, R. (1990). *Economics and Sociology*. Princeton University Press.

Thompson, G.B. (1982). "Ethereal goods: The economic atom of the information society," in L. Bannon et al. (eds.), *Information Technology: Impact on the Way of Life*. Tycooly.

Thompson, M. (1979). *Rubbish Theory: The Creation and Destruction of Value*. Oxford University Press.

Thorngate, W. (1990). "The economy of attention and the development of psychology of attention," *Canadian Psychology* 31: 262–271.

Thurow, L. (1997). "Needed: A new system of intellectual property rights," *Harvard Business Review*, September–October, pp. 95–103.

Tullock, G., and McKenzie, R.B. (1975). *The New World of Economics*. Richard D. Irwin.

Turkle, S. (1984). *The Second Self: Computers and the Human Spirit*. Simon and Schuster.

Turner, S. (1998). "Making normative soup with non-normative bones," in A. Sica (ed.) *What Is Social Theory?*, pp. 118–144. Blackwell.

Tweney, R., Doherty, M., and Mynott, C., eds. (1981). *On Scientific Thinking*. Columbia University Press.

Veblen, T. (1904). *The Theory of Business Enterprise*. Scribners.

Weber, M. (1954). *On Law in Economy and Society*. (Orig. 1925.) Simon and Schuster.

Weber, M. (1958). "Science as a vocation" (orig. 1918.), in H. Gerth and C.W. Mills (eds.), *From Max Weber*, pp. 129–158. Oxford University Press.

Weil, V., and Snapper, J., eds. (1989). *Owning Scientific and Technical Information*. Rutgers University Press.

INDEX

A

Academia. *See also* Universities
  business mentality versus, 5, 6
  grants to, 40
  hyperspecialization, 134
  knowledge society and, 6
  private funding to, 40
  unions and, 7
Academic bullionism, 31, 35, 224
Academic values in corporate
    enterprise, injection of, 44–49,
    197–198
Academics
  accountability, 194
  civil republican agenda for
    academic CEO of
    tomorrow, 229–231
  consensus conferences, 215–
    216
  contract academic workers
    challenge to university's
    republican constitution,
    225–228

hiring, 192
information technology
    avoidance by, 137–138
intellectual rent and, 38–39
journal articles, 177
marketing attitudes, 182
private funding and, 35, 40
publishing and, 174–178
selling expertise to knowledge
    engineer, 137
Accelerating production of new
    knowledge, who's afraid of,
    49–56
Alienating knowledge from knower
    and commodification of
    expertise, 7–8, 106–115
Artificial intelligence (AI), 126,
    130, 131, 136–137, 141, 153

B

Back to basics, 36–44
Bioprospecting, 111–113, 162–163
Bounded rationality, 4, 18

Weizenbaum, J. (1976). *Computer Power and Human Reason*. W. Freeman.

Wenneras, C., and Wold, A. (1997). "Sexism and nepotism in peer-review *Nature* 387: 321–343.

Wenneras, C., and Wold, A. (1999). "Bias and peer review of research pi posals," in J. Smith and R. Smith (eds.), *Peer Review in Health Care*, p 77–87. British Medical Journal Publishing.

White, H. (1981). "Where do markets come from?" *American Journal Sociology* 87: 517–547.

Wicklund, R. (1989). "The appropriation of ideas," in Paulus (1989), p 393–424.

WIHSC (Welsh Institute for Health and Social Care) (1998). "Report of t Citizens' Jury on Genetic Testing for Common Disorders http://www.medinfo.cam.ac.uk/phgu/info_database/Testing_etc/ci zens'_jury.asp

Will, F. (1988). *Beyond Deduction: Ampliative Aspects of Philosophic Reflection*. Routledge.

Williams, Raymond (1983). *Keywords*. Oxford University Press.

Williams, Roger (1971). *Politics and Technology*. Macmillan.

Wittrock, B. (1985). "Dinosaurs or dolphins? Rise and resurgence of tl research-oriented university," in B. Wittrock and A. Elzinga (eds.), *Tl University Research System*, pp. 13–38. Almqvist and Wiks(International.

Woodmansee, M. (1984). "The genius and the copyright," *Eighteen Century Studies* 17: 425–448.

Woolgar, S. (1988a). *Science: The Very Idea*. Tavistock.

Woolgar, S., ed. (1988b). *Knowledge and Reflexivity*. Sage.

C

Capitalized education as ultimate information technology, 191–195
  consumer customization, 193–194
  divided labor, 192
  holistic craft, 191–192
  mass production, 192–193
  stages of, 191
Challenge to knowledge in theory and practice, 23–36
  deconstruction of public goods, 23–30
  disintegration of the university, 30–36
Churches, universities as, 217–219, 230–231
Citations, 207–208
Civic republican theory of knowledge management, x, 113, 196–231
  agenda for academic CEO of tomorrow, 229–231
  challenge of contract academic workers to university's republican constitution, 225–228
  consensus conferences, 213–216
  definition of republicanism, 198
  historical and philosophical bases of, 197–203
  historical threats to republican constitution of the university, 220–225
  knowledge worker unions, 212–213
  liberty and its devolutions, 203
  Polanyi's "republic of science," Michael, 203–211
  republics of science, two, 210

search of republican vehicles for knowledge management, 211–220
universities as ultimate republican institution, 216–220
Computers. *See* Cyberspace and scholars; Human-computer interface, society's shifting; Information technology as key to knowledge revolution
Consensus conferences, 213–216, 247, 248, 249
  extended peer review and, 250
  objections to, 214–216
Consumer customization, 193–194
Consumer demand, 89–93
Copyright
  authors and laws for, 175–176
  bioprospecting and, 113
  Internet and, 190
  patent versus, 102–104
Corporate amnesia, 45, 48
Corporate enterprise injection of academic values, 44–49
Corporate hoarding of knowledge, 45
Credentials race, 114–115
Cyberspace and scholars, 167–191
  conclusion, 189–191
  cyberplatonism versus cybermaterialism, 169–174, 182
  paperless is no panacea, why, 183–187
  peer review, 187–189
  publishing industry as cyberscapegoat, 174–178
  purifying cyberplationism's motives, 189–191
  resistance to frictionless medium of thought, 178–183

D

Deconstruction of public goods, 23–30
Democratic pluralism, 147

E

Economists
innovation viewpoint of, 25, 26
internalization of externalities, 20
knowledge and, 3, 4, 26, 27, 28, 87–88
on knowledge as indivisible, 86
knowledge consumption and, 28, 87
knowledge managers viewpoint versus, 4
knowledge production and, 28, 83, 87
knowledge-power equation, 81
on new knowledge pursuit, 49–50
public goods and, 29, 86, 98–99
sharing information, 73
on wages and research productivity, 39
writing books, 86–87
End of knowledge in practice, 30–36
End of knowledge in theory, 23–30
Engineering versus physics, 92–93
Entrepreneurs, 6, 22, 40
Epistemology to information technology, from, 117–125
Exchange rate, idea of an epistemic, 67–81
Executive Ph.D. program, 47–49, 246, 249
Expert systems, 121–122, 129, 131, 132
customizing, 135–136
expertise to, 143–167

global effects of, 135
human experts versus, 133, 135, 142, 162, 166
hypotheses by, 137
limitation of, 136
pseudo-democratization of expertise and, 154–161
sociology of knowledge systems and the lessons of, 151–154
Expertise
behaviorist, 147, 148
brief social history of, 143–145
cognitivist, 147–148
defining, 146
distribution of, 154
expert systems and pseudo-democratization of, 154–161
knowledge engineers and destruction of, 154–155
knowledge engineers and social character of, 145–151
legal protection of, 161–162
market-driven, 159
politics and, 150–151
relevance, 145
significance of, 146
skills associated with, 145
social character of, 147–148
solution to erosion of, 161
tactics for being in control, 149
as ultimate subject of intellectual property, 161–167

F

Frictionless medium of thought, some resistance to, 178–183

G

Gap between managers and knowledge workers, 8–9
Governance versus management, x, 197

H

Historical myopia as precondition for knowledge management, 5–12

Human-computer interface, society's shifting, 137–142, 193
functional and substantive modes of rationality, 139, 140
intellectual property law and computer definition, 139
mass computerization problems, 142
social relationships of information technologies, 139

I

Infopreneur, 190

Information feudalism, 164, 167

Information technology, intellectualization of, 125–137
alienation, 128
artificial intelligence (AI), 126, 130, 131, 136–137, 141
Bell on, Daniel, 125–126, 127, 128, 130
computer simulations, 127
expert systems, 121–122, 129, 131, 132, 133, 135
expert systems versus human experts, 133, 135, 142

Information technology as key to knowledge revolution, 116–195
access versus possess information, 120
alternate legal-economic models of social relations of, 165
capitalized education as, 191–195

computer interface historical overview, 137–142
consequence of computerization, 124
cyberplatonism versus cybermaterialism, 169–174
cyberspace and peer review, 187–189
expert system, 121–122, 129, 131, 132, 133
from expertise to expert systems, 143–167
intellectualization of, 125–137
introduction, 117–125
as liberator and captivator, 123
mind over matter, 122–123
paperless is no panacea, 183–187
post-industrial dream, 125–137
publishing industry as cyberscapegoat, 174–178
purifying cyberplatonism's motives, 189–191
recapitulation, 161–167
scholars and cyberspace, 167–191
social history of expertise, 143–145

Information versus knowledge, 13, 16–20
classic conception of relationship, 16–17
economists and, 18–19
origin of word information, 16

Innovation, 25–26

Intellectual capital versus social capital, 107

Intellectual property
bioprospecting and global regulation of, 1111
book writing and, 99–100
challenge to attributions of values, 86–88, 89–93

Intellectual property (*continued*)
  challenge to attributions of
    validity, 82–85, 88–89
  challenges posed by dividing the
    indivisible, 82–88
  challenges posed by inventing
    the discovered, 88–93
  computer definition and, 139
  copyright versus patent,
    102–104
  credentials race and, 114–115
  from disciplines and professions
    to law of, 96–98
  expertise as ultimate subject of,
    161–167
  ideas founded on, 81–82
  Internet and regulating, 190
  as landed property, 164
  law, 20, 96–98, 102, 104, 159,
    165
  legal epistemology of, 98–106
  legal promise of, 111
  libertarian approach to, 165, 166
  new category needed for, 159
  as nexus of epistemic validity
    and economic value, 81–93
  obtaining rights as business
    strategy, 25
  peer review and, 243
  proprietary grounds of
    knowledge, 105–106
  recapitulation, 96–98
  research as, 42
  theft, 244–245
  totalitarian approach to, 165,
    166
  trademarks, 104, 105
  U.S. Constitution and, 110
  value of, 243
Intellectualization of information
  technology, 125–137
Internet. *See also* Cyberspace and
  scholars; Human-computer

interface, society's shifting;
  Information technology as key
  to knowledge revolution
cost accounting, 173
prototype of, 173
Inventing the discovered,
  challenges posed by, 88–93
  attributions of validity, 88–89
  attributions of value, 89–93

J
Japan Effect, 159, 161

K
KM. *See* Knowledge management
Knowledge
  accelerating growth of, 54–55
  definition, 61
  embodied versus embedded,
    118, 120
  hoarding, 45
  legal problem of, 101
  much ado about, 2–16
  nature of reality and, 51, 52
  predicting, 54
  in rent, wage, profit, 36–44
  scientific, 55–56
  too much or too little, 93–96
Knowledge and information, 13,
  16–20
Knowledge management
  alchemy of, 10
  civic republican theory of, 113,
    196–231
  historical myopia as
    precondition, 5–12
  military-industrial metaphor of,
    252–253
  mixed root metaphor of,
    252–253
  need for, 94
  original gurus of, 13
  as oxymoron, 2

Realpolitik of, 3, 25
search of republican vehicles for, 211–220
squaring the circle of, 49–56
what's in a name, 12–16
Knowledge management and knowledge, 1–56
accelerating production of new knowledge, who's afraid of, 49–56
back to basics, 36–44
challenge in theory and practice, 23–36
deconstruction of public goods, 23–30
disintegration of university, 30–36
information and knowledge, 16–20
managers and, 24
metapublic goods and injection of academic values into corporate enterprise, 44–49
scientist as enemy, 17–18, 20–23
why much ado about knowledge now, 2–16
Knowledge market(s), 93
creation of, 67–81
likeness to money, 76–79
materializing marketplace of ideas, 75–81
saturated or depressed question, 93–96
unlikeness to money, 79–81
why scientists share, 72–75
Knowledge policy reversibility, 54
Knowledge revolution, information technology as key to, 116–195. *See also* Information technology as key to knowledge revolution
Knowledge society, 13–15, 24, 106–107, 114

Knowledge systems, lessons of expert systems for sociology of, 151–154
Knowledge workers
as consumers, 11–12
gap between managers and, 8–9
manual laborers versus, 8, 10
unions, 212–213
Knowledge's likeness to money, 76–79
abstractness, 78
articulateness, 77
control, 77–78
cool versus hot, 78
creditworthiness, 77
evaluability, 77
invariance, 78–79
mediation, 76
objectivity, 76–77
Knowledge's unlikeness to money, 79–81
diminishing marginal utility, 79–80
scarcity, 79

L
Legal problem of knowledge, 101
Librarians, 134–135

M
Making knowledge matter, 57–115
Management at a distance approach, 9–10
Management's interest in knowledge, 3, 8
Managers and conduct of knowledge worker, 8
Materializing marketplace of idea, 75–81
Metapublic goods and injection of academic values into corporate enterprise, 44–49

Modes of science governance chart, 221
Motivating knowledge workers, 7
Much ado about knowledge, 2–16
   historical myopia as precondition for knowledge management, 5–12
   what's in a name, 12–16

N
Network failure, 45

O
Opportunity costs, 88–89
Organizations, dumb versus smart, x, 33, 43, 85, 229

P
Paperlessness is no panacea, 183–187
Patent versus copyright, 102–104
Patents, courts defining scope of, 109–110, 164
Peer-review processes
   categories difficult for, 234
   challenges to, 249–250
   contract workers and, 238–239, 240
   cyberspace and, 168, 172, 187–189
   defining peers, 235–237
   definition, 232–233
   design purpose of, 176
   extended, 245–248, 249
   future of, 248–251
   goals of, 233
   grant proposals and, 237, 240, 241, 242, 243, 244, 251
   historical aim of, 187
   implications for research and policy, 248–251
   intellectual property theft and, 244–245
   Internet and, 172

judgments in question within, 131
monitoring peer judgments, ethically, 242–245
national registry for, 240–241
in natural and social science, 205
non-academics and, 245–248, 249
as "old-boys network," 226, 236, 238, 239, 250
Polanyi's "republic of science," Michael, 203–211
promises and pitfalls of extended peer review, 248
recording peer judgments, systematically, 241–242
recruiting peers, 238–241
research needed on, 250
scope of peer review, 232–235
sequence, 233
track records, 239–240
what's living and dead in, 232–251
women in, 236–237, 249
Peers
   absolute, 235, 242
   concept of, 236
   defining, 235–237
   recruiting, 238–241
   relative, 235, 242
Philosophical obstacle to knowledge management, basic, 58–67
   conceptualizing knowledge, 59
   consumption of knowledge, 65–66
   definitions of knowledge, 61, 66
   focus of philosophers, 60
   knowledge as exchange function, 64–65
   knowledge as mirror of nature, 63–64
   knowledge as property, 62–63

problems, 61–67
pursuit of knowledge, 66–67
shielding of knowledge, 60–61
value of knowledge, 61–62
Philosophy, economics, and law,
57–115
alienating knowledge from
knower and
commodification of
expertise, 106–115
knowledge markets creation,
67–81
legal epistemology of intellectual
property, 98–106
obstacle to knowledge
management, basic
philosophical, 58–67
recapitulation, 96–98
Physics as gold standard of science,
71–72
Physics versus engineering, 92–
93
Polanyi's "republic of science,"
Michael, 203–211
Positional good, knowledge as, 6,
29, 114, 133–134, 158–160,
163–164, 221
Possessing knowledge and
possessing money analogy,
75–81
likeness to money, 76–79
unlikeness to money, 79–81
Post-industrial dream, 125–137
Printing, 140. *See also* Writing
books
authorship, 171–172
church and, 140, 141
social status, 141
technical journals, 141
Process cost of producing
knowledge, 82–83, 86
Production of new knowledge,
who's afraid of accelerating,
49–56

Profit, value of knowledge in, 36,
37, 40–41, 42, 43, 44, 73
academic ethos and, 41
view of arithmetic and, 41, 42
Proprietary grounds of knowledge,
strategies for studying,
105–106
Public good(s)
access costs of, hidden, 27–28
case example, 28–29
concept of, 29
deconstruction of, 23–30
definition, 27
higher education and, 29
maintenance of, 28
metapublic goods versus, 46
theorists interest, 28
Publishing industry
as cyberscapegoat, 174–178
in cyberspace, 186–187
esoteric publishing, 178–179,
182
paper costs, 183–184
peer review, 176, 177
as proactive, 182–183
as reactive, 183
standardization of scientific
writing, 176
strategy of big versus small
publishing houses, 179–180

R

Realpolitik
of capitalism, 55
of knowledge management, 3,
25
Rediscovering value of knowledge
in rent, wage, profit, 36–44
potential sources, 37
Reductionism, 69, 70, 71
Rent, value of knowledge in, 36,
37, 38–39, 42, 43, 73
intellectual, 38–39
view of arithmetic and, 41, 42

Rent, value of knowledge in (*continued*)
wages versus, 40
Republicanism. *See* Civic republican theory of knowledge management
Research
and development, 20, 25, 26
and funding, 35–36
as intellectual property, 42
outsourcing, 49
Research epistemology, 23

S
Say's Law, 89, 94
Scholars and cyberspace, 167–191
cyberplatonism versus cybermaterial knowledge management, 169–174
cyberspace and peer review, 187–189
paperless is no panacea, why, 183–187
publishing industry as cyberscapegoat, 174–178
purifying cyberplatonism's motives, 189–191
resistance to frictionless medium of thought, 178–183
Science Citation Index (SCI), 207
Science governance modes, 221
Scientist(s), 20
accelerating knowledge growth, 55–56
computer simulations and, 127
cooperation and, 55–56
as knowledge management's enemy, 20–23
knowledge managers versus, 17–18
labor unions and, 7, 212–213

publishing works by, 22
sharing information, 72–75
social, 117–118, 129, 191
universities and, 42
word origin, 20–21
writing books, 86
Scientometrics, 32–33
Social capital, 107–109
Social epistemology, 23, 51–52, 65, 101, 168, 169, 209, 221
Social knowledge, characterizing, 14–15
Social science, 138
challenge to future of, 139
peer review in, 205
Sociology of knowledge
expert systems lessons for, 151–154
philosophers on, 144
start of, 123
Students of power versus students of knowledge, 60

T
Tacit versus explicit knowledge, 26
Trademarks, 104, 105
Transaction costs, 19–20
Turing's Revenge, 115

U
Unions and knowledge workers, 7, 212–213
Universities. *See also* Academia; Academics
academic bullionism, 31, 35
academic CEO of tomorrow, civic republican agenda for, 229–231
administrators, 33
autonomy strategies, 218–219
big names at, 31
British ideal, 222, 223, 224, 225

challenge of contract academic workers to university's republican constitution, 225–228

communitarianism versus liberalism, 220, 221

corporate enterprise injection of values of, 44–49

curriculum design, 217–218

deformations of republican spirit of, modern, 222

disintegration of, 30–36

Executive Ph.D. program, 47–49, 246, 249

expansion and contraction of, 230

fixed-term contracts, 42

French ideal, 222, 223, 224, 225

German ideal, 222, 223, 224–225

historical threats to republican, constitution of, 220–225

information professionals and planning policy, 134

Internet costs at, 185–186

as knowledge trust-busters, 47

knowledge workers loyalty, 9

metapublic goods and, 46–47

network failure redressing, 45

polarized demands, 44

ranking of, in United Kingdom, 34

republican institution, ultimate, 216–220

Research Assessment Exercise (RAE), 34, 35

during Scientific and Industrial Revolutions, 32

scientists in, 42

Stewart on, Thomas, 33

teaching versus publication, 212

vocational training centers versus, 114

V

Value in knowledge production, potential sources, 37, 43

Value of knowledge in rent, wage, profit, 36–44

W

Wage, value of knowledge in, 36, 37, 39–40, 43

rent versus, 40

research productivity and, 39–40

view of arithmetic and, 41–42

Writing books. *See also* Printing copyright foundation, 100

economists and, 86–87

intellectual property and, 99–100

scientists and, 86

KNOWLEDGE MANAGEMENT CONSORTIUM INTERNATIONAL

Managing Knowledge about Knowledge Management™

Knowledge Management Consortium International (kmci) - organizations and individuals coming together to develop a shared vision, common understanding, and aligned action about Knowledge and Knowledge Management.

KM as a Balanced System of People, Processes and Tools
kmci is a non-profit organization founded in 1997 devoted to developing a balanced view of knowledge management from the context of an organization. We seek to establish knowledge management as part of a complex adaptive system involving people, processes, and tools. People manage knowledge, not tools. Tools can help people manage knowledge more effectively. The end result of kmci's efforts is to provide a practical, measurable application of KM to businesses and other organizations.

The KMCI Network
Information and Resources for a Competitive Edge

KMCI is your leading resource for professional development, offering special training and certification programs, as well as access to the latest news, conferences, and educational events for today's knowledge workers.

Our online journal, *Knowledge and Innovation* offers a unique perspective which draws together the concepts and processes of Knowledge Management, Organization Theory, Systems Theory and Complexity.

We offer a variety of membership levels. Benefits include discounts on KMCI Institute's CKM cerfication course and other training and development courses, special offers with members of our network, access to discussion groups, today's news, white papers, featured websites, case studies, and a complimentary subscription to our Knowledge and Innovation online journal. Visit our website for these and other features including links to our affiliates, and corporate sponsors, job postings, and more!

Visit www.kmci.org for more details today!

General Inquiries (860) 280-3394 KMCI P.O. Box 191 Hartland Four Corners, VT 05049

2971 134